THE TETRIS EFFECT

THE TETRIS EFFECT

■■■■■

THE GAME
THAT HYPNOTIZED
THE WORLD

■■■■■

DAN ACKERMAN

PUBLICAFFAIRS
New York

Published in the United States by PublicAffairs™, an imprint of Perseus Books, a division of PBG Publishing, LLC, a subsidiary of Hachette Book Group, Inc.
All rights reserved.
Printed in the United States of America.

PublicAffairs books are available at special discounts for bulk purchases in the United States by corporations, institutions, and other organizations. For more information, please contact the Special Markets Department at the Perseus Books Group, 2300 Chestnut Street, Suite 200, Philadelphia, PA 19103, call (800) 810-4145, ext. 5000, or e-mail special.markets@perseusbooks.com.

Book design by Trish Wilkinson
Set in 11.5-point Adobe Caslon Pro

Library of Congress Cataloging-in-Publication Data

Names: Ackerman, Dan, author.
Title: The Tetris effect : the game that hypnotized the world / Dan Ackerman.
Description: First edition. | New York : PublicAffairs, 2016. | Includes
    bibliographical references and index.
Identifiers: LCCN 2016009855 (print) | LCCN 2016017158 (ebook) | ISBN
    9781610396110 (hardback) | ISBN 9781610396127 (ebook)
Subjects: LCSH: Computer games—History. | Computer games—Programming—
    History. | Pajitnov, Alexey, 1956– | BISAC: GAMES /
    Video & Electronic. | COMPUTERS / Programming / Games. | BUSINESS
    & ECONOMICS / Industries / Computer Industry.
Classification: LCC GV1469.15 .A35 2016 (print) | LCC GV1469.15 (ebook) |
    DDC 794.8—dc23
LC record available at https://lccn.loc.gov/2016009855

First Edition

10 9 8 7 6 5 4 3 2 1

CONTENTS

■ ■ ■ ■ ■

PART I

.....

1

■■■■■

THE GREAT RACE

The airplane lurched into a final descent toward Moscow. Henk Rogers gripped the worn armrest wedged against him. Years of circling the globe chasing business deals and new technologies had left him feeling like a well-traveled citizen of the world, but this was something altogether different.

He looked around the shaking cabin with some trepidation. He had spent the last eleven hours on a flight jointly operated by Japan Airlines and Aeroflot, the notorious Soviet state airline that allowed the Russians a hand in the business of actually carrying paying passengers across the Pacific and over the Russian continent.

Eyes fixed on the seatback in front of him, he asked himself what was worse: going in blind to a strange city in a strange country without speaking a word of the language, or agreeing to enter one of the world's most notorious international flash points under false pretenses?

The paperwork for his tourist visa to Moscow felt heavy in his jacket pocket. Rogers had no doubt that if he was caught lying about his reasons for visiting the USSR, the powerful business interests bankrolling his mission would cut him loose without a thought. They had built enough plausible deniability into the deal that he'd appear to be just another economic opportunist, looking to slice off a piece of Soviet prosperity for himself at the expense of the people.

He wondered how what should have been a simple software licensing deal had taken him from Japan, where he had lived for years, to the USSR, tasked with chasing down a shadowy arm of the Soviet government while staying one step ahead of a pair of powerful corporate mercenaries who would stop at nothing to steal away the prize.

To fly into the heart of the Soviet Union in the late 1980s was to take an uncertain step behind the feared Iron Curtain, a political and psychological barrier that kept 280 million citizens locked away from the Western world. Secret police ears were still everywhere in Moscow during the final years of the Cold War. Visiting tourists, businessmen, and even journalists could expect their phones to be tapped and hotel rooms to be bugged, or even to be tailed around town by a boxy Lada sedan, the preferred vehicle of dark-suited government minders.

Yet a new reality had started to replace the traditional East-versus-West rivalry. A spirit of glasnost, or openness, was the Communist Party's official marching order of the day, and with it came an influence both craved and feared—foreign money.

It was into this charged environment that Henk Rogers flew on February 21, 1989. He was one of three competing Westerners descending on Moscow nearly simultaneously. Each was chasing the same prize, an important government-controlled technology that was having a profound impact on people around the world.

That technology was perhaps the greatest cultural export in the history of the USSR, and it was called Tetris. This deceptively simple puzzle game had circled the globe numerous times in multiple formats before the government realized it was not only a rare cross-cultural Cold War triumph but also an untapped source of much-needed cash.

Street after street of identical gray slab buildings flew by the window of Rogers's taxi on his way into the heart of Moscow from Domodedovo International Airport. Could this really be the epicenter of the fearsome Soviet empire? Long blocks of poured concrete high-rises were broken up by occasional flashes of brilliance, from Saint Basil's Cathedral to the Triumphal Arch, shadows of the city's history as a hub of art, architecture, and even commerce.

And it was commerce that had brought him here, despite his tourist visa. Rogers hoped the checkbook in his pocket and the promise of a hefty bankroll from his unofficial corporate sponsors would be enough to smooth over any ruffles with the Soviet government if his legal status became an issue.

What could possibly go wrong? After all, he was only entering one of the most closed-off societies on earth, looking to coax an Orwellian bureaucracy into dropping its current well-connected partners in favor of an uninvited guest. But he suspected the deal he had to offer might be the exact tool he needed to drill through the impenetrable wall of "no" he expected from the Russians.

Despite the military parades and positive state-run media reports, the Soviet empire was hanging by a thread. A brief era of government-sponsored prosperity in the late 1970s and early 1980s was over. This was a time of breadlines and frustrated citizens with little money and even less to spend it on.

One-half of the USSR's bureaucracy was tasked with luring hard currency behind the frayed Iron Curtain; the other half was equally adamant in its mission to protect the hermetically sealed hierarchy of local privilege and power, by any means necessary. It was as if the country had put up a sign in its front yard that read "Open for Business," and beneath it someone had scrawled, "Now, go away!"

In less than three years, the USSR would be gone, dissolved by Mikhail Gorbachev, the eighth and final leader of the Soviet Union. Even now, the Cold War practices of spycraft and espionage were slowly being replaced, or at least augmented, by the cutthroat capitalism of international business deals. Intellectual property replaced state secrets as the intangible product to be fought over, bought, sold, and even stolen.

Rogers flipped through his pages of handwritten notes as the taxi sputtered toward his hotel. Even securing a room reservation had been a minor victory: customer service remained a novel idea in Russia (a situation some would say has changed little in the twenty-five years since).

But there were bigger problems on his mind. The pages of his notebook contained smatterings of conversational Russian, mostly in the form of simple questions, some back-of-the-envelope calculations on sales and royalty numbers, and a single name, circled for emphasis: Alexey Pajitnov.

Of the mysterious Pajitnov, Rogers knew little. Finding this man could be the key to stealing a multi-million-dollar deal away from his adversaries.

One of those adversaries was Kevin Maxwell, the privileged son of a hard-charging UK media mogul. Anyone who had taken on Maxwell and his well-connected father, Robert, found that the Maxwell family frequently proved the old adage about starting a war of words with someone who buys ink by the barrel.

Rogers's other challenger was Robert Stein, a self-made software magnate with a street hustler's flair. Some would call Stein little more than a calculator salesman who stumbled across a lucky break, but Rogers knew there was more to Stein than simple luck.

During this final week of February 1989, all three men were in a race to Moscow, each aiming to undercut the others and strike a deal worth millions with the increasingly paranoid Russian state for its unlikely prize. Tetris was the most important technology to come out of that country since *Sputnik*.

Tetris had stunning global impact. In 1984, a lone computer scientist at the Russian Academy of Sciences, working in his off hours on painfully outdated equipment, programmed it. Before Tetris and its trance-inducing waterfall of geometric puzzle pieces, video games were brain-dulling distractions for preteens, personified by Pac-Man, Super Mario Bros., and other cartoon-like kids' fare.

Tetris was different. It didn't rely on low-fi imitations of cartoon characters. In fact, its curious animations didn't imitate anything at all. The game was purely abstract, geometry in real time. It wasn't just a game, it was an uncrackable code puzzle that appealed equally to moms and mathematicians.

Today, Tetris is firmly established in the pantheon of the greatest video games of all time, but in 1989 its future was much less certain. The Tetris Henk Rogers pursued was a cult favorite that was starting to generate some real money for some major publishing companies, but like all underground phenomena, it had to either grow or fade away.

At the time, Tetris had yet to meet its perfect counterpart, another new technology that would come to be considered equally groundbreaking. That technology, called the Nintendo Game Boy, was a then-secret project hidden away in a series of R&D labs in Japan. It would form a powerful symbiotic relationship with Tetris: the handheld console and the puzzle game would be packaged together, and tens of millions of units would be sold worldwide.

That Game Boy version is the Tetris people know and love from childhood, and three decades after its birth, Tetris lives on in tablets, laptops, smartphones, game consoles, and more. It's estimated that the dozens of official versions of Tetris have generated more than $1 billion in lifetime sales, and the game's legacy has directly influenced time-sucking moneymakers from Bejeweled to Candy Crush Saga.

But, in 1989, none of that was on Henk Rogers's mind. He instead focused on navigating the shadowy world of Communist trade negotiations, outmaneuvering his better-equipped rivals, and bringing West, East, and Far East together in an unprecedented level of commercial and creative partnership. The future of this game—later a cultural legacy of surprising persistence and reach—hung on Henk Rogers's skillful detective work and backroom deal making. Any misstep on his part, and the game would be little more than another dusty eighties curio.

Striking a deal would not be easy. Tetris was treated like a valuable state secret, guarded by one of the Soviet empire's final creations, a new division in its massive secretive bureaucracy named Electronorgtechnica, or ELORG.

ELORG wasn't tasked with searching for nuclear secrets or flipping consular employees into double agents. Instead, it was officially an arm of the Soviet Ministry of Trade charged with handling the somewhat novel concept of protecting and licensing rights for computer software and other technology created under the government's enormous umbrella.

For Rogers, one key to unlocking ELORG lay with Alexey Pajitnov, who had hand-coded the original version of Tetris five years earlier. The two had never met, never spoken, but perhaps, Rogers thought, they might have a lot in common.

They were both computer programmers at heart. Both outsiders who found themselves in the employ of massive power players, creators in worlds that did not often value the creator's spark. Rogers was beholden to one of the world's biggest entertainment companies; Pajitnov and his singular creation were both wholly owned subsidiaries of the Soviet Union.

Rogers knew enough of the tortured backstory of Tetris to peg Pajitnov as a useful ally to have on his side. Thanks to the byzantine nature of Soviet bureaucracy and fading, but still enforceable, ideas about collective state ownership, Pajitnov had no formal say in the future of Tetris and wasn't entitled to a single ruble of the potential profits. But a vote of confidence in Rogers from the game's creator would carry some weight with the technologically inexperienced negotiators at ELORG. Rogers hoped it might be enough to get the deal he wanted.

This was where Henk Rogers saw himself running into the first of many brick walls. Despite a pedigree in the video game world, he was clearly the odd man out in this three-way race. Both Robert Stein and Kevin Maxwell had previous dealings with the USSR and experience with its opaque business practices. Rogers was not only a new visitor to Russia but also an uninvited one.

He knew his rivals were on their way to ELORG's Moscow offices to meet with its lead negotiator, vice chairman Nikoli Belikov, a broad-chested Russian bureaucrat straight out of central casting, known for shifting between amiable Russian hospitality and cutthroat Soviet aggression at a moment's notice. Each had the goal to win ELORG's blessing on producing and selling new versions of Tetris. In five short years the game had become one of the most-shared software applications of all time. As far as the Russians were concerned, most of those shared copies were unlicensed, which meant that some of the world's biggest technology companies were unwitting partners in financial crimes against the Soviet Union.

Henk Rogers shared the same goal, but he lacked a formal invitation from ELORG and Belikov to take part in the negotiations over Tetris. He didn't even know where in the sprawling city to find the headquarters of the secretive trade group.

Not an auspicious start for someone in Moscow for the first time, and carrying a suspect tourist visa. But that willingness to dive into unknown territory was exactly why Rogers, a thirty-six-year-old with a helmet of black hair and a thick Tom Selleck moustache, had been given the job.

Rogers found that understanding Moscow was not as easy as programming a computer game. The television set in his room seemed to have two modes of operation: shooting sparks from its power cord, or completely unplugged. Even a meal was hard to come by. Restaurants required twenty-four hours' notice for reservations, and room service was as foreign a concept as Rogers's full-tilt salesman's smile.

When he asked about a trade group named ELORG, the hotel clerk's fear-tinged blank stare told him all he needed to know. Asking for information, especially about government agencies in 1980s Moscow, was suspect. Locals assumed that if you didn't know something, you weren't supposed to.

But having earlier in his career talked his way into the executive suites of Japanese corporations—in some ways even harder for outsiders to penetrate, with their carefully constructed social mores of business culture—he would not be so easily deterred. In Japan it was a matter of learning a rigid code of respectful behavior. Here in Russia, it seemed to be a matter of finding the right person willing to bend the rules.

The more he considered the puzzle in front of him, the more the two cultures seemed to share a common denominator. The key to one could be the key to the other, a secret known only to a select few.

Rogers remembered the first time he talked his way into a meeting with legendary Nintendo president Hiroshi Yamauchi. It was 1985, and flush from the relative success of his first game, The Black Onyx, Rogers wanted nothing more than to make his next project for the hugely popular Nintendo Famicom console, known in the United States as the Nintendo Entertainment System, or NES.

But getting in the door to see a major player such as Yamauchi was next to impossible for a non-Japanese small-time software publisher like Rogers. After reading in a magazine that the Nintendo president was a fan of the traditional board game Go, a strategy game dating back to ancient China in which players encircle each other's positions on a game board with black and white stones, Rogers quickly composed a fax to Yamauchi's office. In it, he proposed

to program a version of Go for the Nintendo Famicom, a complex
artificial intelligence task that most assumed was beyond the capabilities of the simple game machine. Less than forty-eight hours later,
he was face to face with Yamauchi, pitching a game he wasn't even
sure he could deliver.

Yamauchi wasn't known for small talk, and even less so with
those outside his very small circle of trusted insiders. But the idea of
releasing Go on the NES intrigued him. "I cannot give you any programmers," he warned.

"I don't need programmers," Rogers said. "I need money." A
hefty publishing advance was the only way he could find the outside
technical talent needed to actually make the game work.

"How much?"

Rogers reached for a number out of thin air, high enough to make
him look like a major player, but not so much as to insult his host.
"Thirty million yen." The figure represented about $300,000 in
American money at the time.

Yamauchi didn't reply. He simply reached over the table and
shook Rogers's hand. The deal was done in minutes, and Rogers had
accomplished the impossible: going from a niche PC game programmer to a licensed publisher for the biggest video game company in
the world.

If the classic game of Go was the key to Yamauchi, perhaps it
could also unlock a way to find Alexey Pajitnov and ELORG.
Though Chinese in origin and especially popular in Japan and Korea,
Go had millions of fans around the world, particularly in Russia.
And, like chess, it was often a way for gamers to socialize across language barriers. There must be a Russian Go Association, there must
be Go players here, he thought. And perhaps one of them is the
game-loving Pajitnov, or at least someone who knows of him.

At the very least, Rogers hoped to connect with a sympathetic
Muscovite who would act as a fixer and tour guide. Asking about
government office addresses seemed to be off-limits, but the locations where Moscow's Go players gathered were easier to uncover.
After a day and a half, Rogers joined in a friendly match against a
man another player had described as "the third strongest Go player
in the Soviet Union."

Predictably, the match ended with a win for the local. Just taking on the challenge endeared Rogers to other players. Though his new friends spoke no English, he felt the first cracks form in Moscow's unfriendly social armor. He was soon able to connect with a young woman who worked as an off-the-books interpreter and guide and who claimed to know the directions to any location he wished to visit.

She operated carefully, because private work for foreigners was a sure way to attract the attention of the authorities. After listening impassively to his so far unsuccessful quest for ELORG, she explained to him the concept her countrymen knew as invisible boundaries: Russians weren't allowed to go places they weren't invited.

But Rogers felt emboldened by his success at getting at least a few steps closer to his goal. He wasn't there to recognize any invented boundaries, he explained. His guide nodded. ELORG's offices would most likely be within the massive Ministry of Trade and a simple matter to find.

In the country for less than forty-eight hours, Henk Rogers had gone from a lost soul on a tourist visa to the talk of the local Go community, and now he neared the moment when he would have to stare down stone-faced Soviet bureaucrats and talk his way into the most important meeting of his life.

But the clock was ticking. By now, Robert Stein and Kevin Maxwell were no doubt settling into their hotel rooms and preparing for their respective meetings with ELORG's director, Nikolai Belikov. Neither was a favorite of the Russian official, but the pair had at least been formally invited to bid on the rights to Tetris.

Only a few blocks from his hotel, his guide stopped. Cars streamed along a main drag known as Kashirskoye Highway, a winding street that bisected Moscow, running south of the Moskva River. On one side stood Henk Rogers and his temporary traveling companion. On the other, a nondescript government building, identical to dozens just like it that ran several blocks in either direction.

Showing this man to a building was one thing; standing next to him when he knocked on the door was another, and she would go no further.

"You don't just show up at a ministry and expect to talk to somebody. You have to be invited," she warned.

But Rogers didn't know how to get invited. And, anyway, here he was.

The odds were long, but Rogers was fairly sure he had arrived at ELORG's offices before either Stein or Maxwell, and that first-mover advantage could prove valuable.

Abandoned by his guide, Rogers dodged the light traffic, barely breaking his stride as he pushed open the outer doors to the sparse Communist-era workplace. Just inside the lobby, he stopped the first official-looking person he saw and said, "I want to talk to somebody about Tetris."

> Tetris was the first video game played in space, by cosmonaut Aleksandr A. Serebrov in 1993.

2

■■■■■

ALEXEY LEONIDOVICH PAJITNOV

The telephone rang in Alexey Pajitnov's Moscow apartment, a modest collection of rooms tucked away on a high floor of a Soviet-era apartment block. The voice on the other end was a familiar one—Nikoli Belikov. It could only mean that there was business about Tetris to be conducted, and Pajitnov's presence was requested.

He was already apprehensive about a meeting scheduled for later that week with Tetris's original licensee, Robert Stein, who Pajitnov disliked. As for Stein's competitor, Kevin Maxwell, Pajitnov knew little about him other than that his father was important, and his father's company was important, so therefore he was important.

During these occasional meetings with Tetris suitors, Pajitnov was invited to act as the public face of his creation. He might also be called upon to answer any technical questions about Tetris. Officially, he was there as the representative of the Russian Academy of Sciences, the government think tank that employed him and to which he had reluctantly signed over the rights to his game.

Because any money they might finally wrangle from Stein or Maxwell would go to ELORG or the Russian Academy of Sciences, Pajitnov was content to sit quietly in the background, unless someone asked him a question.

Over the phone, Belikov threw a wrench into the coming week's carefully choreographed meeting schedule. A stranger from Japan is here, he said, and he wants to discuss something about Tetris. "No problem," Pajitnov answered. "I could come over."

Alexey Pajitnov learned patience early in life, like generations of Soviet citizens before him. Sitting through an extra negotiating session over video game rights was certainly a step above his early years at the RAS, when he spent much of his time engaged in that most traditional of Russian activities, waiting in line.

When he started there as a computer researcher nearly nine years earlier, he was supposed to have access to the latest in Russian technology. Instead, he frequently stood around waiting along with other researchers for his turn to feed a punch card into a wall-sized mainframe, the fearsome BESM-6. Its Russian name literally means "Large Electronically Computing Machine." Set in an American computer lab, such a scene might have played out in the 1960s. In the Soviet Union, the same creaky mainframes were still in use twenty years later.

Had moving over to the RAS been a mistake? He had taken a professional leap of faith in joining the Dorodnitsyn Computing Centre at the sprawling, sometimes rebellious, Russian Academy of Sciences. His previous position had been an enviable one, a safe academic track at the prestigious but ultimately stifling Moscow Institute of Aviation. It was a particularly good gig for a young scientist, trading in the cachet of the aviation industry—a field of endeavor that carried serious weight in Cold War Russia.

Lured by the promise of high-level access to computers, this former math prodigy saw a chance to be on the forefront of research in computer programming. To claim his spot, he started as a summer volunteer, taking courses and becoming a known quantity to the other computer researchers, until he was offered his first on-staff research job.

But his earliest days at the academy were not exactly promising. Pajitnov knew he was lucky to be there, but a machine designed in 1968 wasn't exactly the ideal hardware for the assignments he tackled, researching speech recognition and artificial intelligence. Performing a series of complex calculations was one thing, but recognizing speech or mimicking human thought, those were serious problems that required serious computer time.

How to get enough computer time? Pajitnov considered the dilemma as merely another programming problem to solve. He staked out a desk in the office closest to the mainframe's central location, which gave him the maximum possible computer access time. The extra cycles paid off. After a few years of dutiful work, as computers at the RAS shrank from room-filling goliaths to tabletop units, Pajitnov was rewarded with his own personal workstation.

It was a proud day when he felt the chunky computer keys yield under his fingertips, and he finally knew he had made the right decision to abandon the Institute of Aviation. Sitting in front of his new computer, one of the most advanced machines he had ever interacted with, he could sense a universe of possibilities unfolding. It was a rare feeling for any intellectually curious young man in the early 1980s in a Soviet Union presumed to be at the height of its powers.

Here was a gleaming example of Soviet technology at its most advanced, the Electronica 60, a rack-mountable desktop computer that resembled a clunky piece of midcentury stereo equipment. The bulk of the body was hidden inside a steel rack, and only an off-white faceplate pointed out, instantly recognizable by its Russian name, Электроника 60, in a bold red script across the top and a series of thick, white switches that would not have looked out of place in an episode of *Space: 1999*.

But, like most things in the Soviet Union at the time, scratch away the facade, and you'd find that nothing is what it seemed at first glance.

The Electronica 60, despite a smart-looking space-age industrial design, was just another Soviet knockoff of a more popular, and better-made, American product. In this case, internally it was a clone of the Digital Equipment Corporation's LSI-11 computer. That machine had been state of the art in its day—but that day was in 1975, and anyone at a research facility or university in the West would have considered it a dinosaur.

Not only was this less than the modern hardware Alexey's state-sponsored explorations into artificial intelligence and other advanced computing topics required but also it was somewhat less than the average early-eighties American middle school student had access to in classroom computer labs.

It was not the first time Alexey Leonidovich Pajitnov was faced with the double standard of life in the Soviet Union. He initially experienced it as a child, waiting behind the reassuring figure of his mother, the pair standing in yet another line. But it wasn't basic household goods or cheaply produced clothing they were queuing for. Instead, they eagerly awaited a chance to taste the forbidden fruit of what state-run media regularly derided as the product of the decadent West: foreign cinema.

Westerners of that era liked to imagine a Soviet population full of miserable fur-hatted laborers and Kafka-esque bureaucrats, but the truth is that the country was home to legions of writers, artists, and designers, all part of a long line of Russian creators dating back hundreds of years, with an inquisitive spirit no amount of official repression could stamp out.

Alexey's mother was a writer, specializing in cinema, which was an especially dubious public platform at the time. On one level, the Soviet state revered the cinematic arts, dating back to Sergei Eisenstein and *Battleship Potemkin*. It considered the moving picture a perfect vehicle for indoctrinating audiences into the empire's official version of Communist ideology. But the films of other nations outside the USSR's sphere of influence were immediately suspect.

Alexey and his mother were attending the semiannual Moscow International Film Festival, a special affair that rarely debuted films from the United States but that still showed works from countries as far flung as Italy, Germany, and Japan. This was not merely an opportunity to share in an experience few young Muscovites could even imagine at the time. It was a chance for mother and son to quietly thumb their noses at convention, operating under just enough official cover to avoid suspicion.

That alone was reason enough for Alexey to be nervous and to scan the line ahead and behind him and the cars parked across the street for the telltale signs of state surveillance. Even a youth with no predilection for counterrevolutionary thought knew that the wrong word overheard in the wrong place at the wrong time could mark not just an individual but entire families.

The Pajitnov family wasn't exactly a collection of true Communist believers, but neither were they politically invested in fighting the system. Instead, they were just like the vast majority of Russian families, firmly middle class and preoccupied with day-to-day survival, keeping their heads down and food on the table.

His family did instill in Alexey a worldly appreciation for popular and artistic culture, both foreign and domestic. The smattering of films from non-Communist countries slotted in between locally produced melodramas and the imported copycat work from satellite states such as Poland and Hungary were always especially thrilling. Moscow International Film Festival screenings of works such as *Confessions of a Police Captain* from Italy and *Live Today, Die Tomorrow* from Japan mixed high and low art, connecting film festival attendees to the greater world beyond Moscow.

Sometimes Alexey would take his mother's passes and attend screening after screening, filling his days with back-to-back movies. Often he saw his own austere homeland reflected back, but also he had a rare opportunity to peek past the Iron Curtain and into the world beyond.

Away from the generally tolerated excesses of the Moscow International Film Festival, Alexey had another, guiltier pleasure—the action-packed exploits of James Bond. Following the on-screen antics of the suave superspy was little more than a minor underground indulgence, a small defiance of Party dictates. But it thrilled Alexey Pajitnov to see his early hero rely not just on his fists and charm but more importantly on a priceless collection of innovative science and technology to outthink villains, solve problems, and unravel death-trap puzzles.

At fifteen, Alexey had a chance to spend a lot of time thinking about puzzles and problem solving, but not in a way he would have wanted. It was a cold, snowy February, and Alexey had decided he would still rather spend it outside than stuck in a classroom. Skipping school for the day, he wandered the city, treating himself to a cleanup at his favorite barbershop.

But it was getting late and time to be on his way home. With the cold air against his freshly cut hair, Alexey spotted the trolley bus pulling in across the street. It came to a stop and the doors swung open. He broke into a full run to catch it, leaping over a pile of snow that had drifted up against the curb, but as soon as his left leg hit the ground, he felt it sliding away from him, pulling farther and farther away, until he crashed into the pavement with a sickening crack.

With a broken ankle and twisted knee, an American kid would have been put in a small cast and sent home the same day. Alexey spent five days in a Soviet hospital and emerged with a massive cast that went all the way up his leg. And that was not the worst part. He soon learned he'd be confined to home for two or three months, an eternity for a teenager.

Alexey stared at the walls of his small bedroom, going out of his mind with boredom. He turned inward, endless reading his only break from the monotony, but soon ran through his own limited library. A friend brought him a few books filled with math puzzles, and he was hooked. He completed the exercises as a means to kill time, and it grew into an obsession.

After his leg healed, he held on to that rare passion for math and problem solving, from puzzles to traditional board games to piecing together complex wooden castles—anything to liven up daily middle-class life in Moscow.

But what little entertainment that could be found in the city's modest toy shops was increasingly out of reach for Alexey. His parents had divorced in 1967, just as the USSR's notoriously strict divorce laws opened up, and he spent most of his time with his mother in a one-bedroom apartment.

Still, even the poorest Russian youth could afford an occasional indulgence, and for Alexey and his friends, a set of pentomino puzzle pieces cost only a single ruble and afforded anywhere from a few minutes of distraction to hours of experimentation for a mind open to the right stimulus.

Anyone familiar with Tetris can see an instantly familiar design in pentominoes. Whereas Tetris shapes, properly referred to as tetrominoes, are composed of four square cells arranged in different formations, pentominoes are made of five squares (the more familiar dominoes, of course, have two). That extra segment allows for much more complex shapes, and pentomino designs were used both academically in math classes to explain polyominoes and geometry and as deceptively simple-looking puzzles.

The twelve distinct possible configurations of pentominoes, plus dozens more if you count mirrored or rotated shapes, are most often presented as a brain teaser. Take a handful of shapes, picked to perfectly fill a box or other container, and then figure out how to slot them all in together, leaving no blank spaces or widowed segments.

Pentominoes are made of wood or plastic, and sometimes they were cut out of paper. The idea of manipulating these shapes dates back at least as far as the early 1900s, and the term *pentomino* has been used by mathematicians since the 1950s. Though Alexey was not aware of it at the time, science fiction author Arthur C. Clarke incorporated his pentomino addiction into several works, including the classic 1975 novel *Imperial Earth*.

How much puzzle-solving value was there in a set of pentominoes? To fit all twelve shapes perfectly into a six by ten grid, there are more than two thousand possible solutions, a number which expands exponentially as you change the dimensions of the game field and the number and variety of the pentomino pieces available.

Alexey was mesmerized by these shapes and the things you could do with them. He could spend endless hours taking the five-cell blocks out of their boxes and fitting them perfectly back in, much as generations of families fit themselves and their possessions into cramped Moscow apartments.

But in the early 1970s the world was changing, and wooden blocks were not in the future Alexey saw for himself. The space race, the most obvious metric of competition against the West, had been neck and neck during his childhood. The Russians scored the early goals, putting *Sputnik*, the first man-made satellite, into orbit in 1957, a year after he was born. Later, in 1961, Yuri Gagarin became the first man sent into space. The tide turned when *Apollo 11* put men on the moon for the first time in 1969, and America leapfrogged to the forefront of space exploration, and technology in general, a position it arguably has not relinquished.

The Soviet Union needed scientists and engineers, and armies of trained technologists to support them. A massive push to indoctrinate generations of schoolchildren into science and engineering followed, eventually putting Alexey in front of the machine that would change his life.

Early versions of Tetris included a "boss button" to hide the game at work in case the boss walked by while you were playing.

He was seventeen, the age when lasting impressions are first made on young men, when he first touched his hands to a computer and stared into the green-and-black expanse behind a glass cathode-ray tube screen. The early machine had only eight kilobytes of memory and could be controlled only by way of abstract code.

Was it love at first sight? This was certainly a new world, one far removed from the shelves of Russian novels and Renaissance paintings that lined the walls of his mother's small apartment. But Alexey was no instant computer prodigy, despite a demonstrated talent for math and science. He was torn between the abstract world of numbers, spending part of his time immersed in puzzles and problems, and killing time the same way nearly every other teenager in Moscow did, gambling, drinking vodka, hanging out.

Still, a fuse had been lit. Alexey saw in the computer a canvas for creativity and fun but also something more important: a future. Eventually, he would become his country's first star programmer.

It took him years to get the training he needed to crack the computer's impenetrable code. And he couldn't have known at the time that he had yet to discover one more source of inspiration, something next to impossible to find in Russia at the time: a peculiarly decadent-sounding Western invention called the video game.

3

■ ■ ■ ■ ■

COMING TO AMERICA

Henk Rogers was a teenager when he first confronted a computer. He remembers being a young schoolkid, contemplating a wall-sized IBM mainframe, waiting for his turn to feed the machine a punch card with instructions. It was cutting-edge technology for the mid-1960s, something very few high school students in the United States had access to. Computer time was a rare and valuable resource, with students waiting days for access.

Rogers found the endless waiting unbearable. He watched punch cards being slid into coded storage drawers, where he knew they'd sit untouched for hours or days before being run through the machine. There must be a way to get around this, he thought, already formulating a plan to hack the system.

For Rogers, an unlikely journey all in the space of a few years took him from his native Amsterdam to the halls of New York's Stuyvesant High School, one of the most elite public high schools in the country. Already eleven years old when he first came to New York, Rogers spoke no English; his stepfather spoke no Dutch. They communicated using second-hand German, and Henk camped out in the family apartment in Flushing, Queens, and absorbed what he could of American language and culture from the near-permanent glow of a television.

For the first six months, he subsisted on a diet of animation, combining the Japanese imports that were popular at the time— from *Speed Racer* to *Gigantor*—with classic American cartoons, such as *Looney Tunes* and *Rocky and Bullwinkle*. It was a radical change from his homeland, where children's programming was restricted to a few hours a week at best. Here, you could watch cartoons from sunrise to sunset if you chose, and for a young man trapped behind a seemingly impenetrable language barrier, that's exactly what Rogers did, in the process inadvertently giving himself a deep immersion education.

His first foray into the New York public school system was a class filled with fellow non-English speakers, but that was only a temporary stop. Thanks to a skill for cultural assimilation that would serve him throughout his life, he was speaking English fluently within a year of arriving in the United States. There was less time for cartoon bingeing when his family moved to the Queens neighborhood of Corona and Rogers was sent to Our Lady of Sorrows, a Catholic grade school.

But the rigid atmosphere of the parochial school agreed with him. Rogers graduated first in his class, which paved the way to Stuyvesant and the unusual opportunities that awaited him there.

While some of his classmates were embracing the growing hippie movement, cutting class to play Frisbee in the park, Rogers was drawn to the school's single monolithic computer, occasionally made available to students. It would be nearly twenty years before personal computers, the kind with monitors, keyboards, and mice, would be a common sight, even in elite schools. The mainframe at Stuyvesant was the kind of computer you really had to want to use to even get in the same room with it. Programming was done by punch cards fed into the system, and the results were output on paper sometime later.

And Rogers found that he really wanted to use, and understand, that computer. He liked that the computer would do exactly what he told it to do, and once he got it exactly right, it would do the same thing over and over forever. His family was in the gem business, which was built around the exacting measurements and precise cutting of stones, and in the Stuyvesant mainframe, he saw a chance to apply those principles. If you're clever enough to do something smart and original and perfect with a computer, he thought, then you've created a kind of masterpiece.

The problem was limited access to the school's single computer. There were a handful of standalone punch card machines that students could use to create the paper slips that would be fed into the IBM mainframe. But there was only one central unit and a school full of high achievers who all wanted to be in on the ground floor of the major shift toward computers they could see coming in the high-end science and engineering fields they were drawn to.

That left Rogers with a handful of punch cards and no patience for the system the academic bureaucracy had put in place to ensure equal access for all. The system satisfied no one. Each class had a drawer in a staging room, and students deposited their cards in the appropriate drawer. Later a technician fed those cards into the computer, which ran the simple programs and calculations hidden in the tiny holes punched in the paper slips, and spit out a result.

About two days later, students would receive their results, which usually did not match up with what they were trying to achieve. That's a common enough occurrence in the trial-and-error world of computer programming but much easier to deal with when all you have to do is change a few lines of code on your personal terminal and rerun the program. With a mainframe, the punch card programming had to be reworked and rewritten, often over and over again, with at least a two-day delay between each time. It was an infuriatingly slow system, and Rogers could feel the days slipping by between turns, thinking about how much faster he could master this computer if he could only have something closer to real-time access. He decided there had to be a way to beat the system.

It may have been the first time he went outside the lines to bend a computer to his will, but it wouldn't be the last. Waiting until the rhythms of the school day had everyone distracted, Rogers visited the handful of punch card machines available and made several duplicates of the program he was working on. He took the cards to the special room with the storage drawers and casually deposited one copy of his program in each class's assigned drawer.

No matter which drawer full of cards went through the mainframe first, his work was tucked into that batch, and he then found his results in the output file, sometimes mere hours later. By studying the results, he could figure out which changes he needed to make and produce a new round of corrected punch cards. These cards went back into each class drawer, replacing the older versions, and the entire cycle ran again, over and over again, until he had the exact results he wanted.

> A company called US Foods sells Tetris-shaped tater tots, named "Puzzle Potatoes."

Rogers was burning through a week's worth of valuable computer time in about one day, leaving his teachers baffled about how he was able to create, test, and correct programs so quickly.

But even that accelerated pace only served to amplify his frustrations. The world of Stuyvesant was a rigidly structured one, and the computer class Rogers was enrolled in the only optional elective he had an opportunity to take during four years packed with math, science, and English requirements. Look what I've figured out with a single elective course, he fumed. What if I had two?

Rogers was determined that any college experience he had would be on his own terms. But the draw toward higher education wasn't foremost on his mind; figuring out how to get more hours in front of a computer was. Even in the last days of the 1960s, that was far from a simple task.

He worked through the possibilities. At the time one could interact with computers regularly only in a handful of places. Working at a bank might do it, or getting into the right department in the military, but neither of those career paths appealed to someone who would rather hack a punch card queue than wait in line with everyone else. College appealed to his nonconformist streak, but the actual academics, and the inevitable slog of requirements, did not.

In the end, it mattered little what Henk Rogers wanted, because after high school, his family uprooted themselves and moved their gem business to Japan to be closer to the source of their precious stones. Rogers suspected his stepfather's obsession with the ancient board game Go made the decision to move easier, because Go was especially popular in Japan, a fact he would later use to his advantage when dealing with executives at Nintendo.

Japan wasn't for him, at least not yet. The nation could be downright hostile to young people emigrating from other countries, and he had already worked for years to assimilate into American culture. At age nineteen, Henk was old enough to make his own choices, and the idea of fighting his way into Japanese society didn't sound as good as stopping off halfway, in Hawaii, and taking up the surfer lifestyle. He parted with his parents and made for the beach.

But even the waves at the fabled North Shore of Oahu couldn't keep Rogers from seeking out the nearest accessible computer lab. After a year of beach living, he was taking night courses at the University of Hawaii, only to be locked out again after he ran through the handful of computer-related courses available to part-time students.

A sympathetic teacher saw that what Rogers really wanted was not structured learning, but simply hands-on access. "Look, if you want more computer time, you're going to have to go to school during the day," the teacher told him. But Rogers was deeply suspicious of the full-time-student lifestyle. Still burning over the rigid coursework at Stuyvesant, he was afraid the university would take his tuition and then force him into wasting months and years taking the same core requirements as everyone else.

He worked out a plan to get what he needed from the school. I'm not going to take any core requirements, he thought. I don't even need a diploma at the end. I just want computer time. And that was exactly what he got, taking computer science classes and anything else that interested him for the next few years.

At the same time, a new cultural phenomenon was sweeping through Rogers's peer group, making an impact on nearly every young male in America with a penchant for science fiction and fantasy, a demographic slice that cross-indexed very closely with young men interested in science and computers. It was a new form of tabletop gaming first published in 1974: Dungeons & Dragons.

Rogers had always played games, from competing obsessively at Monopoly as a child to playing Go alongside his stepfather as a teen.

Far beyond any of that, the expansive world and complex rules of D&D, as the game was commonly called, appealed to him.

Created by Gary Gygax, a legendary figure in game design, Dungeons & Dragons grew out of decades of traditional tabletop strategy gaming, where tiny metal figurines moved across paper maps and armchair generals were pitted against each other in what could be days-long campaigns. Gygax applied some of the same concepts to Lord-of-the-Rings-style fantasy, which was especially hot among both hippies and college students in the late sixties and early seventies.

Rogers was taken in, as were thousands of other early D&D players (a number that would grow into the millions as the game became more mainstream over the years), by the delicate mix of established rules and free-form gameplay. The basic tenets of the game were originally laid out in a series of three rule books named *Men and Magic, Monsters and Treasure,* and *Underworld and Wilderness Adventures.* But it was up to each group of players, under the guidance of the chosen omnipotent Dungeon Master, to pick and choose which rules to use and which ones to change and even to make up entirely new rules to suit the mood of the players.

The original books were endlessly photocopied and passed along as Rogers's role-playing game (RPG) group grew and attracted new players. The loose confederacy of elves, dwarves, and human heroes eventually became known as ARRGH, or the Alternative Recreational Realities Group of Hawaii, and massive Dungeons & Dragons games would go on around the clock for days, with players dropping in and out around their class schedules.

For Rogers, starting with those same three little books and evolving from there with no set-in-stone rules or requirements was a perfect complement to his free-form studies of computer science and programming. When he and his friends wanted to push the boundaries of the game's already improvisational narrative, they simply made up their own rules, a move that was both radical and in keeping with D&D's core tenets of player-created worlds.

The game's universe, full of wizards, elves, and sword-wielding heroes, wasn't exactly new, having been built on well-established fantasy tropes from literature and film. But now-common ideas, such as "role-playing" a game's characters and "leveling up" in a game with additional skills and powers, can be directly traced to Dungeons & Dragons. These ideas influenced countless generations of video game designers and programmers, and one of the first was Henk Rogers.

At the time he hadn't yet drawn the mental connection between his two obsessions, but role-playing fantasy games and computer programming would eventually come together, cementing his place in video game history, long before he had ever heard of Tetris.

In between surfing sessions and D&D marathons with his friends, Rogers's college career ran into exactly the problem he had feared all along. Three years into taking classes as a full-time undergraduate, his pick-and-choose approach to course selection attracted the attention of the University of Hawaii's faculty.

"Mr. Rogers, you have a year of core requirements ahead of you," a student adviser told him, outlining the basic science, math, and liberal arts courses he had neglected to take all this time.

"No," replied Rogers, "I don't." And that was the end of his undergraduate career. He had gotten what he wanted out of the school, and those years of early 1970s computer access were worth more to him than any paper diploma.

Freed from the daily class schedule, he cast his attention westward, toward Japan. Going there wasn't a hard decision because much of his family was already headquartered there. He was also following a girl, an English major named Akemi, who had returned to her native Japan after school. He gave chase, and she provided the incentive he needed to stay. After going back and forth for three extended visits to Japan, he simply decided not to return to the United States.

In 1976, Rogers called a friend back in Hawaii and broke the news that he wouldn't be returning. "You can have my car, you can give away my apartment, throw everything away," he said. But he couldn't bring himself to cut all ties to his former life. Rogers asked his friend to go to his apartment and save a couple of specific boxes of computer papers and files, including stacks of punch cards and computer tape. Everything else he was happy to trash.

But if Henk Rogers thought he was about to transition into a ful-filling career in computer programming and development in Japan, one of the most computer-savvy nations in the world, he was mis-taken. After chasing computer time and programming experience across half the world with such fervor, fate would intervene, and he would not so much as touch a computer for years to come.

4

■ ■ ■ ■ ■

THE FIRST BLOCKS

L ike Henk Rogers, Alexey Pajitnov was spellbound by his teenage
introduction to the computer. But, for both men, it would take
years before finding their way as programmers.

For Alexey, first there would be more schoolwork and more training. Enough in fact to crush the creative spirit out of almost anyone.
After finishing the program at the rigorous Moscow Mathematical
School No. 91, often seen as a gateway to the prestigious Moscow
State University math program, known as Mekh-Mat, Alexey instead focused on more practical pursuits, at least for a math wiz, and
worked toward a master's degree in applied mathematics from the
famous Moscow Institute of Aviation.

It was 1979, and Alexey studied and surrounded himself with the
latest advances in science, math, and engineering, all of which
the school applied to Russia's growing aerospace industry, fueling the
technology behind both the arms and space races. Still he was drawn
toward the computer, which remained a rare resource in Moscow at
the time. Even the glamorous (for academia) appeal of aerospace was
not enough to check his curiosity.

Instead, he left the popular, prosperous aviation academy behind
and relocated to the more research-oriented halls of the Russian
Academy of Sciences. Although it was just nine miles away, to the
east across the Moskva River and away from the city center, it might
as well have been on another planet. Unlike the tightly focused aviation institute, the RAS, as it was known, was an umbrella academic

organization that fostered research and development across a wide range of fields.

Despite the fact that it was now essentially a kitchen sink government think tank, the Academy of Sciences was no creation of the Communist collective ideal. Instead, its origin stretched back much further, founded in 1724 in what is now Saint Petersburg by none other than Peter the Great. The academy survived wars, regime changes, and the rise of the USSR, acting as the central hub for the highest-end Soviet science and technology research since 1925.

By the early 1980s, the Academy of Sciences was home to more than five hundred individual institutes. Alexey slotted in to a research position at the little-known RAS computer center, called the Dorodnitsyn Computing Centre. Years dragged by while he shared the primary room-sized mainframe with other researchers before he finally obtained regular access to his own Electronica 60 computer hardware, dated as it was.

He would take a break from programming to peek over the partitions between workstations. The computer lab didn't exactly scream high technology, with tacky wood paneling covering the walls and rows of metal desks. About a dozen similar computers were humming away, mostly by day, a few manned into the evening hours by night owls such as him. His days typically started at ten or eleven in the morning and could easily run until midnight. But he didn't mind or even notice the long hours. Between the weather in Moscow—it always seemed to be winter—and the faltering economy, there was little else but work to occupy him.

Despite feeling fortunate to have access to even this level of technology and the relative academic freedom to push the limits of the hardware, he knew all the silicon in the lab could be outmatched by a single modern computer in the United States or Europe. But even machines nearly a decade out of date had headroom for discovery in the right hands.

Though he had little personal experience with them, Alexey was vaguely aware of the growing phenomenon of video games, a major cultural force in the West and Japan. A curious mix of games slipped past the censors, including Pac-Man and Q-Bert—interestingly, both games built around spatial manipulation in a grid-like environment.

> The original black-and-white version of Tetris is part of the permanent collection at the Museum of Modern Art.

But there was a large gap to bridge between a colorful imported Pac-Man machine and most of the equipment available at the RAS. Any child of the eighties in any country with access to computers is familiar with the bulky cathode-ray tube monitors that dominated computing in the 1980s—a square screen that bulged out toward the user, its background painted a deep black. Text, whether lines of code, experimental results, or early bookkeeping and productivity programs, appeared as glowing green or white characters in tightly regimented lines across the screen.

His Electronica 60, with its monochromatic monitor, was incapable of displaying anything beyond the letters, numbers, and symbols of his computer keyboard. The visual flights of fancy of even early video games were thought to be simply out of reach.

Alexey worked on projects assigned and sanctioned by his department—which was surprisingly forward-looking—concerning speech recognition and artificial intelligence, two areas that continue to bedevil computer scientists today (as anyone who has ever tried to talk to Siri can attest).

He also saw the possibilities of applying the predictable, powerful, and programmable capabilities of his computer lab to the games and puzzles he loved as a child. It was as if the perfect tool for crafting new puzzles had been dropped right in his lap, even if the path from here to there was not yet clear.

To decipher that path would take time and countless hours experimenting with ways to combine the rigid logic of his computers with the fluidity of puzzle design. Despite a generally relaxed atmosphere toward experimentation, there was always programming and debugging to do, no matter how many evenings he stayed late at the center, smoking and guzzling coffee late into the night.

He knew another programmer who was as obsessed with Pac-Man as Alexey had once been with plastic and paper pentomino puzzles. The man talked about the game's artificial intelligence as some sort of alien hive mind that followed and adapted to the player's movements through the two-dimensional maze. To escape the feeling of being observed and manipulated by a machine, his friend attempted to reverse-engineer the game, reprogramming it from scratch and writing a new, nearly identical version just to figure out the programmatic thinking behind it.

That was how software was shared and copied in the days before connected computer networks, USB keys, and online downloads. You'd see a computer program that interested you, and if you couldn't get a copy of the code, or if your computer platform used a different language, you simply tried to re-create the program's behavior as best you could, often ending up with a photocopier version of the original—a recognizable but imperfect copy with its own unique qualities.

Consumed by the idea of re-creating game experiences on his Electronica 60 and the other machines he worked on at the academy, Alexey found inspiration in the sprawling aisles of Children's World, the most famous toy store in Moscow. The shop had been a landmark for decades, occupying a magnificent corner building with breathtaking stone arches, ironically only a short distance from KGB headquarters. It offered the latest in toys and entertainment for Russian children.

When he searched the store shelves, something familiar caught his eye. It was a simple plastic set of pentomino puzzle pieces, and before he knew it, the set had made its way into his hands and soon sat on his desk at the RAS. He spent hours fitting the pieces together, trying to bridge the connection between these simple geometric designs and the programmatic, predictable computer platforms he worked on. He knew there must be a way to translate these ideas from the squares on his desk to the computer screen, even without access to the high-end (for the time) graphics powerhouses used to power Pac-Man and other arcade-style games.

The first results were primitive, but the basic idea for what would become Tetris started taking shape. The problem, Alexey knew, was that his hardware was close to a decade out of date compared with what even amateur game programmers in the rest of the world had access to. Re-creating the effect of a pentomino puzzle required some visual sizzle, and the Electronica 60 had no ability to draw even primitive computer graphics.

His initial imperfect solution was to create a stand-in for shapes using the only paintbrush available, the alphanumeric keys on his computer keyboard. Each shape could be approximated using punctuation keys, mostly bracket shapes, in different combinations, carefully coded across multiple display lines. It wasn't pretty, but it worked.

In this early version, crafted in six days and ambitiously named "Genetic Engineering," the five-segment pentomino shapes were cut down to a more manageable four segments, which could be formed into seven basic shapes he called tetrominoes. His first version was a faithful re-creation of pentominoes—the player simply moved the tetrominoes around on the screen until they all fit. As an initial attempt at a spatial manipulation puzzle game, it was a breakthrough, but even Alexey could tell after a few playthroughs that it was deathly dull. It needed something else.

Computer puzzles were different. Paper, plastic, and wood puzzles could be played over an unlimited amount of time, left to sit while the player thought over new moves and new strategies. But a computer screen and its cathode-ray tube create a more manipulative relationship with the player, beaming light at the viewer's eyes and demanding reciprocal action. A puzzle played on a computer had to be more of a game, and a game required the elements of timing, danger, and a constant push toward action.

For a professional programmer like Alexey, the actual mechanics of creating the game were easy, but the idea of simply dropping these shapes into a square box lacked the addictive quality a good game needed. This early build simply measured how many shapes you could fit into a box, and it took only a few minutes to work out the best solution. Once you did, there was little motivation to play again.

Alexey continued to work on his programming assignments, taking time here and there over the next several weeks to pare his new game to its most basic elements. A strictly enforced design minimalism led to a breakthrough idea. What if you didn't need the entire computer screen? Just because the monitor was square didn't mean everything displayed on it needed to be.

This small innovation changed the feel of the game. Just as he originally trimmed the shapes from five segments to four, Alexey shrunk the playing area from nearly the entire screen to a narrow channel that started at the top and ran to the bottom in order to focus on making fast, accurate choices. But there was still a problem with the game. Once all the spaces along a horizontal row in the new narrow playing field were filled, any area underneath that was permanently out of reach.

Again, the game ended too quickly, leaving little reason to play it again. Alexey stared at the display, hating to see dead, wasted space on his newly improved gameplay field. His brilliant solution would become the one single element of Tetris that has remained constant throughout hundreds of sequels, variations, and knockoffs in the more than thirty years since.

When a horizontal row is filled with tetromino segments, leaving no gaps from left to right, that row simply vanishes in a puff of virtual smoke, opening the downward path for the next set of pieces to fill. The goal becomes not only fitting shapes together and packing them onto the screen but also causing as many lines to disappear as possible.

Whereas Alexey had once spent countless late hours at the RAS computer center working on academic projects or testing new computer hardware, often risking missing the last train in the early hours of the morning, he now spent similar hours working on, tweaking, and playing his new game. Even during the day, he occasionally pretended to be working on a software debugging project while playing round after round of his own game, unable to keep his fingers off the keyboard.

This new invention called the tetromino was at the game's heart, and the constant back-and-forth battle between the falling blocks and the player reminded Alexey of tennis, so he called the game Tetris. In Russian, *Tetris* is Тетрис, and tennis is теннис, making this a conjunction that works across multiple languages (it helps that the name lacks a true Russian origin—the prefix *tetra* is Greek in origin, and *tennis* arguably comes from thirteenth-century Old French).

At the Dorodnitsyn Computing Centre, Alexey's side project had not gone unnoticed. Other students and researchers would gather around the screen to watch or try their hands at the game, patiently waiting for a turn, even while their actual computer center work went undone. It was an experience virtually unknown in Russia, where few homegrown games had gone beyond their creators, and most were probably as compelling as Alexey's early aimless prototype.

Aside from a handful of Pac-Man fanatics, access to American or Japanese game machines was rare, so there was little to compare Tetris with. That was probably for the best, because this version of the game, the first one complete enough to truly be called Tetris, lacked much of what we think of as Tetris today, beyond the shapes and basic rules.

On his green-and-black computer monitor, Alexey's primordial Tetris game lacked music, or in fact any sound at all, with its shapes falling silently, as if in a vacuum. At first there was no score, although the idea that clearing a row of segments by forming a complete horizontal line stood out as an obvious way to count points. There were no separate levels, much less a way to graduate from one level to another. In later years, the "level ninety-nine" problem, where the popular NES version game could go no further, would be one Tetris experts would struggle with, giving rise to a small but dedicated community of professional Tetris players trading new records for highest score and highest level reached.

Nor was the game, in this early stage, decorated with the simple block illustrations of Russian architectural icons that players of any of the classic 1980s versions will remember (along with its plinky Russian folk tune soundtrack). Those window dressings, along with the reversed Cyrillic *R* in the title, all came much later and were exclusively for the consumption of Western audiences looking for a taste of exotic computer technology from behind the Iron Curtain. For Alexey and his colleagues, this was already a Russian game, crafted by a Russian programmer on Russian computer hardware and played, so far exclusively, in a Russian computer research institute. They certainly didn't need a picture of the Kremlin to remind them of that.

Even with the approval of Alexey's peers, Tetris looked as if it would be like any number of reasonably interesting computer projects created by and for a small audience of experts: amusing for a few days or weeks, and then forgotten as the collective moved on to something new. After all, there were no commercially available on-line networks on which to share the game, and few people in Russia, even in Moscow, had access to personal computers.

Even if you were lucky enough to be one of a handful of Musco-vites with access to a personal computer at work or at home, and you had somehow managed to get a hand on a copy of Alexey Pajitnov's code for Tetris, it would likely have done you no good. The Elec-tronica 60 was a rare machine, even at the RAS, and the original 27-kilobyte file was written to work on that specific computer. It wasn't compatible with the IBM PC machines that were starting to become the de facto standard for computing, both in Russia and in the West. Those systems were built on MS-DOS, an operating sys-tem at the start of a tangled evolutionary path to the Windows PCs of today. In the beginning, Alexey's code for Tetris simply wouldn't run on the computers most Russian programmers and technology enthusiasts had access to.

Despite this, word about the game spread within the Dorodnit-syn Computing Centre like a virus, intriguing researchers and an-noying managers for weeks. But for all its incipient popularity within the halls of the RAS, Tetris seemed doomed to burn out once the handful of people with access to an Electronica 60 computer had tired of it. To make the leap from this closed ecosystem to the gen-eral population, Tetris needed the same thing any virus needed: a carrier.

5

■ ■ ■ ■ ■

THE BLACK ONYX

In the late 1960s, Henk Rogers had been one of the only high school students in America with regular access to a mainframe computer. In the early 1970s, he had gamed the system at the University of Hawaii to maximize computer time, still a rare and valuable commodity, while skipping the mind-numbing core course requirements that other college students rolled their eyes at.

But by 1982, Rogers had hardly touched a computer in six years.

His move to Japan in 1976, a combination of spur-of-the-moment action and careful calculation, started off well enough. He had fallen in love with a Japanese girl, and coincidentally, his family's gem business was centered in Japan and the surrounding regions, giving him a perfect excuse to move there permanently. Little tied him to Hawaii, aside from a college degree he had no intention of completing and overlapping social circles of surfers and Dungeons & Dragons players.

The situation soured almost immediately. With no money and no assets, he had moved to a country he was only passingly familiar with. He had no college degree. He lacked even a rudimentary grasp of the Japanese language.

Rogers knew he had no easy way to break into Japan's highly insular high-tech industry, so, gritting his teeth, he joined the family gem business. In a sense, it was his first step toward understanding Japanese social mores. As the eldest son, he was naturally expected to carry on the family business.

Henk and Akemi married in 1977 and took up residence in the Japanese countryside, occupying one of seven small houses in a modest family compound owned by his stepfather and making him even more dependent on the family business.

But if Rogers thought he'd be taken in as a valued executive and heir in a high-profit, high-touch business, he was quickly set straight. He was cheap labor and little more, and with a new wife to support, he was forced to take whatever assignments his stepfather offered.

The next six years crawled by. Rogers felt little better than slave labor, drawing no official salary and being shifted from position to position at whim. He was sent to far-flung corners of the region, unsure where he'd be living from one month to the next. Despite the hardships, children followed, and Akemi was often left to raise them and maintain the household on her own for long stretches at a time at the Rogers family compound.

Henk Rogers was trapped in Thailand and pissed off. It was 1982, and he had been sent because his stepfather had moved a large portion of the family business there in order to be closer to the source of the gems they traded in. Back in Japan, Akemi was about to give birth to the couple's third child, but she would have to do it without Henk. The business was considered more important, and he was forbidden to leave his post.

In that moment Rogers knew he had to get out. He made a decision to bail on the family business as soon as possible and to find something, anything, else to do to support his growing family and his own ambitions.

Six months later, the moment of truth arrived. Rogers traveled back to Japan for a Christmas visit, dreading the idea of having to return to Thailand afterward. It's do or die, he thought. I'm twenty-nine years old, and I have to start my own business, and it has to have something to do with computers.

Japan may have been the center of the technology universe at the time, with companies such as Sony and Hitachi projecting a culture of futurism with portable audio, televisions, and other electronic consumer goods, but Rogers was as far removed from that as someone could get.

Despite his training in computer science and programming—still a rarity for someone of his generation—he had missed out on a half decade of computer innovation. During years of unpaid or underpaid work in the gem business, the closest he came to getting back in touch with his love for computers was when he begged to borrow a simple home computer from a friend. It was one of the first PCs in Japan to support the briefly popular Z80 processor from Zilog, a now-forgotten computer pioneer.

Little better than a toy to most computer enthusiasts at the time, the machine was still a world away from the mainframe at Stuyvesant high school, which already seemed like a piece of ancient history. Rogers applied himself to the system furiously for the short time he had it at home. He had to hack the system to do any serious programming, and he spent hours watching its primitive cassette tape drive spin into action, slowly loading programs from what looked like an ordinary audio cassette for a Walkman.

But he saw the potential in this underpowered little computer and loved its tiny screen, with a then-impressive 200- by 400-pixel resolution, presented in eight glorious LED colors. That alone put it ahead of systems like the Apple II, Tandy TRS-80, and Commodore 64.

Now, at the end of 1982, as he prepared to make a leap into the unknown, leaving the family business and finding a way to break down the doors of Japan's computer culture, he knew it would start with one major investment. But to finance a pro-level computer programming setup, he'd have to get a few freelance programming projects under his belt.

Even this simple plan turned out to be a disturbing introduction to the Japanese business world, where centuries of traditional etiquette sometimes concealed a culture of ruthless backstabbing and theft. It was a learning experience that would serve him in years to come.

Rogers had a friend already doing some programming work on the side for Hitachi, a Japanese corporate giant with a hand in dozens of industries, from consumer electronics to construction materials. It seemed like a golden opportunity to earn a little money and chalk up a credit doing actual computer programming for a major technology company.

But nothing at Hitachi was as it seemed. Rogers went in, at first to simply clean up the coding on work his friend had been doing. But it soon became clear that Hitachi was so large it operated with a very decentralized style. Each Japanese prefecture had its own home office that in many ways acted independently of the company's upper management. The office Rogers worked in started making requests far outside the original scope of his work, and word came down that his next task was something to be kept on the quiet side.

He wasn't asked to work on a top-secret technology project. Instead, he was given a copy of VisiCalc, one of the leading computer spreadsheet programs of the time. But that copy belonged to a different division of Hitachi, and Rogers was instructed to break the copy protection on the software so additional copies could be installed from a single disk. It was an immediate red flag and a sign that his apprenticeship at Hitachi was going down a dark path.

"No, I'm not doing this, and you shouldn't be doing this either," he told the friend who had brought him onto the project. "This is a dead-end thing, being a hacker and breaking people's software." On top of that, Rogers was incredulous that one group within Hitachi was trying to essentially rip off another group within the same company. The whole thing didn't smell right, and Rogers could see his dreams of making a living in the computer industry fading away.

He objected, loudly, and the company back-burnered this request and came back with another assignment. This one offered at least a modest chance to make some real money. The task was to create a custom accounting program for software retailers of Hitachi Basic, the company's branded version of the Basic computer programming language. Basic, in its many forms, was one of the earliest programming languages and was the first look at coding for several waves of students in the 1970s and 1980s. The language's use was still incredibly widespread at the time, despite being, as the name implies, basic.

Rogers's friend was more of a hacker than a programmer, and his first stab was a mess. Jumping in to rewrite much of the code, Rogers built the program out of the very same Hitachi Basic programming language the project was designed to help sell. The two programmers found themselves invited to Hitachi headquarters in Tokyo to present their creation.

This was no local office branch, but a glass-walled home base for a business empire, and Rogers was ushered in to a large conference room filled with executives and, to his surprise, a lawyer. The shady under-the-table approach to circumventing copy protection used at the local offices wouldn't fly here, and it quickly became clear this meeting would be more of an interrogation than a sales pitch.

The lawyer barked questions at Rogers. "Did you get permission to use Hitachi Basic?"

What kind of stupid question is that, he thought. "You guys asked us to program for your machine, and it only comes with Basic. Doesn't it go without saying that you gave us permission to use your programming language?"

The meeting was not going well, and Rogers was glad he had taken some precautions with the software he was presenting. The original code was on a floppy disk, those once-ubiquitous little squares of plastic with tiny round magnetic storage strips inside. Floppy disks were inexpensive, portable, and the most common way to transmit data or files at the time, long before the creation of the commercial Internet. But floppy disks were also very easy to copy and distribute, which gave Rogers cause for concern.

A different division of the same company, after all, had asked him to crack the copy protection and make unauthorized copies of Visi-Calc, and here he was, about to hand over a floppy disk with his own proprietary accounting software on it. As the cocreator of the software, he stood to make some extra money depending on how many copies of his accounting program were sold to software dealers. But Hitachi also had a history of hiring people exactly like Henk Rogers to crack and make unauthorized copies of software. He had no confidence that the company wouldn't simply take his master disk and churn out extra copies without ever reporting sales numbers to the software's creators.

Before presenting the program, Rogers had done some hacking to the physical disk his master copy lived on. In his workshop, he crafted a carefully spaced pair of strong magnets. Magnets were dangerous to floppy disk data, and even just touching a disk with a magnet could wreak havoc on the contents. But by applying the magnets carefully, with foreknowledge of just where on the spinning disk the most important data were, there was a lot you could do with a disk and a couple of magnets.

Rogers positioned the first magnet on the outer edge of one side of the disk. He touched the other to a spot near the center of the disk, leaving a small magnetic landmine at each location. The directory of the disk's contents, required to make it run, was written between those areas, so disrupting a few magnetic particles on the inner and outer edges wouldn't affect the ability of the software to launch and operate. But where he had touched the magnets to the master software disk would cause any program attempting to make a copy to crash as soon as it reached one of those bad sectors.

It was an ingenious bit of physical hacking, and unlike the behavior he had encountered at Hitachi, Rogers was up front about what he had done, explaining that he would only turn over the program with his copy protection in place. The executives were incredulous. "We don't take any programs that use copy protection," they insisted.

The conversation continued to spiral downward from there. This is just too weird, Rogers thought, and he knew he had to extricate himself from this entire situation and try something else.

But what else? Hitachi was a major technology company, and Rogers, fretting over his questions about the ethics of software copying, didn't see why another tech giant would be any better. The only thing left was to leave any hopes of being a programmer at a big company behind and go into business for himself. But what would he do? Build computers? Write accounting programs?

At least he knew where to start. When you're in Japan and you want to take the pulse of what's going on in technology, there's only one place to go: Akihabara.

The name alone sets off a Pavlovian response in techheads the world over. The streets of this tiny district in Tokyo are lined with stores selling the latest electronics and games. The closest parallel may be the dozens of camera and electronics shops that used to line the blocks around Times Square in New York City. Whereas only a handful of these camera shops remain, Akihabara has only grown over the past few decades and is now the global hub for Otaku culture, a worldwide community of hardcore fans of computers, video games, Japanese animation, comic books, and everything in between.

This bustling neighborhood, ideally located for trade right where the Kanda River connects to Tokyo Bay, has been known as a technology sales and distribution hub since the 1940s. Starting with vacuum tubes for early electronics, it has evolved with Japan into a leader in sales of computers, stereos, and gadgets. By the 1980s, it was ground zero for the growing personal computer revolution that was sweeping through the United States, Japan, and Europe.

Rogers trawled the streets and alleys of Akihabara searching for inspiration. In 1983, the tone in the district was a mix of glowing neon signs and bombast, and studious computer hobbyists searched for components, cases, and rare imports. In later years, Akihabara became a mashup of a Disney cartoon and *Blade Runner*, filled with costumed anime fans and gawking tourists, but for now it was a perfect research lab for Rogers to figure out what the trends were in the computer industry and where he should take his next, and possibly last, shot.

As he looked over what was selling in the different computer shops, a common thread emerged. Some computer hobbyists had Apple II computers; some had the infamous low-rent Tandy TRS-80, better known as the Trash-80 and sold in the United States in RadioShack stores. More serious programmers and hackers used expensive NEC machines. Indeed, the Russian computer Alexey Pajitnov was working on in Moscow at nearly the same time was a locally made knockoff of an older NEC computer.

But no matter the platform, nearly all of these computer enthusiasts, including several of Rogers's friends in the small expatriate community in Tokyo, used their hardware to play games. Japanese gamers preferred action and puzzles, and especially popular was a genre of game called Sokoban, presented as a top-down view of a warehouse with tiny digital workers pushing boxes and crates around.

But Rogers also had a unique insight into what was going on outside of Japan, thanks to his computer-savvy Western friends.

He would sometimes take the train to visit what he called his *gai-jin* friends, and that's where he first played games like Temple of Apshai on the TRS-80 and Wizardry on the Apple II. These were role-playing games not far removed from the pen-and-paper Dungeons & Dragons games he had immersed himself in back at college in Hawaii.

There were epic quests, dragons, sword-wielding heroes, and monster-filled dungeons to explore. Rogers looked over these early computer role-playing games and realized he had seen nothing like them in a long time. During his years in Japan, one of the many hobbies he had given up was Dungeons & Dragons. Although it was more popular than ever in the United States, the game was virtually unknown in Japan, outside of a very small circle of players who imported the English-language game manuals.

A plan started to come together. Games were the most universal language of computer users in Japan, and that business was dominated by big companies such as Nintendo, with little room for a newcomer, especially a foreigner, to break in. But, despite their incredible enthusiasm for computers, games, and fantastic storytelling, most young Japanese had never seen anything like Wizardry or Dungeons & Dragons. It was truly an untapped market, and Henk Rogers decided he would bring fantasy role-playing games to Japan.

There was only one problem. He had never programmed a game before, much less something as complex as an RPG.

Nevertheless emboldened, Rogers marched back to Akihabara and purchased an NEC PC-8801. It seemed like the most advanced of the big personal computers at the time and the best suited for creating, rather than just playing, games. It was a major investment, the equivalent of $10,000, but he knew this was his one chance to start a computer career and break away from the family gem business for good.

It was a good thing Rogers had never programmed a game before or thought too much about why good D&D-style role-playing computer games were so few and far between. If he had, the very idea of fitting an epic sword-and-sorcery adventure in the 64 kilobytes of memory available on his NEC would have seemed insane.

Rogers threw himself into the project, designing the characters, settings, and storyline. As a one-man shop, he'd be responsible for not only the technical coding of the game but also the art and script.

There was an immediate problem to overcome. The popular Western RPGs of the time, such as Wizardry, assumed that players were reasonably familiar with the basic tenets of role playing. There was a pretty much 100 percent overlap between pen-and-paper Dungeons & Dragons players and early computer RPG players. But, in Japan, role playing as a hobby was practically nonexistent, and for his project, Rogers would have to write a game for people who knew nothing about role-playing games.

The first challenge was the art of "rolling" a character. The term comes from the old analog D&D days when players would literally roll many-sided dice to randomly generate the numbers to create a new adventurer, with his or her individual statistics for strength, intelligence, and so on. Still a staple of RPG computer game series today, from Fallout to World of Warcraft, rolling a character could present a steep learning curve for Japanese players, potentially scaring them away.

To fit character creation into the game itself would have squeezed out much of the room for gameplay and monsters, so Rogers created an entirely separate program that walked players through the process of choosing their avatar's head, clothing, and name and setting its starting stats. That character was saved to a magnetic cassette tape and then loaded into the main game separately.

That was only one of the many shortcuts Rogers crafted as he worked, instinctively finding new ways to do things to save time and computer memory space. His monsters were particularly troubling. Each was a unique design, and the animation required to make them come to life ate up precious space and computation cycles. He looked at the popular action games in the market at the time. The monsters in those games were wonderfully animated, with up to a half-dozen distinct movements. But that meant you could fit in maybe five of them at most. For a hack-and-slash fighting game, that might be fine, but an epic adventure into the deepest dungeons of a faraway magical land needed a bit wider cast of characters.

Keep it simple, he thought. Take each monster and work it down to a single animation. That would be enough for players who were more focused on exploring and managing their characters. The experiment in stripped-down monsters worked beautifully, and the game soon had thirty different beasts wandering its dark halls.

Today, 3D graphics are standard in nearly every game. The powerful computers and consoles used to play video games render the entire environment and all the characters in three dimensions anywhere from thirty to sixty times per second and present the player with an ever-changing view, all in real time.

In the early 1980s, that was so far beyond the pale as to be unimaginable. Instead, Rogers and other early RPG programmers essentially tricked their computers into presenting a faux first-person view of a dungeon corridor, redrawing the walls of the dungeon from scratch with each move. Even though the view was little more than a few white lines against a black screen, it was incredibly taxing on Rogers's computer. He thought the effect was so slow that it looked like a set of curtains opening and closing rather than walls moving past an adventurer exploring a dungeon.

The problem, he realized, was that he was writing the entire game in Basic, the standard programming language he had been using since college. He knew there had to be a better way, and he found it by loading up an assembly language program cassette that enabled him to access a much more efficient programming language, and one that was better suited to generating simulated 3D images. It was as if the floodgates to creativity opened, and the game started to fly. He split the tasks required of the game, routing the text, story, and internal game logic to Basic, and sending the first-person point of view of the dungeon to the assembly language.

His game was coming together, but it needed a name. All Rogers had known for the past six years had been the gem business, and despite his antipathy toward it, he decided to call the game The Black Onyx.

At this point, the game was entirely in English, which would not do for the Japanese market. Despite living in Japan for years, being married to a Japanese woman, and raising his children there, Rogers's grasp of the language was still barely functional, if that. He hired a few local students proficient in both English and Japanese to translate the game's text and to write a manual with playing instructions.

Designing and programming The Black Onyx turned out to be the easy part. The real challenge was getting it into the marketplace, and for that Henk Rogers would have to dive back into the dark waters of the Japanese business world. Working for the family business for years had left him with surprisingly little in the way of relevant experience. His stepfather handled most of the buying and selling, and the books were kept in his stepfather's head, so there was little in the way of formal accounting. Rogers had been set to physical and engineering tasks, such as building the specialized furnaces that could change the color of rubies and sapphires by heating them to 1,900 degrees Celsius.

To support his family during the long months of game coding, he had to bring in an investor and exchange half the proto-company for about $50,000 in capital. It was the first of many rookie mistakes that would almost sink The Black Onyx. The next crisis came when he searched for a publishing partner to help manufacture and distribute his game. With little understanding of software publishing, he was virtually unarmed, as if he had wandered into his own game's dungeon without a sword.

An early meeting with a small company took an odd turn. Rogers went into the family-owned software publisher and presented a prototype of The Black Onyx. The room seemed impressed, so he proposed a deal to the president of the company. "You subtract all of your costs," he said. "You subtract the marketing. You subtract the PR. You subtract the cost of goods, everything, advertising, and then we'll split what's left over because I'm doing the work, and you're putting up the money."

It was atypical, especially for a first-time programmer like Rogers, but it wasn't outrageous. And besides, he had an ulterior motive for structuring the deal like that. Keeping an eye on the costs associated with each phase of the process would give him an insider's view of software publishing and would help him with his next goal, to set up his own publishing company and shut out the middlemen.

Rogers and the president shook hands on the deal, and the matter seemed settled. From somewhere in the back of the office, a woman came flying out. "I'm the one who makes the decisions because I'm the one who put the money in the company," she announced. She told Rogers the terms of the handshake deal were off the table. She would give him a straight percentage of sales and that was all. The money might not have been much different, but he wouldn't get access to the accounting and cost information he wanted to learn enough to start his own publishing company.

> The closing ceremony at the 2014 Winter Paralympics in Sochi, Russia, was built around a Tetris theme.

Rogers was essentially living off of the generosity of his in-laws, so he felt pressure to agree to the new terms. This was more than a deal to sell some games; it was a deal to feed his family. Anyone else in the same situation might have taken the revised deal and hoped to sell enough games to cover his costs and maybe make a bit of a profit. But Rogers knew selling one software program through a publisher wasn't the long game he needed to play. Without knowing where he'd turn next, he said, "If we don't have a deal, we don't have a deal," and walked away. It was an incredible gamble, for a first-time game maker working on his own with no track record, to leave even a compromised publishing deal on the table.

But luck was on his side, and Rogers found a friendlier set of ears at SoftBank, the next company he approached. Later a major media company, at the time SoftBank was just a midsize distributor of computer software. Rogers went into a meeting, Black Onyx prototype in hand, and asked for an introduction to a publisher he could work with. In the shorthand of the day, a publisher produced software disks and provided advertising and marketing for a new game or application; a distributor handled the physical task of storing the retail product in warehouses and shipping it to stores.

The advice he got was unexpected. You don't need a publisher, he was told. "All you need to do is get your wife to answer the phone. We'll introduce you to a company that can duplicate your game for you, and then you can pay them when we pay you." It was an intriguing idea. Rogers could simply pay to have Black Onyx floppy disks made, and SoftBank promised to buy three thousand copies of the game to sell through to stores. Akemi helped him incorporate as a business, and she answered the phone to make this one-man operation appear at least a little like a Japanese software company.

By the time Rogers had gone over every bug and error his game-testing friends had found and the game was completed, it was getting late in 1983. Christmas, although not as big a deal as it was in the West, was a popular season for gift giving, and that was the targeted date for putting The Black Onyx on sale. Rogers was confident enough in his efforts that he made the risky decision to price his game at a significant premium over other Japanese computer games. It would cost 7,800 yen rather than the more common 6,800 yen. You could play this game for at least forty hours, he thought. That ought to be worth something extra.

With that settled, the final steps were to commission some eye-catching cover art and buy advertisements in Japanese computer magazines.

For the art, he turned to a college friend back in Hawaii, who was able to turn in a glorious-looking painting straight out of a 1970s dorm room poster. In the style of cult fantasy artist Frank Frazetta, it pictured a muscled, bare-chested hero swinging a sword atop a pile of fallen enemies. It was an impressive image but wouldn't tell anyone, especially Japanese audiences unfamiliar with epic fantasy storytelling, what the game was really about. When the art went into magazine ads, using the last of Rogers's capital, it elicited almost zero response.

SoftBank had promised to order three thousand copies by Christmas, but that promise also vanished into thin air. "Sorry, we can only order six hundred copies," he was told, and Rogers felt a cloud of doom falling over his all-or-nothing enterprise. Worse still was sitting by the phone, waiting for orders to come in. During the first month after the game's official release, the company received only a single phone inquiry.

Rogers went into crisis mode, changing up his game plan in a desperate attempt to get anyone in Japan interested in The Black Onyx. He ripped up the existing advertisements, threw out the epic but unrepresentative art, and replaced it with simple screenshots. If only people could see what the game actually looked like, from the custom characters to the simulated 3D look of the maze-like dungeons, someone might take a chance on it.

The changes were a step in the right direction, but only a small one. The next month, Roger sold four copies.

With his savings and seed money gone and cartons of game disks sitting around collecting dust, Rogers had one more desperate shot before he'd have to return to the gem business and beg the family to take him back.

At the time there were about five major computer magazines in Japan. Some specialized in games, but others were general-interest magazines for computer enthusiasts that included game coverage and other topics. He had purchased advertising space in a few, but that had been no guarantee any of them would write about or review the game, and in fact, none of them had.

In January 1984, Rogers hired a translator and went door to door, visiting the offices of each computer magazine and offering to give the editors a hands-on demonstration of The Black Onyx. The game was different enough that the magazines all agreed to at least see him, unsure of what exactly to expect.

It was a long shot for a foreigner who hardly spoke the language to walk into a series of editorial meetings with a new type of game none of them had ever played before. Working out a new plan of attack to pitch the dubious magazine editors, Rogers called forth a natural salesman's instinct.

At the start of each meeting, Rogers and his translator greeted the magazine editors. "What is your name?" he asked each subject, entering the response into the Black Onyx character creator. He then asked them to pick from the body and head options to create the most similar-to-reality personal avatar for the game. If these journalists play a game with a character that looks like them and has their name, Rogers reasoned, they might be more likely to keep playing.

Speaking through his translator, he taught the editors to play the game, and then left them on their own to discover the massive virtual world he had created. Back at home, time crawled by with little movement. SoftBank wasn't ordering any more copies, and the phone was hardly ringing.

Then the April issues of the major Japanese computer magazines hit newsstands. Each one carried a long, detailed, and enthusiastic review of The Black Onyx. His hands-on gambit had worked. Within a month, ten thousand copies of the game sold. The next month, another ten thousand copies, and the month after, still another ten thousand. Japanese gamers could not get enough.

By the end of 1984, The Black Onyx was the best-selling computer game in Japan, and Henk Rogers was hard at work on a sequel. But the entrenched major players in the Japanese gaming world would not slumber for long while a one-man company run by a foreigner took top honors in their industry. Over the next two years, games such as Dragon Quest and Final Fantasy took The Black Onyx's success and appropriated it, becoming enduring hits that would go on for decades. The Black Onyx, though pioneering in its time, is remembered today only as a footnote, the first fantasy role-playing game in Japan.

Rogers had to find a new niche in the competitive game publishing world; otherwise, he'd be little more than a one-hit wonder.

6

■ ■ ■ ■ ■

GOING VIRAL

By the time the ideas for Tetris were first coming to life on Alexey Pajitnov's Electronica 60 computer, the game's creator was already twenty-eight years old. Well past the age when most twenty-first-century dotcom CEOs founded their first company, Pajitnov was still considered a young go-getter by the conservative standards of the Russian Academy of Sciences. But that didn't mean there wasn't a motivated new generation, one that had come of age in the era of the modern microcomputer, waiting in the wings to make a mark.

One such eighties digital native was Vadim Gerasimov, a Moscow high school student with an interest in computers far beyond what the limited equipment available in his high school classroom could satisfy. For a sixteen-year-old hoping to land on the cutting edge of the Soviet technology industry, it was frustrating to see glimpses of advanced computer technology in snippets of foreign television shows and movies and to know the latest hardware was so far out of reach.

He was a gifted teen, perhaps picking it up from his scientist mother. People around him tended to notice this, and a high school teacher named Arkady Borkovsky took it upon himself to act as a mentor to this young man, introducing Gerasimov to people he knew at the Dorodnitsyn Computing Centre. During their first visit, the computer lab must have seemed like a science-fiction movie set to the high school student.

He became a frequent visitor to the center. In fact the staff programmers couldn't keep him away. Vadim took an instant shine to the slowly growing rows of IBM PCs available there, and after ingratiating himself with some of the researchers at the center, he started learning how to code for those MS-DOS machines. Teaching himself advanced coding at a rapid pace, Gerasimov soon caught the attention of the researchers at the center.

One of them was Dmitry Pavlovsky, a colleague and friend of Alexey Pajitnov's who had provided invaluable coding and testing feedback on the original version of Tetris. Pavlovsky was impressed with Gerasimov's work on a directory encryption program and confided to his new friend that he had been working on some computer game programs, still a somewhat heretical idea at the time. But Pavlovsky's games to date had a fatal flaw, even before considering their value as entertaining games: they had been programmed not on consumer-level hardware but instead on the center's massive mainframe computers, the kind of room-sized machines that were already painfully outdated.

Pavlovsky waved the young student over. Perhaps I could show you some of my games, he offered, hoping to enlist Gerasimov's help in converting the software to work on MS-DOS systems. Then as now, few computer-savvy sixteen-year-olds wouldn't jump at a chance to work on video games, and Gerasimov quickly agreed. Together they ran through a few of the projects, and Pavlovsky provided Gerasimov the source code for one of them.

Less than twenty-four hours later, Gerasimov was back. In one day the teen had a nearly identical version of Pavlovsky's program up and running on one of the center's IBM PCs, an impressive feat in translating software between two completely different computer ecosystems.

Having an IBM-compatible version of one of his programs was certainly satisfying for Pavlovsky, but this had been more than a simple coding exercise. In reality, it was a test, with the subject unaware that he was being vetted for an opportunity to work on a much more important project.

With Gerasimov having successfully proved his skills, Pavlovsky felt confident introducing the high schooler to another programmer at the RAS, Alexey Pajitnov. Emboldened by his special status as a teenager with access to an advanced postgraduate computer lab, Gerasimov could hold his own in technical conversation with his older colleagues, and in fact already looked and acted the part of a veteran programmer, hunching over his computer keyboard with singular determination, unkempt curly hair shaggily hanging down to the top of his wireframe glasses.

Even in those early conversations, both Pavlovsky and Pajitnov could tell Gerasimov had already surpassed their own technical skill, and he spoke the language of coding as only someone born into the computer era could. By the age when Pajitnov had only just touched his first primitive computer, Gerasimov was fluent in programming languages such as Pascal and Basic, and the MS-DOS platform, and he displayed a special talent for debugging the work of others. He could find coding errors that stopped software from operating properly and correct the thinking and syntax so that it worked as intended.

Pajitnov sensed he was talking to the right guy to help him take his own game development to the next level. Gerasimov had developed a reputation as a troubleshooter, and he even made a habit of debugging the work of the older computer scientists in exchange for a few bucks in pocket money.

The team of Pajitnov, Pavlovsky, and Vadim Gerasimov brainstormed ideas into the night at the Dorodnitsyn lab. None of them aimed to be hardcore capitalists or even to buck the Soviet system more than any other overeducated and curious young person. But the idea of actually producing and selling computer programs lurked in the backs of their minds. Perhaps a series of games could be packaged together into one bundle that would have commercial value, they thought. Gerasimov even called this umbrella package the Computer FunFair, which showed initiative, if not exactly a keen ear for entertainment marketing.

But the barriers—legal, bureaucratic, and psychological—seemed insurmountable. Gerasimov in particular found the idea of producing and selling a work of intellectual property, an ethereal concept compared to selling a painting or a bookcase, difficult to get his head around. It would all be looked at as highly irregular, he argued to his compatriots, having had few if any examples in his own life of entre-preneurial risk taking.

Instead, the trio tabled that idea for the moment and focused on honing their respective skills at designing, tweaking, and program-ming games. Pajitnov watched his young friend carefully, holding his own work on what would eventually become Tetris close to the vest until he was sure Gerasimov was up to the task of working on such a potentially important project.

Some of what they worked on were re-created versions of the handful of Western computer games that had snuck behind the walls of the computing center. Other times, they added to a growing li-brary of code snippets and techniques for adding pseudographics, text, and sound to game programs. One of the only projects from that era that still exists, called Antix, was spearheaded by Pavlovsky.

Even behind the Iron Curtain, content creators shared the same dirty little secret: they copied the work of others. Imitation was not only the sincerest form of flattery but also the best way to kick-start your own creative endeavors, by starting with something already considered successful and morphing it to your own needs.

That's exactly what happened with Pavlovsky's game, Antix. It was, depending on who you ask, an homage or a knockoff of a West-ern PC game named Xonix. In fact, the project was coded under the original name Antixonix, just in case anyone was unclear about what Pavlovsky and Gerasimov were working on.

If you've never heard of Xonix, originally released in 1984, don't worry; few have. The game was itself a version of a much more pop-ular game from the early days of the video arcade, Qix. Although it's largely forgotten now, Qix was a reasonably reliable B-list entry in standup arcade game cabinets for years after its 1981 release by Japa-nese video game publisher Tatio, itself best known for the arcade classic Space Invaders.

Somewhat more abstract than the overly literal ghosts and giant apes of contemporaries such as Pac-Man and Donkey Kong, Qix appealed to an older, arguably more intellectual crowd. The appeal to Pajitnov and his crew was obvious—like Tetris, the game was one of spatial relations and improvised architecture.

A game of Qix, or Xonix/Antix, starts with a blank field. In the original arcade version of Qix, the player's on-screen avatar is a small diamond shape, which travels the screen making only 90-degree turns. The diamond-shaped avatar leaves a trail behind itself, in the form of a thin white line, little more than a linear series of white pixels against the black screen background.

By using those vertical and horizontal lines to close off space within the larger rectangular playfield, the player seals off sections of the screen, which are then filled in with a solid color, indicating that they are off-limits for the remainder of the level. Making this more than an exercise in drawing a gigantic box is the titular Qix. An enemy that won't make it into the video game bad guys hall of fame anytime soon, the Qix is a simple, short, one-pixel-wide line that twirls end over end like a possessed majorette's baton as it traverses the screen. Touch the randomly flipping and flopping Qix, and it's game over.

It gets harder and harder to avoid the Qix as you shrink the field. Seal off 75 percent of the screen and you move to the next level.

Other challenges and enemies come into play, but that's the game at its most basic. For an industry that even in the late seventies and early eighties was locked into rote fantasy and sci-fi tropes, from Defender to Bubble Bobble (the latter being Tatio's only other major hit), it's surprising something so abstract made it past a pitch meeting, much less became a staple of arcades and taverns for a short time.

The reason you probably don't remember Qix, assuming you're old enough to have stepped foot in a genuine 1980s video game arcade, is that its initial novelty wore off quickly. With little new to be found on subsequent levels and no colorful characters or backstory to keep players engaged, it lacked legs. Tatio executives would later lament that this abstract game—essentially a series of colored lines and blocks—was simply conceptually too mystifying for most gamers.

Nevertheless, the game maintained a small cadre of loyal followers, many of whom apparently programmed their own versions and unofficial sequels, hence games such as Xonix, Antix, Styx, Fortix, and others. The idea of using a video game to play with space and structure, with no distracting narrative elements or cartoonish mascots, was a good one. It just turns out that Qix and its successors were not the right formula at the right time. And without the contributions of Dmitry Pavlovsky and Vadim Gerasimov, Tetris may have suffered the same fate.

But with a ready audience of computer science and math types with access to at least some computer hardware, Antix made sense as a project for the RAS programmers to practice on. Xonix, the game it was based on, was one of the few mainstream video games people at the computing center had access to and were able to pass around freely. It became a minor viral hit well before Tetris did, ending up on nearly every compatible computer at the Dorodnitsyn center, and it even filtered out onto some of the very small handful of personal computers in Moscow at the time.

Alexey Pajitnov was impressed with Gerasimov's programming skills, especially considering he was just a high school student. His friend Pavlovsky had impeccable timing, introducing them to each other just as a key new idea was coming to fruition. After they first started working together, Pajitnov took Gerasimov aside and offered to show him a special project, something unlike anything any of them had worked on before.

Tetris, both the name and the final idea, was still months away. But Pajitnov already spoke endlessly of puzzles and games, and how the two disciplines could come together. Gerasimov was intrigued by this kind of talk and eager to see and try a fully functioning game designed and programmed by Pajitnov, to learn whether the result could live up the rhetoric.

But, on the screen, it was clear that this game, currently closer to Pajitnov's original pre-Tetris Genetic Engineering prototype, was not the answer. Gerasimov tapped on the cursor buttons to move the four-segment tetromino pieces around the screen, assembling different shapes, but the whole exercise seemed pointless to him. He wasn't sure what the goal of the game was, and besides that, the execution felt dull.

Gerasimov shrugged. Not every idea is a great one, and the trio of programmers had many other paths to explore. If Pajitnov was disappointed in the lukewarm reception, he didn't show it. In fact, he knew quite well that his initial version of the game didn't quite click.

But there was still something to the idea of combining a child's pentomino puzzle with an interactive computer experience, and he had latched on to it like a pit bull. The wheels were already turning in his head on a revamped version of the game, a project that would eventually come to be called Tetris.

A few months after Genetic Engineering's disappointing showing, and after Pavlovsky, with Gerasimov's help, had completed their Antix version of the Qix/Xonix game, Pajitnov was ready to give the tetromino another shot. At one of the trio's regular brainstorming sessions, he announced a new concept that included some of the elements of the earlier game but in a more pointed, challenging version.

Take the tetrominoes, he explained, and picture them falling into a tall, narrow, rectangular glass and piling up at the bottom. The idea certainly sounded better than the listless assembly of shapes in Genetic Engineering. But, at least for now, Pajitnov wasn't looking for programming input from his friends. The next time Gerasimov and Pavlovsky heard more about the tetrominoes and the glass container, Pajitnov had finished his solo coding marathon and had the first version of the game up and running on his Electronica 60 computer.

This time, everything that felt wrong about the first prototype now felt right. The game was as simple as a game could be, lacking color, sounds, anything but the most rudimentary improvised graphics, and without even a scoring system. But the key elements were there. Gerasimov and Pavlovsky watched as Pajitnov, wired after weeks of frantic late-night coding, walked them through the game he called Tetris.

The tutorial was unnecessary. As much as video games themselves might have been a foreign language to most Russians, even computer programmers, Tetris defied such barriers, presenting its meaning and methodology through pure design, requiring nothing in the way of written instructions or diagrams. Start playing, and the game's rules and features became immediately evident, tapping into the same basic primordial instinct that leads toddlers to stack blocks into ever-higher towers.

The name sounds a bit strange, Gerasimov commented. Even after Pajitnov's explanation of the contraction of *tetromino* and *tennis*, his friends never quite got why such a level of abstraction was needed.

And besides, it sounded more than a bit foreign, and 1984 in the Soviet Union was not the time or the place to come off as less than committedly patriotic.

Pajitnov insisted. Just as he had kept the development of Tetris away from his collaborative efforts with Gerasimov and Pavlovsky, the name of the game would also be his personal stamp on the project.

But now that the first official version of Tetris was fully coded and stable, Pajitnov had a problem. Although still not publicly espousing the tenets of capitalism, the idea of having a salable product had never completely left his mind. Yet, the game in its current form, though hypnotizingly fun and already building some word-of-mouth buzz around the computer center, wasn't something anyone would pay a single ruble to own.

The complications with Tetris were manifold. First, although the design and gameplay elements were brilliant, both because of and despite its forced minimalism, any version that might be a commercial success would need a substantial amount of polishing.

Films and television had become increasingly sophisticated over the past decade, especially in how they presented special effects. Even if most Soviet citizens had not had a chance to see *Star Wars* and its sequels—which never received widespread release in the USSR—they were aware of the imagery and the larger cultural phenomenon. And the USSR had its own proud tradition of high-concept science fiction, first in novels and later in films (often based on the same novels) such as *Solaris* and *Stalker,* which made economical but effective use of the country's limited expertise in cinematic special effects.

In the face of this, Pajitnov's version of Tetris, with its tetromino shapes constructed of special keyboard characters strung together like ASCII illustrations (those dubious works of early computer art, often jokey, constructed entirely of letters, numbers, and symbols), felt primitive. The primary purpose of a game, computer-based or otherwise, was a competition of some sort, either pitting one player against another or a player against the game itself (in that sense, Tetris is similar to solitaire). But the lack of score recording and record keeping meant each game was an island unto itself, offering no historical record of extraordinary performance or memorable feats.

Even as early as 1981, video game players in America were recording and sharing their high scores on arcade machines. Score-keeping organizations such as Twin Galaxies celebrated top players with a kind of low-level celebrity and, more importantly, kept the focus of eighties gaming firmly on this kind of man-versus-machine (or man-versus-man) competition.

Another factor was that the most successful games imported from Japan or America were built around fanciful storylines and cartoon-like characters. Pac-Man was already making his way from arcades to home consoles to cereal boxes and television screens, and even an early minimalist classic such as Space Invaders pretty much spelled out its B-movie sci-fi plot in two brilliantly chosen words. It lent drama and energy to a stripped-down shooting game, a marketing feat worthy of Roger Corman.

Tetris could have succeeded missing one or two or more of these features. But lacking graphics, scoring, sound, a storyline, and characters, it was simply too abstract to appeal beyond the very narrow audience of fellow computer programmers to be found in the halls of the computing center.

And there was a further problem beyond all of that: Pajitnov had programmed his game on his Electronica 60 computer. Tying the game to this very idiosyncratic computer, itself a knockoff of an already-outdated Western computer, made it very hard to share Tetris. Few people, even at the RAS, had an Electronica 60, and certainly no one purchasing a computer for the first time would choose this machine or platform. Pajitnov had essentially programmed a brilliant first draft of a game that only he and a handful of others could play.

The tide was turning toward computers created by IBM that ran MS-DOS, which presaged the Windows operating system that still runs on a vast majority of the world's personal computers today.

More importantly, the IBM ecosystem was widely shared. Unlike the early Apple computers, which had found a cult following in the late 1970s and early 1980s, the first IBM PC (released in 1981) was simple enough that creative computer entrepreneurs could effectively reverse-engineer it. They could create their own computers that looked and behaved like the more expensive official IBM versions and, above all, ran the same software. Thanks to a loosely defined licensing agreement between IBM and a then-unknown software company named Microsoft, these newer computer companies, such as Compaq and Texas Instruments, could build and sell desktop machines that came to be called IBM clones, described with the ubiquitous phrase "IBM-compatible."

Besides being cheaper to produce and easier to use, these IBM-style systems had BIOS (basic low-level instructions that define many of the computer's underlying functions and behaviors) firmware that allowed software to communicate with hardware in a faster and more efficient manner than ever before, effectively cutting out a middle translation step earlier types of computers required. That made the IBM and other MS-DOS computers a fast new favorite of amateur and professional game programmers, because the systems could react to much more complex instructions and user input instantaneously.

These machines could also display code output with basic graphics and colors. They broke free of the monochrome displays of older machines, which were nearly all limited to the same 128 alphanumeric characters first codified in the original ASCII standard of 1963 (with some variations for different countries, such as the Cyrillic alphabet used in the Russian language).

For better or worse, the IBM style of computer was becoming the new standard around the world and in the Soviet Union, and Alexey's Pajitnov's Tetris game code was completely incompatible with it.

Fortunately, Pajitnov had a secret weapon: sixteen-year-old Vadim Gerasimov, who had already proven himself adept at translating software to the MS-DOS platform and who often added his own improvements and ideas along the way.

Although the final stable code was only a few days old, Tetris was already an underground hit among Pajitnov's small circle of computer engineer colleagues. They lined up to play the game on one of the few compatible computers at the center or else obtained a copy of the original code if they were lucky enough to have an Electronica 60 or another DEC computer clone to work on.

When Pajitnov first approached Gerasimov, the idea of putting together a collection of games and somehow finding a way to sell them as a commercial product was still hanging in the air. Some of the games up for consideration had been joint projects (most lost to history), and some, like Antix, were primarily the work of Pavlovsky. But Tetris was Pajitnov's project from the start. He had conceptualized and coded the original version as a one-man show, talking little to others about the game's in-progress development after the initial disappointing feedback that his Genetic Engineering prototype received.

Tetris needed to break free of its original limited audience and go live on the increasingly popular IBM and IBM clone platforms. This was a task that seemed well suited for someone like Gerasimov, with a natural talent for translating ideas between computer languages. But it was more complex than it might have seemed. Whereas modern computer programmers can take the highest-level source code for a project and compile different versions to run on different hardware, hence Mac and PC versions of the same software, or even video games that run on both the Xbox and the PlayStation platforms, eighties programmers faced a much more involved process.

In modern translation, some additional work is required to get the program working on different devices, but the bulk of the coding remains unchanged. Back in the mid-1980s, translating a program from one computing platform to another was a decidedly more analog affair. Gerasimov couldn't simply recompile Pajitnov's source code to run on MS-DOS; instead, he had to observe the first-draft Tetris game in action, pore over the original code line by line, and quite literally re-create the game from scratch, hoping to make his new version look and run as similarly to the original as possible. It was reverse-engineering, eighties style, and for years remained a standard way to copy simple software from one platform to another.

Gerasimov could tell the original version of the game was already highly playable and even addictive, despite its minimalist design and lack of features that most games included automatically. But even with his deep skill set, creating the next version of the game was a nerve-wracking task, especially working under Pajitnov's watchful eye. The teenager was not overly familiar with the Electronica 60 hardware and had in fact never actually programmed one.

He got to work immediately. The IBM-compatible version of Tetris would be written in Pascal, a programming language the most serious of hardcore coders looked down on, but one well suited for flashy consumer projects. Pajitnov pushed his young friend, and the first version of Tetris on an IBM PC was up and running in only a few days.

But a mere translation wasn't enough for Pajitnov, Gerasimov, and Pavlovsky. This prototype IBM version didn't stay the same for more than a day or two at a time, and new ideas and features were added to a growing list of improvements.

Even on more advanced hardware, the IBM version of Tetris, with Gerasimov as the lead coder, didn't offer computer graphics on par with what PCs and home video game consoles were capable of at the time in the West. But it eventually did offer a splash of visual design, much more appealing than the monochrome bracket-and-space representations on the Electronica 60, thanks to a new feature that was among the most pivotal ever added to the game, and one that remains one of the most recognizable elements of Tetris, even decades later.

After several weeks of updating, recording, and testing, Gerasimov implemented the breakthrough idea of representing the tetromino pieces in color, using on-screen spacers filled in with primary colors. Even today, the current Tetris visual brand language and official game rules define the pieces by color just as much as by shape, and sharp-eyed players can zero in on a piece and its optimal placement almost from the first flash of color, before their eyes can discern which of the seven distinct tetromino shapes it is.

Gerasimov's color palette was darker and more subdued (and perhaps more Russian) than the modern version's. The long four-segment bar was represented by a deep red color, like dried blood, and the troublesome Z shape was the dark cyan of a stormy Moscow sky. Today, in contrast, the official standardized colors approved by the game's owners run from bright orange to lime green.

Along the way, the team added new elements and features, numbering subsequent builds in a haphazard way that somehow ended with version 3.12 after dozens of distinct evolutionary versions.

Besides Gerasimov's colorful blocks, Pavlovsky made a prime contribution by adding a behind-the-screens data table that recorded and presented high scores. This was an important competitive element that lured players into playing over and over again in hopes of beating a high score and recording their own for posterity.

Pajitnov played through version 3.12 of the game. Two months after work started on the IBM version of Tetris, this felt like a good place to stop and try to find a larger audience. Although similar in its broad strokes to Pajitnov's original Electronica 60 version, the IBM version had been coded from scratch and was vastly superior in every way. It looked better, played better, kept score like a standard video game, and, more importantly, worked on a much wider range of computers.

Most of the raw code for this build came from Vadim Gerasimov, but despite the additions and new ideas he and Pavlovsky added along the way, the core DNA of the game still belonged exclusively to Alexey Pajitnov. It still played like a modern version of the pentomino puzzles that had captivated Alexey as a child.

Gerasimov was intrigued by his older friend's interest in commercializing Tetris as well as some of the other games the informal team had worked on but always kept such ideas at arm's length. His position as a favored visitor at the computing center was somewhat tenuous; even as a gifted programmer, he was underage and the Russian Academy of Sciences could not offer him an official position even if it wanted to. So, he was essentially a ghost employee, working in the margins, just as Pajitnov was dedicated to a ghost project, one not sanctioned by the computing center's managers. And, in any case, if there was a way to turn Tetris—clearly the star of any of the games they had developed—into something that could be bought and sold, the academy would have the most legitimate claim to its ownership.

Even working through the permutations of such ideas made Gerasimov uncomfortable. The kind of private business arrangements required to form an agreement to manufacture or distribute software were simply unheard of.

That would all change soon enough. The following year, 1985, brought to power a new general secretary of the Communist Party of the Soviet Union, an unexpected reformer named Mikhail Gorbachev. Within three years, Soviet citizens would be legally allowed to form their own commercial ventures and reap the potential profits. But Tetris arrived just a few years too early to be a test case for economic liberalization.

So, to Gerasimov, any talk of commercialization was purely hypothetical, and that was probably for the best. He had already gotten an advanced personal curriculum in computer programming and access to a wide range of hard-to-find equipment by spending his free time at the computing center, and that made the entire experiment more than worthwhile.

Despite his lack of interest in commercializing Tetris, Gerasimov was pleased to see that the early versions of the game on the IBM PC bore the following credit line on the title screen, just below the bright red Tetris logo: "game by A. Pajitnov and V. Gerasimov." It was an on-screen credit that would not last, but for a while, it was payment enough for the high school student.

For Pajitnov, the idea of turning an idea that lived only in the recorded memory of the computer into a product that could be sold was far from hypothetical. But where to begin? His experience with the business world, even the limited Soviet version of it, was practically nonexistent. His personal history was little help: both his parents were writers, and like successive generations of Russians, he had little in the way of positive role models of entrepreneurship to look up to or learn from.

In true Soviet style, it was better, he concluded, to operate via backchannels, informally. There was no doubt that Tetris had the addictive qualities of a great game. Pajitnov's fellow researchers clamored for a turn at the game, and some demanded their own copies of the code, on 5.25-inch floppy disks, to install and run on their computers.

Thanks to Gerasimov's continuous code fixes and troubleshooting, the IBM-compatible version of Tetris had arrived at such a stable state that it would work across the vast majority of MS-DOS computers floating around the computing center at the time, even though those machines had different internal components and even ran at different clock speeds. The unsung hero of the 3.12 build of Tetris was a series of timer delays that ensured the Tetris pieces would fall at the proper rate, even on a faster computer.

Guinness World Records recognizes Tetris as being the "most-ported" game in history. It appears on more than sixty-five different platforms.

That was especially important because each successive generation of computer hardware ratcheted up processor speed, a silicon arms race that continues to this day. It got to the point that very early PC games often sped up to comical levels when played on even slightly newer systems. On-screen avatars would race around like characters in a Benny Hill skit, and in-game cues for user input would fly by too quickly for any human to react to in time, rendering many games unplayable on computers that were even just six months newer.

For Tetris, the fact that a game so dependent on split-second timing would work identically on nearly any of the growing number of IBM-compatible computers was a clincher. Without those timer delays, the game might have vanished as quickly as tetromino segments in a completed line.

The successive requests for copies of the game gave Pajitnov an idea, and it was one that feels very modern, even today. He would copy the executable code for Tetris, along with Antix and few other games he had worked on with Gerasimov and Pavlovsky, onto a series of disks and hand them out to those who showed the most interest in his work.

Still starstruck by the older programmer, Gerasimov helped him with the laborious process of making copies of their game disk, one at a time, and handing them out to trusted colleagues and friends. The name might have long since been abandoned, but in some sense the Computer FunFair concept would live on.

In the thirty years since, little has changed in how creative works from independent artists or small companies are distributed. Music is handed out freely, played without cost on streaming services such as Spotify, or given away as free download cards from Starbucks. Games, especially those played on mobile phones or tablets—the biggest growth area of the industry by far—are essentially all free to play. The modern twist is that most now use a model called "free-mium," which offers a basic version of a game for free, with the promise of added features for those who pay to unlock or download them.

If the backend technology had existed at the time, perhaps Alexey Pajitnov would have distributed Tetris as a freemium game. It was certainly addictive enough to draw players in for hours at a time. A version of the game that allowed only a certain number of levels or tetromino shapes or that limited playtime to fifteen minutes or even an hour at a time could have been a powerful narcotic for early players. Of course, those players would need a way to pay to unlock the full version of the game, and reliable, trusted methods of conducting such microtransactions are a relatively recent invention, only becoming accepted in the last several years.

So, without the business model for selling his game, or the technology to allow players to buy it, the only option open to Pajitnov was to simply give it away. And when you give something addictive away for free, there's always a chance it will spread out of control, like a wildfire. Fueled by the beginnings of the widespread personal computer era, the first inklings of glasnost in the Soviet Union, and the perfect combination of Pajitnov's concepts and Gerasimov's programming skills, Tetris did just that.

It was an especially amazing feat because it wasn't as if Moscow, or any other city in Russia, was teeming with personal computers. Such devices were commonplace in homes and classrooms in the United States and Europe, thanks to cheap, mass-produced PCs. But in the USSR, computers were largely restricted to universities and research institutions, plus a few government offices. If you were lucky enough to have a personal computer in your home at the time, it was very likely acquired through black market backchannels, with all the added legal risk and inflated prices that accompanied any such smuggled consumer goods at the time. It's been estimated that up to 90 percent of the PCs in Eastern Bloc countries in the eighties were obtained in this manner.

But still, in a country as large as the Soviet Union, tens of thousands of computers were in operation at the time, and a large percentage of those were in Moscow, within easy reach of Tetris game disks, which were largely distributed by hand, palmed off between meetings at workplaces or cautiously carried to a friend's apartment after hours. Today, we call that method of distribution "sneakernet," which means to physically carry a hard copy of a program or file to a recipient. With only the most basic level of early computer networking available on a handful of machines at the top research think tanks and military facilities, sneakernet was a surprisingly effective way to distribute digital information right under the noses of the authorities.

Vladimir Pokhilko didn't consider himself "the authorities," but nonetheless, he had a problem. He was a clinical psychology researcher at the Moscow Medical Center and a casual acquaintance of Alexey Pajitnov. He was an early recipient of one of Pajitnov's hand-copied floppy disks with Tetris on it and soon fired the game up on one of the computers his team used at the medical center.

The addictive nature of the game was immediately obvious to him. Manipulating the tetrominoes with his keyboard, Pokhilko experienced the satisfying high of completing a line and watching it vanish from the screen as well as the vexation of misplacing a piece and trapping himself in an inevitable pileup that soon reached the top of the playing field and brought the game to an abrupt halt.

As a psychologist, he could intellectualize what was happening to his brain and how he was being manipulated by what he called the game's "emotional dynamics." For a researcher primarily interested in the analog vagaries of the human brain, the idea of using computer games, with their rigid rule sets and pitiless progression, suddenly felt like an undiscovered country ready for exploration.

Pokhilko was not the only one who felt that way. In his early excitement about the game, he had made copies of the original disk and passed them around the medical center to fellow researchers. He should have known better; his team was soon hooked on Tetris, a response propagated around the city in tech-centric enclaves, where people had access to computer hardware and copies of the game were starting to pass freely from person to person.

The next time he saw Pajitnov, Pokhilko cornered him, saying, "I can't live with your Tetris anymore," with mock seriousness. One night, after the last round had been played, and another day's work had gone half-done, Pokhilko tarried at his desk. Checking around each workstation to make sure no Tetris addicts were still lurking, he quickly gathered every copy of the Tetris disk he could find and destroyed them all.

But that was not the end of Pokhilko's involvement with Tetris. The game was not so easily banished from his lab, and new copies turned up in short order. At least the staff was slightly more circumspect about balancing playtime with work the second time around. Pokhilko would use the game in psychological testing of patients, and over the next couple of years, he worked with Pajitnov and Gerasimov to create a unique two-player version of the game, with an eye toward observing how players interacted with each other as well as with the game itself.

In that build, similar to competitive modes still found in some versions of the game, the long, narrow playing field had no true top or bottom. Tetrominoes floated down from the top for one player and up from the bottom for the second. They competed to stack shapes in the shared center, each experiencing space and gravity in opposite ways. Pokhilko was the first to use Tetris as a tool for medical research, recognizing its unique properties early on, but he wouldn't be the last.

Outside the Dorodnitsyn Computing Centre and the Moscow Medical Center, Tetris continued to spread, by word of mouth and by game disks traded hand to hand like precious bootleg movies or books from the West. The difference was that this was an entirely homegrown phenomenon, and something Russian computer programmers could be proud of. From Moscow, where it was played day and night under the noses of supervisors and administrators (many of whom were undoubtedly addicted to the game themselves), copies filtered to Saint Petersburg and any other Russian city where more than a handful of computers could be found.

Pajitnov kept tabs on the second-hand stories of Tetris's success and was amazed by the viral nature of the game. He had never seen anything like it. And though the reports he received were spotty and infrequent, Tetris generated a definite buzz among those lucky enough to be part of the select club of computer-savvy Soviets.

But for all the unexpected success of the game, Pajitnov's primary payoff was in the form of his name, with Vadim Gerasimov's, on the title screen of the IBM-compatible version. Copies may have been traded for favors between friends or colleagues, but not a single one was sold, officially or otherwise, and not an extra ruble came into his pockets.

In short order there would, in fact, be plenty of money to be made from the game, but those rubles, dollars, pounds, and yen would line a great many other pockets before Alexey Pajitnov's. And for that money to start flowing as unceasingly as falling tetromino pieces, Tetris would have to slip past the Iron Curtain out into the world.

7

■■■■

THIS IS YOUR
BRAIN ON TETRIS

The shapes and colors form out of nothing, flaring against the empty sky like falling meteors, only to fade back into the ether a moment later.

The phenomenon doesn't end there. New shapes replace the old, rotating through variations and permutations, never staying long enough to snap into full focus. To some, this feels like nothing more than a desert mirage, a half-remembered impression of something seen in waking life. To others, it's the aftereffects of a fireworks show playing against the negative space of closed eyes.

This is the mind's re-creation of light and movement, fired off from synapses fueled by the two most important codebases of human consciousness, repetition and time. This is the Tetris Effect, a term used in both medical and popular literature to describe the result of repetitive, pattern-based activity that eventually begins to shape the thoughts and imagination of an individual. Before the Tetris era, we may have called it a kind of hypnagogic imagery, literally a waking dream.

Vladimir Pokhilko, the clinical researcher forced to hide copies of his friend Alexey Pajitnov's new game from his coworkers at the Moscow Medical Center, was among the first in the scientific community to recognize the addictive qualities of Tetris. Even he could not have predicted that it would be addictive enough to literally alter the minds of long-term players.

The game, in its early days ricocheting around Moscow, proved itself to be a primary example of viral electronic content. Its addictive qualities were evident from the very start: Pajitnov spent extra days and weeks supposedly polishing and finishing his initial version of Tetris simply because he couldn't stop playing his own creation.

It's precisely because Tetris imprints itself as both procedural memory, which guides frequent repetition of action, and as spatial memory, which deals with our understanding of 2D and 3D shapes and how they interact, that the game is a singular trigger for the effect now named after it.

If while packing a car for a vacation you've seen the suitcases and coolers as tetrominoes slotting perfectly together, you've experienced a mild version of the Tetris Effect. If after playing Tetris, or one of its descendants, such as Bejeweled or Candy Crush Saga, you still see falling shapes or colored blocks in the periphery of your vision, you're one level deeper in. The most extreme examples literally re-wire the brain's ability to record information and retain memories, sometimes for good and sometimes for ill.

Despite its scientific bona fides, the name *Tetris Effect* has its origins not in an academic journal but instead in the pages of a publication that's done more for the popular acceptance of science and technology in the past twenty years than any other: *Wired* magazine.

Many people have experienced a lost weekend, sometimes lost to drugs and alcohol, sometimes to simple meditative contemplation. In 1990, writer Jeffrey Goldsmith lost six weeks to Tetris, and in doing so, he came to understand the powerful pharmatronic effect certain kinds of technology could have on people. It was a feeling so pronounced, he called it the Tetris Effect, a simple name that stuck and now has expanded to cover a wide variety of psychological phenomena.

Shortly before his descent into the depths of Tetris addiction, Goldsmith was just another member of Generation X, drifting and exploring different avenues of art and culture. At twenty-three, he moved from New York to Mexico for the same reasons so many leave the crowded urban centers: to find the solitude and inspiration to write a novel.

But something else found him in Mexico. His temporary home, a small town near the center of the country named Guanajuato, was host to the annual Festival Internacional Cervantino, a collection of theater, dance, photography, and more. It was there Goldsmith saw a performance by Natsu Nakajima, a Japanese performer of Butoh, a type of dance performance typified by ghostly white makeup and deliberately controlled slow-motion movements. It was enough to drive Goldsmith to move to Japan, where he delved further into Butoh culture and ended up working in advertising.

During a 1990 trip to New York from Japan, something unusual caught his eye amid the hustle of the city. Goldsmith paused to watch a man sitting in a parked car on a side street in Tribeca. The man was unaware he was being watched, instead engrossed with something small and gray held tightly in his hands. Leaning closer, Goldsmith could see the man was holding a Nintendo Game Boy device, still a relatively new invention, and was furiously concentrating on a game, which turned out to be Tetris.

Goldsmith was fascinated. After this initial encounter he was suddenly seeing the game everywhere, with Tetris zombies staring down at handheld game machines just as mobile phone addicts do today. He thought it was an interesting cultural moment, but nothing more, and filed it away in his head.

Goldsmith prepared to return to Japan. He planned to retreat to the countryside to work but first arranged to stay with a German friend in Tokyo for a week. To pass the time while his friend was at work, he impulsively picked up a Japanese version of the Game Boy machine he had seen people playing in New York. At the time, the Game Boy came packaged with a single game cartridge, Tetris.

The moment Goldsmith fired up Tetris on his very own Game Boy, things changed. His one-week visit bled past a month. He was chained to the game. He sat in a small but well-appointed guest room, at times venturing out only for food and batteries. He was self-aware enough to notice the effect the game had on him: when he would visit a convenience store, he'd buy snacks and other small items, and then nonchalantly toss a pack of AA batteries on the counter at the last minute, even though replenishing the power supply for his Game Boy was the real reason he was at the store in the first place.

Goldsmith wasn't quite sure what he hoped to get out of the experience, nor did he think about it in terms as concrete as achieving a certain high score. Instead, he progressed, level by level, battling the game day after day. But, on his occasional walks around Tokyo, he discovered he was mentally fitting cars, people, and buildings together. Not only did the game have an addictive hold over him but it was altering how he saw reality. The effect was not strong enough to blur the line between real life and fantasy, but his perception was being altered in a way that scientists had begun to understand. Goldsmith was not alone in his observations, and in the following years, several groups of researchers independently discovered Tetris as a perfect tool for cognitive research.

And then, after six weeks of an unquenchable Tetris addiction, Goldsmith experienced something completely unexpected. After he surpassed an incredibly high score—where the puzzle pieces descend so rapidly only someone who has spent countless hours honing his skills at the game could possibly react in time—the game ended. It didn't end with a crushing defeat at the hands of an errant tetromino. Instead, the tiny monochromatic screen of his Game Boy informed Goldsmith that he had won. He had beaten Tetris. The game celebrated his achievement with a short animation of Russian dancers kicking their way through a traditional folk dance, followed by another animated scene, this time of a space shuttle—an oddly American-looking space shuttle, just shy of having a giant NASA logo printed on it—lifting off from a launchpad and rocketing into the sky.

And that was that. Tetris was over. Goldsmith felt a great weight lifting from him. He couldn't believe it, but there was nothing left for him to accomplish in the game. While he was in the throes of addiction, the game provided something between a high and the wired feeling of climbing a steep learning curve. But once that learning curve was conquered, the need to play was over. He put the Game Boy down. From that moment on, its spell on him was broken.

He soon departed for the Japanese countryside, seeking solitude and creative inspiration. Although his Game Boy made the trip with him, it stayed stowed away and was not turned on once. Since those six weeks, Goldsmith has played Tetris a few times over the years, but only in the most casual way. That singular triumph in Tokyo was essentially the end of his Tetris-playing days. Once that space shuttle took off, the obsession to play never returned.

But, even though his days as an obsessive Tetris player were over, the questions the experience raised continued to bother him. How could he have become so addicted to a simple video game? What sort of mind was capable of conceiving such a deceptively simple puzzle? How was Tetris affecting other people? Was there really such a thing as Tetris addiction, or was he simply an outlier?

"I wondered if Tetris wasn't really some sort of electronic drug, a pharmatronic," he would later write, coining another term still used today, if not as widely as *Tetris Effect*.

Goldsmith eventually moved back to the United States and gave the game little further thought. About two years after his extended lost weekend of Tetris addiction, he was doing well as a freelance journalist, working for glossy newsstand magazines such as *Details*. After trading pitch ideas with the editors of one of the most forward-looking magazines in print at the time, he picked up an assignment from *Wired*. That monthly, combining elements of pop culture, science, and technology, was one of the only publications in the early 1990s where you could read about the growing interaction of technology and culture. It was written for a mainstream audience but without any dumbing down.

His *Wired* assignment started out simply enough and spoke directly to his personal experience—it was to interview Tetris creator Alexey Pajitnov.

But what seemed like an easy assignment turned into more of a bust. Goldsmith interviewed Pajitnov, who was by then living in the United States, several times by phone, spending a couple of hours trying to draw a compelling narrative about the game out of its creator. Totally nice guy, Goldsmith thought after his sessions with Pajitnov, but just not that interesting of an interview.

Goldsmith hunkered down with Kevin Kelly, *Wired*'s longtime executive editor, and the pair looked for ways to salvage what might have turned into a forgettable pop-culture interview. Kelly suggested converting the feature into a thought piece, driven less by Pajitnov, and more by Goldsmith's personal experiences and a further exploration of the nature of Tetris addiction.

Jumping at the idea, Goldsmith reached out to Pajitnov's old friend Vladimir Pokhilko, who had run into so much trouble with Tetris at the research clinic at the Moscow Medical Center. By then, Pokhilko had moved to San Francisco, where he briefly partnered with Pajitnov in a technology start-up called AnimaTek. Goldsmith also called on Dr. Richard Haier of the University of California, Irvine, who was simultaneously working on cognitive research projects that used Tetris as a tool to alter brain energy consumption and mental decision making.

He went back and asked Pajitnov specifically about the idea that Tetris is uniquely addictive among video games. Pajitnov denied it, telling Goldsmith, "Many people say that, but my feeling is it's more like music. Playing games is a very specific rhythmic and visual pleasure. For me, Tetris is some song which you sing and sing inside yourself and can't stop." And perhaps Pajitnov was right. But what is a catchy summer earworm that replays itself in your head over and over again if not a type of addiction?

Goldsmith's end result became one of the most-cited mainstream media articles on video games ever published. "This Is Your Brain on Tetris," from the May 1994 issue of *Wired* is credited with introducing both the concept of the Tetris Effect, or at least the modern version of this kind of persistent visuospatial memory effect, as well as the term *pharmatronic,* the idea that technology addiction could be laid squarely on the technology itself, not merely on the addict. Not bad for 775 words in a glossy newsstand magazine.

Since then, Goldsmith has continued to work in technology and media, usually giving no thought to his important place in the history of understanding the intersection between technology and cognition. But a couple of years ago, he was reminded of that while waiting in line at a grocery store in San Francisco. A woman at the checkout fitting groceries into paper bags with expert precision caught his eye, and he asked her how much she consciously thought about the process, or even if she saw grocery shapes fitting together in her sleep or while walking down the street.

Oh, no, she replied, I don't get the Tetris Effect from doing this job. Goldsmith was shocked to hear the term he coined in 1994 quoted back to him nearly twenty years later—and by a San Francisco grocery store clerk, not a scientist or game industry type.

"'Tetris Effect'? Where did you hear that term?" he asked.

"Oh, I learned about it in college," she said.

"What do you mean you learned about it in college? I think I coined that." Goldsmith went home after the grocery store encounter and Googled "Tetris Effect." Whereas those who study video games and technology and effects on long-term users had been using the term off and on for years, this was the first inkling Goldsmith had that it had crept into the mainstream public consciousness and, more, that he was widely credited with its naming, by sources from Wikipedia to *The New Yorker*.

But for those who study human cognition or the long-term effect of technology on people, the concept Goldsmith named has had a long and useful shelf life.

■■■

When we refer to Tetris or other games as addictive, it's not simply a clever turn of phrase to describe the pull toward achieving just one more level of Tetris, playing one more round of Candy Crush Saga, or winning a dozen more matches in multiplayer Halo. Because, as much as you might feel like playing some more instead of going to work, making dinner, or talking to friends and family, there's a big difference between playing a video game and sucking on a crack pipe, right?

Maybe. But there's a reason why many compelling online experiences, be they games or social media mentions, are often compared to drugs. That's because, far from being a harmless diversion, there's an identifiable addictive quality to some aspects of technology, which include gaming experiences. Perhaps that's why we all know people who claim to be "addicted" to Facebook, or their phones, or other technology hardware and services. It's not just a bit of colloquial wordplay, it's that each of these experiences can be classified as having a pharmatronic quality. That key descriptor refers to a technology experience, typically software-driven, that exhibits the same addictive qualities as a drug.

There are times when this pharmatronic quality is deliberately triggered, such as with high-tech contraptions for relaxation and meditation that use binaural sound and flashing or strobing lights. Usually the subject wears a set of goggles and headphones so that certain parts of the brain are activated for therapeutic effect.

The efficacy of these devices, typically found lurking in the back pages of Sharper Image or SkyMall catalogs, is debatable, to be generous. Over the years it's the unintentional pharmatronic effect, as exhibited in Tetris addiction, that has demonstrated real power and that has led to missed classes, late arrivals at the office, blown-off social outings, and long nights in bed, staring at a mobile phone or tablet, while your partner sleeps or stews next to you.

There are other types of technology addiction, to be sure. Social media addiction is one of the most commonly cited today, and saying you are addicted to Facebook carries varying levels of social stigma, depending on how your friends and family feel about your oversharing timeline updates. But Facebook addiction is driven by social pressure and a pull toward conformity as well as the anxious wait for a dopamine hit upon receiving a new "like" or notification. The pharmatronic effect of Tetris is better explained by the hypnotic rhythms of the game and its simple, geometric patterns, with the constant stream of immediate closed-loop feedback hooking unconscious triggers into the waking mind.

Humans are always looking to rewire their thinking, whether by drugs, therapy, or meditation. Some are looking for a competitive edge, a sharper connection to consciousness, some for creative inspiration, and others for relief from the physical or mental aftereffects of trauma.

So, the warning that Tetris can change your mental state and can literally rewire memory or perception, sometimes permanently, can be seen as an opportunity by some. For scientists and doctors, the Tetris Effect is a chance to explore the brain's plasticity, or its ability to change and adapt to new input. This is especially true if that input hits certain metrics, namely, that it's simple, repeated for long periods of time, and directly jolts the primordial brain centers responsible for our most instinctive perceptions of reality—our ability to recognize and navigate patterns and manipulate objects or shapes within an ordered system.

The earliest mention of this idea using a name we would recognize came two years before Jeffery Goldsmith's *Wired* article. In 1992, University of California, Irvine, professor Richard Haier called a phenomenon he found the "Tetris learning effect." That version is related to, but different from, the idea of seeing and manipulating persistent tetromino shapes even when not playing the game. In Haier's findings, the brain becomes more efficient at playing Tetris the longer a subject is exposed to the game.

Haier had been studying this larger concept of brain energy for years, long before he crossed paths with Tetris. Starting in 1988, he would inject test subjects with a radioactive sugar solution while giving them a series of nonverbal abstract intelligence tests. The purpose was to track the rate of glucose metabolism in the brain to show a correlation between how well the subjects did on the test and how much energy their brains used.

The procedure for figuring this out in the late 1980s, however, was slightly more arduous than simply quizzing subjects hooked up to a few wires. The subjects were injected with the solution, and then they had to climb inside a PET (positron emission tomography, a kind of nuclear imaging technique) scan machine, a giant horizontal tube somewhat like a CAT scan machine. Once the subject was inside, the radioactive solution enabled Haier and his team to monitor where the injected material had traveled inside the brain while the subject was working on the test.

Haier assumed he'd find a commonsense result. He would scan the subjects once while they were "learning" the intelligence tests. After some training, they would be asked to take harder tests and to do them faster, and he would scan them again. He expected to find that working harder on the tests and doing them faster required more brain energy.

Instead, he was shocked to find a negative correlation. During the second test, while working harder and faster, the subjects actually used less brain energy. Put another way, the harder the brain worked, the less well it did on tests of intelligence. At the time, this was a shocking and surprising result. Was it universal, or was it specific to that type of old-fashioned intelligence test?

Simple pen-and-paper visual puzzles just weren't challenging enough, so Haier searched for a new and novel task for the brains of his student subjects to work on. Why not try using a computer game? he thought.

> According to the record-keeping organization Twin Galaxies, the first "perfect" score of 999,999 in the NES version of Tetris was recorded in 2009 by American gamer Harry Hong.

So, in early 1992, Dr. Richard Haier pulled into the parking lot of an Egghead Software store in Irvine, California. He was searching for a computer program that could replace the old paper-based tests and challenge the intelligence of subjects in a learning study.

Maybe a flight simulator program, he thought, because most people don't know how to fly an airplane. They could learn to fly, and as they got better and better, they could fly more complex routes, and we could scan them before and after they developed some expertise at this game.

The store was relatively new at the time, as was the consumer software business. This was back when shopping mall software outlets, from Egghead to Software, Etc., stocked entire stores with row after row of boxed software, from games to accounting programs to applications for creating greeting cards and organizing recipes. All were packaged in large, colorful cardboard boxes, oversized compared to the small floppy disks inside, to both catch the retail customer's eye and to discourage shoplifting.

Because the industry was still novel, you could walk into a software store in the late eighties or early nineties and get an exemplary level of customer service. Clerks would happily open a software box and demo a program for you, an idea that feels far removed from the state of retail media sales today.

Haier had the clerks at the Egghead Software store load up a flight simulator for him to try out. The task of flying the plane across a pixelated skyline was certainly challenging, but in practice it wasn't exactly what he wanted, which was a visual task that required quick thinking and reflexes, without too much conscious thought or reading. No, the flight simulator was too intellectual an exercise. He needed something more visceral.

Not sure where to turn next, he explained to the store clerks the most basic outline of his study, hoping to get a suggestion from the employees, who had a much better idea of what the different games in the store were like.

"Well, what about this game?" one of the clerks said. He was stacking boxes on top of each other for a floor display. "This just came in. It looks like an interesting game. We haven't tried it yet. Let's open it and take a look."

Haier and the clerks cracked open one of the red cardboard boxes. Inside was a floppy disk named Tetris from a company called Spectrum Holobyte. Within minutes of loading it on a PC and watching the first few lines of tetromino shapes cascade down the screen, it was obvious to Haier that this was exactly what he was looking for. This is the perfect game, he thought, the rules were simple—you could explain them in a minute—and as the game progressed, the pieces sped up, making it harder to play.

With a new boxed copy of Tetris in hand, Haier left the store and returned to his colleagues, but not everyone was as impressed as he was. This would be a terrible test in psychology, warned some of the experimental psychologists he worked with. It was visual-spatial problem solving, there was motor coordination, you could rotate the shapes—there was just too much going on for a psychological experiment.

What those psychologists were looking for was a test in which everything was controlled except for one variable. But, for Haier, multiple variables just made the game even more of a potential home run.

"I wanted a task that would light up lots of brain areas, not just one, because the brain doesn't work that way," he later told me. "There's no one area in the brain that exclusively lights up when you do one task. The brain is like an orchestra; there's a lot going on."

Because Tetris was still relatively new, he was able to find enough UC Irvine students who were not already familiar with it to form a test group. Few, if any, had personal computers in their dorms back in 1992, so he could control not only their introduction to Tetris but also how much practice they got playing it by inviting each student for set Tetris training sessions using his office computer.

Once again, it was time for the PET scans. At around $2,500 each, it was a risk using an untested methodology like playing Tetris, but Haier managed to get each of his subjects to learn the basics of the game, injected them all with the radioactive glucose, and then positioned them inside the PET scanner after a thirty-two-minute play session. Next, he took each of his test subjects and subjected them to an intense Tetris training regimen. The goal was to create an army of Tetris experts, with each student's brain so attuned to the game that by the time they were scanned again, they would be playing Tetris at peak efficiency.

The relatively small number of computers available on campus could have been a hindrance, but Haier turned it into another way to control for variables that could cloud the experimental data. He scheduled students one after the other to visit his office and practice Tetris on his university computer. One hour at a time, five days per week, for fifty days. If he was worried about taking up too much of the students' time, he shouldn't have been; at the end of each practice session, most didn't want to leave. The hooks of Tetris had already snagged them, and he could see them becoming addicted.

Ten weeks later, the fifty-day Tetris training period came to an end. Haier watched over the shoulders of his subjects as they completed their final rounds of practice. He knew they had been getting very good at the game, and by now the pieces were moving so fast he could hardly believe a human was playing in real time.

It was time for the next step in the experiment. Students came to the testing lab, where they were again injected with the radioactive glucose solution before they played another round of Tetris. They blasted through the levels like nothing.

The timing needed to be precise. Exactly thirty-two minutes after the injection, the glucose solution was metabolically fixed in the brain and ready to be tracked. Students walked across the hall to the massive PET machine, where they slid inside and waited while Haier and his colleagues were able to get a detailed picture of what their brains had been doing for the previous half hour.

Today's advanced brain imaging equipment makes the way Haier gathered and analyzed the data, down to reading through long print-outs of glucose levels in different parts of brain and comparing them by hand to the subjects' Tetris scores, seem primitive by comparison. But analysis clearly showed that the now-advanced Tetris players interacted with the game in a way much different from how they did before fifty days of intense training. The same negative correlation appeared in the data, and the Tetris learning effect was born.

It's not necessarily that the player simply gets better at the game or racks up higher scores—although that's inevitable, as anyone who's watched a novice become an overnight Tetris expert knows. Instead, the *Tetris learning effect* refers to the actual efficiency of the brain when playing Tetris.

If the brain of a beginning Tetris player is a gas-guzzling SUV, with the Tetris learning effect, after a certain number of game hours (typically long, uninterrupted spells) the brain turns into an eco-friendly compact car, using its engine and form more efficiently to travel longer distances on a single tank of fuel. For those exposed to the game in extreme doses, the effect becomes more pronounced. The brain of a true Tetris master, when engaged in the game, is an electric car: driving the same roads at the same speed, but using even less energy to do so.

That's the idea of brain plasticity at its most basic. As the brain engages in certain actions—simple, repeated, spatial tasks are the most obvious—the behavior moves from being conspicuously powered by conscious thought to largely automatic. Connections between shapes, repeated moves, and strategic analysis become easier, and each of these actions requires less brain energy. It's as if by driving the same commute to work every day, your car eventually becomes more efficient on that route and uses less fuel to cover the same distance.

It doesn't work for relatively simple machines such as cars, but it does work for the most complex machine of all, the human brain.

PART II

8

■ ■ ■ ■ ■

FROM BEHIND
THE IRON CURTAIN

Despite its viral popularity in the USSR, Tetris was stuck. By 1986, nearly everyone with access to an IBM-compatible personal computer in Moscow and the handful of other more-cosmopolitan cities where you could find a large number of PCs had already played the game.

They might have received a disk from either Alexey Pajitnov himself or one of his close associates, or else they had made their own gray market copy of the game program from someone else's disk. If not that, they had access to the game at work or at school, where computers could sometimes by found in that era.

There was certainly still a novelty factor, and no new game had come along to displace Tetris as the preferred high-tech addictive time-killer for Russia's computing class. But even being installed on every PC in and around Moscow meant Tetris had a fairly small footprint, and not a single one of those copies of the game had been officially bought or sold. If any money or favors had changed hands, none of it found its way back to either Pajitnov or the Dorodnitsyn Computing Centre.

This problem wasn't in the least bit uncommon, because the Soviet Union had little precedent for the enforcement of intellectual property rights, the mechanics of starting and running a small business, or a concept as capitalistic as the collection of software royalties.

For Pajitnov, the idea of breaking through simple computer programming to become a software entrepreneur might have ended there but for a palpable sense that Tetris was meant for greater things, beyond an Iron Curtain already fraying under pressure from glasnost.

Among Tetris's many fans was Pajitnov's manager at the computing center, a man named Victor Brjabrin, who led a team of about twenty independent-minded researchers. Some bosses, especially in the Cold War–era Soviet Union, may have done everything in their power to stamp out unofficial projects and personal enthusiasm of the kind Pajitnov demonstrated for his powerfully addictive game. But Brjabrin was proud of his charge and similarly believed that Tetris could travel farther, given the right breaks. He looked for opportunities to make it happen.

One of the copies Brjabrin personally helped distribute was a floppy disk with the IBM-compatible version of the game. He sent it to some colleagues at the SZKI Institute of Computer Science in Budapest, Hungary, an academic center primarily concerned with energy studies.

The effect Tetris had at SZKI was the same as at the RAS and the Moscow Medical Center. Researchers and academics, not accustomed to seeing their computers as anything more than work tools, were entranced by the hypnotic action of the falling blocks. Hungary was not the Soviet Union, and despite being in a smaller country, the researchers had access to more mainstream personal computer brands that Americans might recognize rather than corporate IBM clones or dated knockoffs like the Electronica 60.

Inevitably, just as Vadim Gerasimov had coded the IBM version of Tetris from scratch using Pajitnov's Electronica 60 version as a guide, so the student programmers in Hungary took the much more advanced IBM version and re-created the game, this time for the machines they customarily worked on.

In this case, they coded for the Apple II and Commodore 64, both among the most popular computers in homes in the United States and elsewhere in the West. IBM-compatible machines were used in business and sometimes scientific research, but Apple and Commodore PCs were what people used at home and students used in grade school. These systems made a lasting impression on the first generation of American public school students who used personal computers in the mid-1980s.

The fact that the Hungarian computer programmers could access the same common computers as consumers in the United States and Europe speaks volumes about Hungary's unique role in the Cold War era as a bridge between East and West. It was among the earliest Soviet bloc nations to experiment with economic reforms and political liberalization, even before Gorbachev and glasnost began to reconfigure the DNA of the USSR.

This model of limited reform had already had a huge impact on the state of play around the world, as evidenced by the intense popularity of Rubik's Cube, a puzzle toy designed by Hungarian architect Erno Rubik and licensed internationally starting in 1980.

Hungary was the perfect weak spot in the armor of the Soviet bloc. It was Tetris's escape route to the West. But it would take someone who understood both Hungary and Europe, both software and good old-fashioned retail salesmanship. That someone was the first Western businessman to take a serious interest in Tetris, Robert Stein.

Born in Hungary in 1934, Stein was a refugee of the post–World War II era, eventually arriving in the UK in 1956. Like many refugees, he had no money, had few possessions, and spoke no English. But he did have some background in engineering, which enabled him to get steady work, doing everything from toolmaking to selling adding machines and calculators. Stein, a bulldog of a man, with a round, fleshy face and large protruding ears, may have lacked refined English charm and good looks, but he had a seemingly natural salesman's flair that compensated for much.

How best to apply his skills evaded him at first. He had tried his hand at an almost endless list of trades over the years, supplemented by night classes to augment his marketing skills and improve his English. His proficiency at buying and selling technology in his adoptive homeland developed alongside a recognizable English accent. Almost sidelined by a difficult bankruptcy in 1979, he made a pivotal decision to move from selling calculators and office equipment to selling early computers and even some video game hardware such as Pong arcade machines.

By the early 1980s, Stein was selling truckloads of one of the most popular consumer-level computers of the era, the Commodore Vic-20. Much more so than Steve Jobs and other eighties computer pioneers, Commodore founder Jack Tramiel understood the importance of video games as a Trojan horse that could bring personal computers into American and European homes.

The Vic-20, released in 1981, was a huge hit; it offered color computing and a decent library of compatible games all for the then-unheard-of price of $299. Ever the promoter, Tramiel said, "We need to build computers for the masses, not the classes." The sentiment was correct, and this was the first computer to sell one million units and later in the 1980s was followed by the even better-known Commodore 64 and Commodore 128.

Robert Stein was moving a decent amount of hardware, but selling computers has always been a high-cost, low-margin business. Even smaller PCs for home use were big, heavy, and hard to import and distribute. An inexpensive system such as a Vic-20, although less than the $1,000-plus IBM systems found in schools and businesses, was still considered a long-term investment for families, and that left Stein with little in terms of recurring revenue from repeat customers.

But, he reasoned, every computer sold, whether by him or someone else, needs software to run. In fact, computers have an almost inexhaustible appetite for new software, from games to productivity programs, and his own sales figures confirmed that machines with deep libraries of available applications simply sold better.

Major software developers and publishers had already cornered much of that market, including a UK-based giant named Mirrorsoft, part of the sprawling Mirror media empire of mogul Robert Maxwell. But, an enterprising salesman, he hoped there might be some margin around the edges to slip inside.

The key for Stein was how to get new software products to bring to market in a way that made sense. Hiring programmers and developing original work was hard enough for deep-pocketed market leaders with huge budgets and teams, and simply reselling existing commercial software would mean competing for a tiny segment of an already thinly sliced pie.

The solution presented itself in an unexpected way. Impressed with how Stein was hawking Vic-20 computers in the UK, Jack Tramiel's Commodore reached out to him when the company was preparing its follow-up, the Commodore 64. Commodore knew that more software titles on shelves meant more hardware sales, and the company wanted Stein to take on a new challenge: finding inexpensive software that could be sold in the UK alongside Commodore 64 machines.

Just as furniture and clothing manufacturers turn to lower-cost countries to produce their wares, Stein suspected he could find cheaper programming talent abroad. There was likely a lot of computer programming talent available outside of the United States and Europe, he reasoned, but there had, to date, been little opportunity to bridge the divide between East and West.

As a native Hungarian, Stein figured the relative openness of Hungary made it a reasonable place to start his search. He traveled to Budapest to scour universities and what few high-tech businesses he could find, searching for native computer programmers and half-decent locally produced software. If anything looked like it might have cross-cultural appeal, he attempted to strike a deal to license it for sale in the UK and other territories. The Hungarian programmers were happy with a small fraction of what software development would cost Stein at home, and the programs he found to import could be sold for less than the competition. On paper, it sounded like a win-win scenario for all involved.

In 1982, spurred on by Commodore, Stein founded a new company named Andromeda Software and began a series of excursions to his birthplace, attempting to satiate the West's growing hunger for computer programs. He would find software, arrange for a license to be sold to a publishing company such as Mirrorsoft or a computer maker such as Commodore, and typically keep one-quarter of the sales total for acting as an agent between the Western companies and the Hungarian programmers.

He scored a major hit right out of the gate. Popular business programs such as Lotus 1-2-3, a spreadsheet application for bookkeeping and record keeping, could cost up to $500, but Stein found a viable Eastern European alternative, which became known as Quattro Pro, and struck a deal to have it distributed by a big California software publisher named Borland. Quattro Pro sold for between $50 and $129.

Hawking cut-rate Hungarian software in the UK was an unglamorous role for an unglamorous man, but it was still a reasonably successful venture that put Stein in an important supporting role for the explosive growth of the personal computer.

By 1986, Stein had become a regular visitor to technology hubs in Hungary. It was during one such visit to SZKI, the Budapest-based Institute of Computer Science, that Stein noticed the normally staid programmers distracted and buzzing around more than usual. People were crowded around computer terminals, watching each other play what appeared to be a simple game. If Stein had been at the RAS in Moscow the previous year, he might have seen a very similar scenario play out as Alexey Pajitnov's colleagues got their first hit of Tetris.

Stein was not a gamer, nor did he have a particular interest in computers as entertainment tools. But he was a salesman, and seeing young, educated Hungarians lining up to try out a computer program got his attention. He cautiously approached it, and after getting a few turns at the keyboard himself, he was impressed.

Even the best computer games of the day had primitive, blocky designs and limited gameplay, held back by computer hardware that was only a few generations removed from spinning wheels of magnetic tape storage powering room-sized computers. This was a game that didn't attempt any kind of representation of familiar characters or objects, whether monochromatic, squared-off aliens descending on an unsuspecting human population or race cars speeding down a chunky, stuttering track.

Instead, Tetris was a game that embraced the limitations of computer graphics hardware. If curves and rounded shapes were hard for computers to draw, this was a game that was built around straight lines and rectangles. If game characters looked like simplistic, jagged cartoons, Tetris skipped them, making the puzzle pieces the star. Unlike nearly every other computer game at the time, Tetris didn't look like a rough draft of what a really cool future game could look like—it was supremely matched to the hardware of the time, taking a handful of features and executing them perfectly. Even the name—Tetris—was familiar yet abstract enough that it would need no translation for foreign audiences.

Stein played round after round, watching the colored blocks line up and disappear and concluding that, if even a nongamer like him couldn't stop playing, then this must be a very special game indeed. Tetris was clearly miles beyond anything else he had considered importing before. He didn't want to tip his hand too obviously or prompt the Hungarians to expect a big payday from their colorful set of interlocking blocks that fell down the computer screen, so he set about quietly investigating the provenance of the game.

He cornered the director of the computing center at SZKI, hoping to figure out who was responsible for Tetris and who stood to gain from its success if he could strike a deal to bring it out of the country. The answer was not the simple explanation he was looking for. The director described how some months previously Victor Brjabrin, a colleague in far-off Moscow at the Dorodnitsyn Computing Centre at the Russian Academy of Sciences, had sent a disk containing his employee's game code, hoping the side project could find a larger audience among computer enthusiasts in other countries.

But, the director added, his own charges weren't simply playing Tetris. In fact, the enterprising Hungarian computer programmers had gone to work almost immediately translating the IBM-compatible version of the game they had received into new code that would work on Apple and Commodore computers.

For Stein, hearing that the game already worked on Commodore machines must have been like hitting the lottery. The version of Tetris he had played was certainly compelling, but if it were locked onto IBM-compatible computers, used mostly for business and rarely found in homes, it would be a challenge to market and sell.

Stein could gladly put together a licensing deal for a Hungarian programmer who had created a product like Tetris, as he had done many times before, and then sell those licensing rights to a larger UK software publisher, keeping his normal 25 percent for acting as the border-crossing middleman.

But although the Hungarians had done good work in terms of re-creating the game for more popular home computing platforms, there was a problem: they had not created the original game. To strike a deal for the underlying intellectual property for Tetris, he would have to cross a much more imposing border than the one between Hungary and the West. He would have to deal directly with parties in the Soviet Union.

That was not as simple as hopping a flight to Moscow or striking a bargain via long-distance telephone call. The Russians, despite being one of the world's two superpowers, were not nearly as sophisticated when it came to negotiating and executing business deals with private companies as the Hungarians were. Whereas Hungary was a gateway between worlds, the USSR was firmly on the other side.

Stein knew he could angle the relative lack of business sophistication he was likely to encounter to work in his favor. The key was to find the person at the Russian Academy of Sciences who could make a deal for this addictive new game and to get that person to agree to having Andromeda license Tetris before any of the many arms of the tangled Soviet bureaucracy could wrap itself around the deal, inevitably strangling the life out of it.

Dealing with the Soviets, particularly by a nongovernmental entity such as himself, could be like shouting into a black hole. Fortunately, Stein had a vitally important lifeline. He knew where the game had come from and who had sent the original disk to the Hungarians.

Stein returned to London, already excitedly thinking about how Tetris would require little to no work in what software engineers called "localization," or rewriting software to be understandable to audiences in different countries. That potentially very expensive process usually required translating written text into other languages or, in the case of entertainment properties, changing references that might be too specific to a single culture or country to be understood around the world. But, in the case of Tetris, little was needed. The game had no story, no dialogue, no characters. Its abstractness made it universal.

> The familiar Tetris theme music in the most popular versions of the game is based on a nineteenth-century Russian folk tune called "Korobeiniki."

Once back in his adopted homeland, Stein wasted no time sending a message via telex machine—a kind of early fax system composed of printers connected to telephone lines—to the computing center at the RAS. If the Hungarians had given him accurate information, he just might be able to sneak Tetris through a discreet opening in the normally impenetrable Iron Curtain.

In his office at the RAS, director Victor Brjabin, the man who had originally sent the game to SZKI, translated Stein's telexed message, written in English. He was impressed that someone would reach out, from outside the Soviet Union even, to inquire about Tetris, but selling a game on behalf of Alexey Pajitnov was far outside his experience or authority. So, he passed the telex on to Pajitnov, hoping the developer would at least be flattered by the attention.

For Pajitnov, this was an unexpected development. After taking the Electronica 60 and IBM versions of Tetris as far as he could, he had moved on to other work. He continued to investigate the ways in which a computer could mimic the appearance of artificial intelligence, an idea put to practical effect in a new program he called Biographer, which provided cookie-cutter psychological therapy advice based on detailed input from a patient.

Pajitnov was shocked to be pulled away from that work to respond to an unexpected message, in English, from a foreigner proposing a licensing agreement for Tetris. The nearly forgotten dream of selling Tetris suddenly came roaring back to life, quite literally landing in his lap on a sheet of paper.

But like most of his colleagues at the RAS, Pajitnov's English was sketchy at best. He understood the telex was a proposal from someone offering to act as a middleman to selling Tetris in England and beyond, with some of the money coming back to the RAS, the Russian government, or Pajitnov himself.

Pajitnov was thrilled but cautious. He would have to tread carefully to avoid offending any Communist sensibilities or drawing too much attention to himself. To officially respond, even in the most general, noncommittal way, he would have to navigate multiple levels of Soviet bureaucracy, tackling a system that in no way represented the neatly ordered world of computer programming he was accustomed to.

The first step was to compose a response to Robert Stein with a mixture of affirmation and caution, being careful not to dig himself too deeply into a hole he could not escape from. He debated the basic outline of what he should say and started writing, in Russian. He began with polite gratitude for Stein's interest in Tetris, then offered a generally positive impression of the proposed deal (not that Pajitnov or his RAS colleagues at this point knew a good international software licensing deal from a bad one), and finally opened the door to further negotiations.

Reply in hand, he then had to find someone he could trust to translate it into legible, official-sounding English, a process that began by getting the center director to sign off on an approval form to have another center employee translate the text from Russian to English.

Days ticked by, and even after getting his English translation back, Pajitnov still had to figure out how to actually send it to Stein. Computer center employees didn't have telex machines sitting on their desks, and even the original proposal he received from Stein had been received by a machine somewhere else in the facility, passed on to Brjabin, and then passed on again to Pajitnov. Simply retracing those steps was harder than it seemed, and incoming and outgoing communications via telex were closely monitored.

Like anything else in Russia, multiple levels of official approval, in the form of signed and stamped paperwork, were required for nearly any undertaking. Getting authorization to send his reply via a telex machine operated by a different division of the RAS required signoff from both his superiors as well as those in other departments. Days turned into weeks before he was able to transmit what he believed was a simple, clear message.

But between Russian and English, and between Stein's impatience and Pajitnov's caution, something went wrong.

Perhaps one of them missed or misinterpreted an important language or cultural cue. Or possibly each side read what it wanted into the back-and-forth communication. Or maybe Stein, after waiting weeks for a reply, simply decided that the Russians were backwater rubes uninterested in making some serious money with Tetris but that that was not going to stop him.

In any case, Pajitnov has since stood by his assertion that his message to Stein, which read in part: "Yes, we are interested. We would like to have this deal," simply meant he was interested in opening negotiations. Stein instead took this response as authorization for him to proceed as the official licensor for Tetris.

And, in fact, Stein wasted no time trying to find a deep-pocketed partner to bring the game to English-language audiences. His ideal target was a fellow immigrant from Eastern Europe, but one who had achieved monumental success as a newspaper owner, politician, and then as a newly minted software publisher.

His name was Robert Maxwell, and despite his long-standing reputation as an international media mogul and multimillionaire, he was hiding a dark secret that would eventually bring down his empire and take him to an early grave.

9

■ ■ ■ ■ ■

INTO THE MIRROR

Jan Ludvik Hoch left his birth name behind in Slatina-Selo, Czechoslovakia, where he was a one of seven children born into a poor Jewish family that had the misfortune to live on land that would change hands multiple times over the decades, never for the good of families like the Hochs. When Hungary annexed the area in 1939 (it would later be occupied by the Nazis and eventually become part of Ukraine) he was just sixteen but could already see the dark clouds of the Second World War gathering on the horizon.

Hoch made his way to France as the war cast a shadow over the entire continent, joining up with what remained of the Czechoslovak army. Routed on the battlefield, his division escaped to England when the Germans swept through France in 1940. It was there that Jan Hoch remade himself—and not for the last time—by joining the British Army at the rank of private and taking on the appropriately British-sounding name of Ian Robert Maxwell.

Maxwell prospered in his adopted army, his talent for languages leading him to intelligence work and a series of battlefield promotions. After fighting through the Normandy Invasion in 1944, he rose to the rank of captain, was awarded the Military Cross, and took on the difficult task of mopping up some of the last pockets of German resistance.

If he took to his work with a ruthless streak, shelling German towns to force their surrender, even reportedly executing the mayor of one town after surrendering German troops fired on his men, it was with good cause. During the course of the war, word had filtered back to him about the extended family he had left behind in Slatina-Selo. Nearly every one of his relations either had died at Auschwitz or, in the case of his mother and one sister, were summarily executed by the Nazis in occupied Czechoslovakia.

The war remade him, stripping away the Yiddish-speaking boy who used to peddle wares in small towns in Czechoslovakia and leaving a man who adopted the persona of an English army officer with the passion of the converted. The attitude of sometimes brutal retaliation he brought to the German soldiers he fought would not disappear either; Maxwell the future businessman was as ruthless and combative as Maxwell the soldier.

He spent his first couple of postwar years in Berlin working for the British Foreign Office as part of its press section. Maxwell detested the Germans, but the assignment in the ruined capital opened doors that led to the birth of a global empire. Like many army officers, he used connections formed while working with the occupying Allied armies to break into business.

In his case, his business was finding locally produced scientific books and acquiring the publication rights so that he could resell them at a profit. When he returned to England, Maxwell rolled his earnings into a small scientific book publisher, renaming it Pergamon and using it to launch a series of publishing ventures that would make him a media figure on a level since matched by no one save the similarly larger-than-life Rupert Murdoch, who was Maxwell's sometime rival in the world of tabloid newspapers.

Just as Andromeda's Robert Stein came to the UK fleeing the aftermath of World War II, Robert Maxwell came from similarly humble beginnings. But unlike the young engineering student who landed on the shores of England with no money and no status, and speaking little English, by the end of the 1940s Maxwell was already a decorated war veteran and a growing book publisher.

Those advantages, and Maxwell's ability to turn adversity into opportunity, would be put to the test in the decades that followed. His beloved Pergamon was lost to accusations of financial impropriety, later regained, and eventually sold for good. He tried his hand at politics, serving in British Parliament as a member of the Labour Party between 1964 and 1970, but later lost his seat to a conservative rival. He would go on to buy newspapers and publishing companies, eventually consolidating much of his expansive holdings in the Mirror Group, which at various times included the best-selling British newspaper the *Daily Mirror* as well as the *New York Daily News* and book publisher Macmillan. Through it all, he used the clout of his newspapers to get close to powerful figures around the world, from successive British prime ministers to Soviet leader Mikhail Gorbachev.

Maxwell was a walking series of contradictions. An avowed socialist, yet a millionaire who ruthlessly cut human costs at his businesses; a brilliant businessman who was never far from allegations of financial impropriety; a war refugee who remade himself as an English gentleman; and even a purported Mossad agent, funneling information to Israel, which he came to consider his adopted homeland just as much as the UK was.

His entry into the world of video games marked yet another contradiction. As a World War II veteran firmly entrenched in the world of newsprint, Robert Maxwell may have seemed an unlikely pioneer in the very modern industry of software publishing. But for Maxwell, *publishing* was the key word, whether it was software programs, newspapers, or books, so he dove in. He founded a new software subsidiary, Mirrorsoft, in 1982 with a fellow veteran, a British Royal Navy officer named Jim Mackonochie.

A square-jawed military man who developed a taste for using the first few generations of home computers to create authentic flight simulators, Mackonochie was keeping it in the family in a sense, because his father had been a test pilot. Flight simulators exist in a parallel world to computer games, far removed from Mario and Master Chief. Fans of the genre are among the most obsessed, slavishly devoted to accuracy and the smallest iterations of in-game physics and the re-creation of real-life aircraft. Mackonochie's game series, with names such as Flanker and Falcon, are legendary in that rarified field.

By teaming with Maxwell to start a new software development house and publisher, Mackonochie was able to combine the best of his military and sim-building experience with the deep pockets of a major media publisher as well as the keen eye of someone trained by years in the trenches of the tabloid news game to see what could catch the public's interest and sell.

It was Maxwell's influence and news connections that allowed for one of Mirrorsoft's early nongame hits. The desktop publishing program was named Fleet Street Publisher, after the stretch in London where many of the biggest newspapers were headquartered. Anyone looking to create an original newsletter or fanzine on a dot-matrix printer suddenly could do so, with all the design flair of a 1980s grade school newspaper.

But besides flight simulators and newsletter layout programs, Mirrorsoft needed a bestseller. By 1986, there were rumblings throughout the Maxwell empire that things were not as rosy as the corporation portrayed. In fact, the wide-ranging series of companies Maxwell controlled was an elaborate facade, already crumbling around the edges but with enough perceived power to keep the wolves at bay for at least a few more years.

When Robert Stein walked in the door, Jim Mackonochie was presented a golden opportunity to get in on the ground floor of what would become one of the most successful video games in the history of the industry. Stein, though not a major player in the field, had enough of a reputation to be taken seriously and established contacts in Hungary and other Eastern European countries to back up his claims to controlling a pipeline that could bring cheap, marketable software to the UK and the United States. Mirrorsoft and Andromeda had done some business together previously, mostly on forgettable Eastern European games, including Caesar the Cat, a literal cat-and-mouse chase game Stein had picked up from a Hungarian programming group named Mikromatix.

At Stein's urging, Mackonochie tried his hand at Tetris. For perhaps the first time in the game's history, a first-time player was unmoved by the experience. It wasn't that Tetris was a bad game, or that it was poorly programmed, just that for someone so deeply involved in simulators and other programs dedicated to re-creating real-life experiences as closely as possible, Tetris simply didn't compute. His initial gut reaction told him it simply wouldn't sell with the kind of numbers that Mirrorsoft needed.

Stein was undeterred. For him, Maxwell and Mirrorsoft were the ideal partners for Tetris, and he knew there had to be another way to get in with the company. He kept digging around, looking for information that could help him get a deal done.

It turned out that Robert Maxwell had more than one software brand. The second, run as an independent company out of California but with a long series of tangled ties to Mirrorsoft, was called Spectrum Holobyte. It might be best described as the US arm of Maxwell's Mirrorsoft software venture, but it was technically an offshoot of his original Pergamon publishing company, and making things even more complicated, it was partially controlled from afar by a charitable trust in Liechtenstein, a tiny slice of a European country best known as a haven for those with an aversion to financial disclosures. As with most of the corporate entities Maxwell controlled, this became a family affair, with Robert Maxwell's son Kevin sitting on the board of directors.

They each developed their own catalog of games and other software titles, and Spectrum Holobyte and Mirrorsoft also published each other's wares. It was a relationship that worked well enough for all involved, at least at this early stage of the consumer software business, when the competition still wasn't completely formed.

Stein's enthusiasm had planted a seed in Mackonochie. The English Mirrorsoft head knew Tetris wasn't his cup of tea, but it was impossible to deny that there was something about the game that got under your skin, making it impossible to forget. Unable to shake the feeling that he might be missing out on something that had a slim chance to be a moneymaker, Mackonochie went to his corporate cousins at Spectrum Holobyte and sought their input.

Running Spectrum Holobyte at the time were a pair of game industry veterans named Phil Adam and Gilman Louie. Louie, then the CEO, was a multifaceted genius, changing career paths at will, starting with design work on the Falcon flight simulators that did so well for Mirrorsoft and Spectrum Holobyte.

He had started his own software company, named Sphere, while still a student at San Francisco State University. His parents had provided some of the seed money by taking a second mortgage on their house. After Sphere demonstrated some initial success, Kevin Maxwell bought it, and with it Louie, and merged his acquisition with the existing Spectrum Holobyte.

Fortunately, as far as Gilman Louie was concerned, the company's absentee landlords were little seen or heard. Although Kevin Maxwell and various members of the Maxwell clan served on the board of directors, there was little in terms of a management structure pointing back toward England, something Louie was reminded of every time he called for a board meeting and no one showed up.

Later, Louie was recruited by the Central Intelligence Agency to run a new program to connect the CIA with technology start-ups. Called In-Q-Tel, it took the form of a not-for-profit company, with Louie as its founding CEO, and invested in organizations working on technology that could be of use to the US intelligence community. In practical terms, it could be considered the venture capital division of the CIA.

Today, as a well-known Silicon Valley venture capitalist, Louie is far removed from both the worlds of video games and government work. But back in 1986 he was just another game maker moonlighting as a software company CEO, about to enter a series of tangled deals with his semiremoved corporate cousin from across the Atlantic. The sharp eye that would later serve Gilman Louie as a VC investor was well honed even back then, because he was an instant convert to the Tetris cause.

His partner, Phil Adam, then the president of Spectrum Holobyte and a games industry advocate with a zeal for sales and marketing, saw and played Tetris first. During one of Adam's regular business trips to London to confer with the mothership, Jim Mackonochie from Mirrorsoft handed Adam a copy of the game disk he had received from Robert Stein.

At first Adam wasn't sure what to make of the strange new game. It came from Hungary, or maybe Russia—the backstory was already sounding a little complicated, but the game itself was anything but; Tetris sank its hooks in him after just a few plays.

Tetris threw every rule of computer gaming out the window. There were no aliens, no dragons, and nothing even vaguely approaching a storyline. The graphics were simple, primitive even, and after the first thirty seconds, you had seen pretty much everything the game had to offer. And yet, Adam couldn't stop playing.

In London the hour was getting late, and he had dinner plans with colleagues. But playing the IBM version of Tetris on a computer in the guesthouse he was staying in, the time seemed to creep by. When Adam looked up at a clock, he had missed dinner entirely; his companions returned to the house to find him still sitting there, glued to the screen, moving and rotating tetrominoes. He was eventually urged away from the keyboard, under duress.

Adam knew he was playing something special, and he wondered why Mackonochie hadn't made a bigger deal of showing it to him. Perhaps he was just downplaying it so the game would have a bigger impact. It certainly seemed inconceivable that Mirrorsoft didn't realize the combination of the game and its unique backstory was as close to a guaranteed hit as could be imagined in the world of 1980s video games.

Adam went back to Mackonochie singing the praises of Tetris. He shook his head in disbelief when Mackonochie said that Tetris "could be a great five-dollar coffee table piece," describing it as essentially a cheap throwaway game that would end up in software stores stacked with a pile of other filler material somewhere near the cash register. For Mackonochie, Tetris was no better than a stocking stuffer, even though the president of his sister company had just missed a dinner appointment and spent all night playing the game.

"No, this is a big deal," Adam told Mackonochie. "This is the first intellectual property ever to come out of the Soviet Union." He added that for Spectrum it was especially interesting because "there's never been a Soviet commercial product, to my knowledge, that ever has been commercialized in North America."

"Well, I can get Stein and sign this. Stein has it," Mackonochie said, still not convinced. Yet, he began to wonder whether his American counterpart was seeing something he simply could not.

Mackonochie said he wasn't confident enough in the game to go it alone, but if Adam and Louie would take on the licensing rights for the United States and Japan, the territories Spectrum covered, then Mirrorsoft could do the same for the UK and the rest of Europe, thereby spreading the financial risk around a bit.

A copy of Tetris returned to California with Phil Adam, who passed it on to Gilman Louie. The two compared notes. Against all conventional wisdom in the computer game industry, this smelled like a sleeper hit. Louie quickly called Mackonochie. His advice was simple but pointed and laid the groundwork for the savvy pop-culture approach Tetris would take to grab the eyes of millions of players in America and Europe.

The game had come to them from the UK and Mirrorsoft, and before that, Robert Stein's Andromeda company had found it in Hungary—but its true origins lay behind the Iron Curtain, in Russia. For the Spectrum partners, this seemed like the single greatest marketing gimmick they could ask for. The game's rigid logic and sharp-cornered architecture already mirrored the common Western view of the Soviet Union, so why not play up that angle and give this unassuming little game—one that admittedly had little in the way of flash to entice window shoppers—a fighting chance?

Louie told Mackonochie that he should sew up the rights to Tetris immediately. Mackonochie was warming to the game, and the idea of playing up the game's Soviet origins sounded like a smart one. In 1986, the Cold War was in full swing. The Berlin Wall stood. Ronald Reagan was president. But things were changing, too, and there might be room to position a Russian game as something more like a stolen view of an alien culture than a totem of a political and military enemy.

The first signs of a Cold War thaw, or at least a slowing of hostilities, had come at the beginning of that year. President Reagan and Soviet General Secretary Gorbachev had opened the year by speaking directly to each other's citizens in a pair of five-minute televised New Year messages. Direct commercial airline flights between the United States and USSR had resumed for the first time since 1978, and the two leaders were planning the historic Reykjavik Summit that would occur later that year.

The upshot was that, although relations between the West and the Soviet Union had a few gaps of sunlight peeking through, the marketers at Mirrorsoft and Spectrum Holobyte had to carefully play up the Russian story of Tetris without crossing a political line in the sand. They didn't realize it at the time, but the parties they were in the most danger of offending were the Russians, not the game-buying Americans whose opinions they were so carefully seeking.

Despite all the effort Robert Stein had put in hauling himself across Eastern Europe, shopping Tetris to publishers, and trying to get past the language and cultural barriers of the USSR, making a deal with Mirrorsoft and Spectrum Holobyte didn't exactly lead to a major payday.

> In 1992, UK music act Doctor Spin scored a top-ten hit with a dance remix of "Korobeiniki," the main theme from Tetris. Doctor Spin was a stage name for composer Andrew Lloyd Webber.

Mackonochie offered about £3,000 up front as an advance against future sales, and once that was earned back, a fluctuating royalty rate from the high single digits to the low teens. For the larger American market, Phil Adam was ready to cut a check for $11,000 to cover an advance against future royalties. To their minds, it covered all the rights they'd need to fully exploit Tetris and paid for the peace of mind that Andromeda would take care of anything owed to the Soviet Union.

It wasn't a windfall, but for Stein, it was enough to make him feel better about shopping Tetris around on the basis of nothing more than a few sketchy, poorly translated telexes with some computer programmer in Moscow named Pajitnov.

Still, there was more potential money in Tetris than just this. Stein held back the rights to publish Tetris in arcade cabinets, hoping to sell those to a company that specialized in that still very profitable space. Dealing with Mirrorsoft, Stein was primarily concerned with home computers, with at best half an eye toward home video game consoles.

The Atari line of consoles, starting with the classic Atari 2600, which had ruled the seventies, had already spectacularly flamed out, the first of several boom-and-bust cycles the video game industry would go through over the years. The next industry-changing device, the Nintendo Entertainment System, was just finding its legs.

Known as the Famicom, or Family Computer, in Japan, the NES had made its way into US toy stores the year before and was just starting to turn up in Europe in the second half of 1986.

Stein was happy to have a deal in place, plus the promise of a modest cash advance when all the paperwork was signed. The fine lines and legalistic definitions between home computers, game consoles, mobile devices, and other types of machines that might someday play Tetris seemed like a remote concern at the moment.

More importantly, while Stein expected to sign his deal with Mirrorsoft and Spectrum Holobyte shortly, he still had nothing on paper from the Russians, aside from a few telexes that were, to be charitable, open to interpretation.

The clock was ticking, and he was running out of time to go back to the source and get a retroactive contract signed with Tetris's creators. If the Soviet government realized he was reselling game rights he didn't yet control, all bets were off.

10

■ ■ ■ ■ ■

THE RUSSIANS
ARE COMING

On November 5, 1986, Robert Stein attempted to pick up the thread of his negotiations with the Soviet Union to secure the licensing rights to Tetris.

It should have been a formality, according to Stein. He already had an agreement in principle in place with the Alexey Pajitnov, who he believed to be both the original author of the Tetris game code and the authorized representative of the Dorodnitsyn Computing Centre at the Russian Academy of Sciences.

After all, Stein reasoned, he had managed to send a direct telex to the head of the Dorodnitsyn center, an impressive act of pre-Internet sleuthing, outlining what he thought was a perfectly clear understanding of what he was offering to do for Tetris's creators in exchange for entering into a standard software licensing arrangement with his company, Andromeda.

Even better, he had received, after a fairly long wait, a positive reply from Pajitnov. For Stein, that was as good as a handshake deal, enough to allow him to go find a publishing partner for Tetris.

As Stein had suspected, all he needed to do was get the right people in front of a computer monitor to simply play Tetris, where a few minutes of product sampling could turn into hours of intense gameplay. He quickly had a deal sketched out from Mirrorsoft and its American sister company Spectrum Holobyte for a few thousand pounds of advance money. Now, it was just a matter of ironing out the formal details with the Russians and figuring out where to eventually send a check when their part of the sales royalties kicked in.

And, if he got stuck in an endless loop of Russian bureaucracy, or if Pajitnov simply vanished into the air—maybe shipped off to the computer programmer equivalent of Siberia for violating some unwritten Communist rule—there was another source for the game's code.

Stein had licensed and sold numerous software programs from Hungary in the West, he had forged a close working relationship with Commodore and other computer companies, and he had been working in the technology and computer industries for years. As far as Stein was concerned, the game he discovered could easily be credited to the programmers at SZKI, who created the Apple and Commodore versions he had played.

If the Russians went incommunicado, he could always simply license the versions of Tetris programmed from scratch by the Hungarians.

Pajitnov would later argue that his reply to Stein's telex proposing a software licensing deal—which admittedly took several weeks to process through translations, permissions, and finding a telex machine to send from—was simply an acknowledgment of receipt and an offer to open a more formal set of negotiations. Not that Pajitnov was especially attuned to the legal side of the back-and-forth paperwork. He was, after all, a computer programmer with little business experience and certainly no concept of how to negotiate international software licensing agreements.

Stein knew he had the upper hand with the Russians, at least when it came to explaining to them how a deal should be structured. His next telex offered a generous-sounding 75 percent royalty on sales, although that was 75 percent of whatever Andromeda had left over after the publishers and distributors had taken their cuts. He also offered a lump-sum advance that would work out to about $10,000, which he expected would be a strong inducement, because the Soviet Union was known to be always in search of hard international currency.

Much to his surprise, Pajitnov responded relatively quickly, less than ten days later, again by telex. The Russians were clearly on the hook, Stein thought. The letter, cosigned by Pajitnov and Yury G. Evtushenko, the director of the computing center, indicated that they were ready and willing to make a deal.

Slowly reeling in the big fish on his line, Stein fleshed out his side of the deal in further back-and-forth messages. Sensing the Russians were eager to do business, he pushed them to accept partial payment in the form of Commodore computers he had sitting around in London. Amazingly, the Russians didn't balk at that, and Stein sensed he had found a goose that was completely unaware of its potential for laying golden eggs.

Pajitnov and his colleagues might have dozens of other programs he could acquire on equally favorable terms. If he could get a direct pipeline of other Soviet-made software to license in the UK, and any of it was half as good as Tetris, he'd be set for life.

As far as Stein was concerned, the affirmative response from Pajitnov and Evtushenko was as good as a final deal, and all that remained was to write it up in contract form and get it signed, but even that was just a formality.

Pajitnov had a different view. He believed he was simply attempting to engage this mysterious foreigner in a polite manner while he tried to figure out the best way to navigate the largely unfamiliar waters of commercial software licensing. He and his superiors at the RAS were generally receptive to Stein's ideas and told him so, but this back-and-forth was simply cocktail party small talk, and the hard work of ironing out an agreement lay in the future. It didn't help that Pajitnov was already operating outside of his very limited level of authority, even with Evtushenko backing him up.

And it turns out that the lumbering machine of the Soviet State was not about to sit quietly by while a low-level computer programmer started making international business deals, even with the approval of his immediate superiors. The Soviets moved slowly, especially in unfamiliar territory such as this, but they did eventually move. The first step took place within the RAS, when a modest inhouse publishing and licensing group, known by the Western name AcademySoft, took over control of the final deal with Robert Stein.

That would not be the first change of control on the Soviet side over the rights to Tetris, and with each move, Alexey Pajitnov would be eased further and further away from the action and, very deliberately, further away from any hope of sharing in the revenue Tetris could potentially bring in.

Whether he was dealing with Pajitnov directly or with AcademySoft, Stein still wasn't getting the kind of actionable response he needed from his new Soviet partners, only more questions on minor issues, such as a sudden insistence that the deal under discussion was for the rights to the IBM-compatible version of Tetris only and that versions that would work on other platforms were a topic that could be picked up later.

For Stein, that was of little consequence. IBM-compatible computers were the mainstream in the UK and elsewhere in the West. And besides, he had functioning versions of Tetris for Commodore and Apple computers standing by, created by the Hungarian programmers who first introduced him to the game. If push came to shove, he could just pay off the Hungarians and have working game code and a reasonable paper trail of ownership. If the Soviets didn't like that, good luck trying to take him to court in the West. After all, all that talk about KBG agents quietly taking down enemies of the state with poison-tipped umbrellas was just Cold War hype, wasn't it?

Still, the need to get all this down on paper and signed by Pajitnov, Evtushenko, someone at AcademySoft, or really anyone in authority in the Soviet Union pressed on Stein. Mirrorsoft had a tentative deal with him, as did Robert Maxwell's American software publisher, Spectrum Holobyte. Both sister companies had done so under the assumption that Robert Stein's Andromeda company had officially acquired rights to Tetris from its Soviet creators. Phil Adam of Spectrum Holobyte was especially insistent that any deal he was a part of would have to be directly traced to the game's Soviet creators, as playing up that behind-the-Iron-Curtain mythos would be a big part of the marketing plan Adam and Gilman Louie were cooking up for Tetris.

Of course, the Soviets had signed no such deal with Stein, but he expected to get all that messy paperwork squared away in short order. For him, this was just an issue of timing, and the way it turned out, he had simply presold his goods to a third party before fully acquiring them from the source. Working across the Iron Curtain could be complicated like that, and if he waited around for all the formalities to work themselves out in the proper order, the moment for Tetris might pass before anyone could capitalize on it.

But, as his entreaties to Moscow to move forward with a final signed contract were met with either silence or time-wasting back-and-forth, Stein began to suspect that no one was really minding the store at the Russian Academy of Sciences. And that concerned him, because Mirrorsoft was moving ahead with its version of the game, and despite the generally lengthy period of time between when a game publishing deal was signed and when the product was ready for store shelves, it was getting closer and closer to a potential ship date.

And if that came to pass, what would he do? Tell Mirrorsoft, a company controlled by one of the biggest media moguls in the UK, to hold off on shipping Tetris because he didn't actually yet own the very rights he had already sold them? Or else, he could simply let things come to pass in whatever order they happened, and let Tetris go on sale in the UK and the United States, and simply hope the Russians either wouldn't notice or wouldn't mind.

Neither answer was satisfactory. Stein, for all his bravado, didn't want Tetris selling in retail stores before the final contract with AcademySoft was signed, at the very least because he didn't yet know how much money he'd have to eventually kick back to Moscow.

But 1986 dragged into 1987 with no real progress made, at least not the kind Stein wanted, with contracts being signed and money handed over. By April 1987, a more direct approach was called for. It was time to put a few of his cards on the table.

In a message to AcademySoft that month, he announced that there was exciting news to report from their all-but-finalized partnership. Two major software publishers, Mirrorsoft in the UK and Spectrum Holobyte in the United States, had agreed to release Tetris.

No need to worry, Stein assured them. The initial release of Tetris would be restricted to the IBM-compatible version. But, of course, with the growing popularity of family-friendly computers from companies such as Apple and Commodore, there would be an eventual need to bring out new versions of Tetris to run on those systems, for which there could be a separate advance royalty payment.

Dangling additional money for other versions of Tetris might hook the Russians into finally getting a formal contract signed. Stein was tacitly saying that the additional advances he was discussing in more concrete terms would never happen until after this deal was done.

By getting so explicit about buying Tetris for other computer operating systems from AcademySoft, Stein was essentially burning his Hungarian connections, who might have been a backup licensing source. But it was a worthwhile sacrifice if it meant getting the Russians to the table.

Even for someone with plenty of experience putting together deals with Eastern European countries, trying to work within the actual borders of the USSR was proving especially maddening, and he couldn't tell whether the programmers and administrators he was dealing with were completely ignorant in the ways of business or playing some sort of brilliant long game with him.

Solving that riddle grew ever more important as the spring of 1987 wore on. Mirrorsoft and Jim Mackonochie were coming at him from the other end, finally ready to put pen to paper and get the formal contract for Tetris signed with Andromeda.

Even though he had not yet reached a final agreement with the Soviets, Stein went ahead and signed the contracts in June 1987, after he could no longer put them off.

That paperwork included several ticking time bombs with the potential to explode in Stein's face if he couldn't find a way to defuse them. For one, the language in the contract was unclear about the platforms it covered. The IBM version was explicitly mentioned, but a line about the contract covering the game on "any other computer system" was open to interpretation.

But there was another, more important one: the clause where he claimed to already control the game's copyright and licensing rights.

But it wasn't clear that he did. The contract with the Russians was still unsigned, and in fact the overall deal outline existed only in a series of telex messages and couriered paperwork, most of which was vague enough to leave anyone going through it without a clear idea of who owned which parts of Tetris and how much they would receive for agreeing to allow the game to be sold in the West.

As 1987 drew to a close, Stein had ink-on-paper contracts with Mirrorsoft and Spectrum Holobyte, both of which were predicated on the fiction he had woven about having a similar signed deal with AcademySoft. But it was a minor shuffling of calendar dates as far as he was concerned. In his best-case scenario, the Russian deal got done sometime in the very near future, hopefully before the newly upgraded version of Tetris for home computers was commercially released. Everyone would get their cut on time, and no one would worry too much about whether one set of papers was signed some months before the other.

Besides, it wasn't as if Robert Maxwell's people really wanted to look too closely at how the deal with the Soviets was structured. East-West business arrangements could still be a potential third rail in the Cold War atmosphere of the day. That was exactly why Western companies worked with international fixers like Stein. He could handle all the messy work of making sure—or at least making assurances—that everything was legally imported and of navigating any difficulties with the bureaucratic black hole that was the Soviet Union, where the state was everywhere and, at least theoretically, owned everything.

While all this was going on, Mirrorsoft and Spectrum had been prepping Tetris for a still-unsuspecting public. There was much work to do, because Mackonochie, Adam, and Louie knew the game would require some creative marketing to sell. It lacked flashy graphics and of course had no characters and no protagonist. There was no pop-culture movie or book franchise to tie into, no heroic military history to hook war buffs. Even the name, Tetris, was a made-up word that would have to be explained to potential buyers.

Other minimalistic, very low-tech games had done well without fancy graphics, but for the most part those were text adventure games, such as the Zork and Hitchhiker's Guide to the Galaxy games from a company called Infocom. They were essentially choose-your-own-adventure novels played on a computer screen, with sharp, clever writing making up for a text-only presentation. And while the original Electronica 60 version of Tetris programmed by Alexey Pajitnov was similarly restricted to text and symbols in place of rendered color graphics, the parallels ended there.

On the plus side, there was little in the way of translation or localization to do to make the game understandable to Western audiences. Part of the reason someone who wasn't a serious game player, such as Phil Adam, could get hooked on Tetris right away was that it required little in terms of instruction. Sixty seconds or so of experimentation was usually enough to give new players the basic lay of the land, and from there it was just a question of honing their skills.

The question remained, how do you take such a simple program and dress it up in such a way that US and UK computer aficionados would shell out as much as forty or fifty dollars for a copy? With Mackonochie still leaning toward packaging Tetris as a throwaway five-dollar novelty, it was up to Gilman Louie and Phil Adam to make Tetris about more than just fitting blocks together.

Knowing that the game could be traced all the way back to the Russian Academy of Sciences in the Soviet Union was the leaping-off point for Adam. The big marketing hook, he proposed, was that this was the first product from the Soviet Union ever commercialized in North America. Even if that wasn't strictly true, it made for good promotional copy.

But their UK counterparts at Mirrorsoft were of little help initially in playing up the Soviet angle for the game, and there was still a lot of work to do. As had happened with each step in Tetris's development since the original Electronica 60 version, a new version of the game would have to be programmed from scratch. The original code, as well as Vadim Gerasimov's code and the versions from the Hungarian programmers, was all ditched in favor of a ground-up approach, which gave Mirrorsoft and Spectrum Holobyte a chance to rewrite some of the game's DNA. Ironically, the idea was not to make Tetris more universal feeling but instead to play up its origins as an exotic import from behind the Iron Curtain.

At Spectrum, Gilman Louie's team added the first examples of Russian folk music, a sound style forever tied to Tetris. Louie also championed the idea of putting the game in a red box with Moscow's iconic Saint Basil's Cathedral on it.

Beyond the box, the game inside also needed a healthy dose of Russian imagery, and not only to sell the game to red-fearing Westerners. One of the odd things about Tetris has always been the disconnect between the shape of the game field and the shape of the computer monitors it was played on. Tetris is essentially about filling a narrow jar with blocks, but that narrow jar sits inside a larger square or rectangular screen, leaving big chunks on the left and right of the playfield as wasted real estate.

Nearly every version of Tetris ever created fills these spaces with background art. Some Tetris background art is abstract, some is animated, some is self-promotional. But for Phil Adam and Gilman Louie, it was just one more place they could brand the game as mysterious and foreign, so the space in that first commercial version of Tetris was filled with colorful backgrounds of life in the Soviet Union. Many subsequent versions of the game stuck with that theme, using different illustrations of Russian themes and locations. But for this version of the game, the backgrounds included Lenin Stadium, a submarine base at Murmansk, May Day celebrations in Red Square, and a view from inside the Russian Salyut space station, with a cosmonaut looking down on Earth.

The Spectrum team also redid the color coding of the blocks, creating a strong identification between each tetromino shape and the color representing it. Adam pointed out the correlation between the seven tetromino shapes and the widely accepted idea that the human mind can remember at most seven variables at a time, which is why it's possible to remember a seven-digit phone number but longer strings are harder to recall. His theory was that with strong identification between the individual shapes and their assigned colors, players would get better the longer they played, and eventually they would see a flash of color as a new piece appeared on-screen and instantly know what shape it would be before the brain could even process the arrangement of the four-segmented tetromino.

Marketing materials to match the Soviet-influenced look and feel of the game were prepared, and Adam planned a launch event that played off of the current Cold War fever, pitching Tetris as a bridge-building measure between two diametrically opposed cultures. If Tetris couldn't end the Cold War, at least it could sell a few boxes of software while showing the Russians weren't all that different from us, after all.

With this new version of Tetris heading to stores in the United States and the UK, Robert Stein was still trying to get the Russians to sign on the dotted line. By December 1987, he had done everything short of boarding a plane and flying directly to Moscow. He did offer to go to them at any time to meet with anyone required to get, if not a final contract, at least a signed deal memo outlining his basic rights to license the game to other publishers, and specifically to Mirrorsoft and Spectrum Holobyte.

> Toymaker Hasbro makes a Tetris-themed version of the stacking game Jenga.

January 1988 rolled around, and for the two companies, it was time to promote their cross-cultural roll of the dice. For American audiences, the rollout was handled with more fanfare and showmanship, and Spectrum Holobyte president Phil Adam rented out the Herbst Theatre in San Francisco for a history-filled launch event.

Part of San Francisco's War Memorial and Performing Arts Center, the Herbst Theatre was an especially apt spot for the launch of a Soviet computer game in the United States. Thirty-three years earlier, when the theater was still called the Veteran's Auditorium, the very same stage played host to President Truman and other world leaders as they came together to sign the original United Nations charter on June 26, 1945.

Now, in early 1988, the Herbst Theatre was playing host to a press event introducing Tetris to the computer and video game press. In a particularly savvy marketing move, Phil Adam invited the Russian ambassador from San Francisco's Soviet consulate, which was located near the neighborhood of Russian Hill and which was long accused of setting up shop in the middle of Silicon Valley in order to spy on American technology companies. The light-hearted video game launch event was a good opportunity for the Russian ambassador to cozy up with the tech community.

But, rather than enjoying his moment, the ambassador was not happy. He chased down Phil Adam to demand changes to the game, lest it further damage delicate East-West relations.

The previous year, in May 1987, a young West German pilot named Mathias Rust flew his Cessna 172 into the heart of Moscow, landing near Red Square and the Kremlin as Soviet Air Defense forces watched and waited for permission to shoot the intruding aircraft from the sky. That permission never came, but Rust was nevertheless arrested and tried on a series of charges, including "hooliganism," in a Russian court. He became an instant international celebrity but remained behind bars until he was released fifteen months later as a goodwill gesture during US-Soviet negotiations over intermediate-range nuclear weapons in Europe.

Early versions of Spectrum Holobyte's Tetris included an art reference to the single-engine plane landing in Red Square, and the ambassador told Adam that his superiors were not pleased that this still-recent embarrassing episode was included in the game.

"You have to understand," Adam told the ambassador, "most people view communism and the people in Russia as very lacking in personality. We see it as very flat. You know how we blame you for all the propaganda that you put out? Well, we put out the same propaganda over here, it's just we don't call it propaganda, because we're a democracy, we're not a communist country. But it's the same thing."

"You're right. The only difference between our children and your children when they're born is that when it's our day it's your night," the ambassador replied, referring to the ten-hour time difference between Moscow and the West Coast of the United States.

Adam picked up on the thread to salvage the moment. "Exactly, everything else, we teach them. This gives the American people some sense that there is some kind of a personality behind the Soviet citizens. It gives flavor. This is very good for international relations rather than very bad."

Apparently mollified, the Soviet ambassador nodded in agreement. Sensing this continued tension between the USSR and the West would be nothing but good for business, Phil Adam doubled down on pushing the Soviet nature of Tetris. He went on to hire a series of Ronald Reagan and Mikhail Gorbachev lookalikes to accompany the game and the Spectrum sales team to industry trade shows.

Although Robert Stein might have preferred to wait to launch the game until all the deals were finalized and the contracts with the Russians were signed, there was little he could do now. Tetris had been unleashed upon the world in its first-ever commercial release, and all he could do was sit back and wait for the public reaction. Tetris would either be a big hit or a total flop, and he couldn't be sure how the Soviets would react to either outcome.

11

■ ■ ■ ■ ■

"A DIABOLICAL PLOT"

A strange new computer game had appeared on the shelves of retail software stores across the United States. It came in an oversized red box and carried a sticker price of $34.95.

With no consumer-level Internet to speak of, and no way to download games from the cloud or order them up through an app store, finding and buying new games required a trip to shopping mall brick-and-mortar chains such as Babbage's and Software Etc. That's why, despite the fact that most games were contained on paper-thin 5.25-inch floppy disks, they came packaged in large cardboard boxes, usually garishly decorated. Much like early compact discs that came in long cardboard sleeves, the purpose of the oversized packaging was to stand out to retail shoppers browsing row after row of similar-looking products.

For Tetris, it was the big red box, the Cyrillic lettering with the instantly recognizable backward *R*, and the unmistakable Moscow architecture that made such a bold first impression. But Tetris had something else going for it. It didn't look and feel like any other computer games of the day. Many of the early players were not people who considered themselves serious gamers or who would ever be caught dead playing the standard alien-and-dragon-filled games competing for shelf space with Tetris.

For that reason, and because of the game's unique pitch, Tetris was embraced by mainstream newspapers and magazines that would have never considered devoting even a single column inch to a fantasy role-playing game or sci-fi shooter.

Word of mouth and favorable media coverage fed off each other almost immediately in the wake of the game's launch. In January of 1988, the *New York Times* called it "simple and addictive" in an article written by Peter H. Lewis, which focused on the game's Soviet origins.

"The new computer game, called Tetris, is believed to be the first Soviet-developed computer software to be sold in this country. According to officials of Spectrum Holobyte, the American company that will start distributing it today, Tetris was written on an International Business Machines PC by programmers at the Computer Center of the U.S.S.R. Academy of Sciences in Moscow."

Interestingly, the *New York Times* was one of the few early media outlets to credit both Pajitnov and Vadim Gerasimov, transliterating their names as "Vagim Gerasimov, an 18-year-old computer student at Moscow University, and Alexi Paszitnov, a 30-year-old researcher at the Academy of Sciences."

Even the reference to Mathias Rust and his unauthorized flight to Red Square, which had so bothered the Russian ambassador in San Francisco, got some ink.

"Colorful graphics that evoke images of the Soviet Union, including an opening scene of a Cessna aircraft buzzing past Red Square, were added to the program in this country to make it more appealing to a sophisticated audience."

Meanwhile, the *Chicago Tribune* announced "Glasnost reaches computer games," and said that Tetris was "a game so good that you won't be able to say *nyet* to it." The rest of its coverage is equally groan-inducing (though, to be fair, these jokes may have seemed fresher in the 1980s).

"Tetris is so simple to learn that you'll know all the rules five minutes after opening the box. But it's so intriguing to play that once you've started you'll be spending many hours in front of the computer screen—so many that you'll begin to wonder if Tetris isn't really part of a diabolical plot hatched in the Evil Empire to lower worker productivity in the United States."

The one-hundredth issue of *Electronic Gaming Monthly* magazine ranked Tetris as the greatest game of all time.

Reuters managed to get Alexey Pajitnov's boss, Victor Brjabrin, on the phone for comment, and he told the news agency, "The idea of commercializing [Tetris] in the West only came recently when the game became quite popular, first of all in the Soviet Union and then in the East Bloc."

Some of the early news accounts of Tetris gave a surprisingly accurate outline of the game's tangled path from the Russian Academy of Sciences to Hungary to Andromeda and Robert Stein to Robert Maxwell's Mirrorsoft and Spectrum Holobyte, and several properly credited Pajitnov (and occasionally Gerasimov), but there was a distinct lack of specificity about whether the game's creator would be receiving any money from the growing Western sales of Tetris.

Of the news reports that accompanied Tetris's 1988 launch, the *New York Times* comes closest to addressing the issue, saying, "It was unclear how the money would be returned to the programmers." To the Soviets, it was actually very clear. Pajitnov's own government went to great lengths to make sure his share of the Tetris royalties would amount to exactly zero.

Although Tetris had what marketers call "crossover appeal," it made immediate inroads with journalists and reviewers who specifically covered the competitive video game industry. This so-called enthusiast press has always been suspicious of games that appealed strongly to nongamers, and for many, the worst sin a game could commit was to be too popular.

At the time, news and reviews of computer games were found primarily in print magazines. Although largely extinct today, in a time before e-mail and websites these newsstand and subscription staples were a key way members of the computer community communicated and kept up with the latest developments. And unlike the simple online bulletin boards the most tech-savvy of eighties computer users could access with early dial-up modems (most of which required you to plug a telephone receiver into a pair of black rubber cups), these glossy print magazines provided color photographs and slick layouts. The style is carried over today in the myriad of magazine-like websites that serve legions of video game fans.

A long-gone glossy print magazine named *ACE*, or *Advanced Computer Entertainment*, called Tetris "a fascinating geometrical oddity . . . that turns the obscure mathematical topic of packing into a cult game." It goes on to note that Mirrorsoft had already managed to rewrite the basic game code to work on a variety of computer systems, including the Commodore 64 and Commodore 128, the Atari ST, and the Amiga, a more advanced system from Commodore that became a favorite with gamers and programmers despite its $1,200-plus price. These were sold alongside the original IBM version, sometimes for $24.95 versus the $34.95 price for the IBM version.

This kind of multiplatform strategy was a common industry practice but would have come as a surprise to the Soviets, who had earlier been very explicit about authorizing, even in principle, only an IBM-compatible version of the game to Robert Stein and Andromeda.

Compute, another magazine for computer enthusiasts, called Tetris "one of the most addictive computer games this side of the Berlin Wall" and warned, "Tetris is not the game to start if you have work to do or an appointment to keep."

In its review, *Compute* also noted a hidden feature in the Commodore and IBM versions of the game that took into account Tetris's addictive nature and the threat that many workplaces might have tried to ban the game from office computers, as had already happened in Moscow: "If you're in the middle of a championship round and you hear the boss coming, a quick press of the Escape key displays a replica of a Lotus 1-2-3 spreadsheet. Press the Escape key again, and the game's on!"

There has always been a web of connections among computers and computer games and the wide-ranging world of science fiction and fantasy novels, films, television programs, and even comic books. Fans of one tend to be fans of the others, and they form a close-knit inner circle of people who "get it," which was especially important during the eighties and nineties, when nerd icons like the Lord of the Rings and the Avengers were the furthest thing from mainstream movie tent poles.

That's what makes a love letter to Tetris from sci-fi author Orson Scott Card so notable. In one of his regular columns in *Compute* magazine, shortly after Tetris's original release, he wrote: "Every now and then a game comes along that is so dangerously addictive that it sucks your brains out through your fingers. . . . I have played until I see these dumb little concatenations of four tiny squares sliding down before my eyes as I'm trying to read, as I'm watching TV, as I'm driving."

He also pointed out an interesting quirk in the original PC version of Tetris. In the publisher's haste to get the game to market, the home computer version included no copy protection, making it as easy to duplicate and pass around as the original code was back in Moscow.

To run, many programs, especially computer games, required a code key that was printed in the game manual, making it hard, but not impossible, to share. Infocom, famous for its funny, talky adventure games, took this to another level, packing game boxes with printed accessories, including maps of game locations or fake newspaper clippings, each with a vital piece of information required to complete the game.

Tetris required none of that and had a viral quality that screamed out for the game to be freely copied and shared. The program was small. Even if you just had an unlabeled disk copied by a friend or coworker, you didn't really need any printed instructions because Tetris was intuitive enough to just pick up and play.

To Orson Scott Card, this suggested that Tetris was part of a nefarious Communist plot to take over every computer in America. "If the Russians were sincere about Perestroika-style game marketing," he wrote, "they'd copy-protect this sucker eight ways from Tuesday, like true-blue, red-blooded American game designers do."

With copious coverage from the mainstream media and equally appealing write-ups from notoriously hard-to-please computer game magazines, Tetris launched to plaudits from seemingly every corner, something virtually no game has accomplished since. Even the best-selling modern games, from BioShock to the Call of Duty series, rarely rate mainstream media mentions beyond business news reports on holiday sales figures.

There's no doubt Phil Adam and Gilman Louie at Spectrum Holobyte were pleased, as was Jim Mackonochie from Mirrorsoft, although sales and general enthusiasm in the UK lagged behind the Tetris mania brewing in the United States.

Robert Stein should have seen this as a triumph of his Eastern Bloc strategy, importing inexpensive programs from Russia and its allies and reselling the rights to deep-pocketed Western publishers. But, if anything, the sudden success of Tetris on home computers only served to attract more attention from the wrong corners of the Soviet Union. He was having enough trouble penetrating the dense bureaucracy of AcademySoft and the Russian Academy of Sciences, but now a new arm of the state had appeared on the horizon to take over the Tetris negotiations, seemingly intent on playing Western-style hardball. From now on, Stein was informed, he'd be dealing with a new organization staffed by hard-nosed professional trade negotiators, a group ominously named ELORG.

12

■ ■ ■ ■ ■

WELCOME TO ELORG

Alexander Alexinko didn't know what to make of this very disturbing Tetris situation. Some computer programmer named Pajitnov had apparently concocted a software application, some kind of game, that had attracted both interest and the promise of money from Western companies. This was, of course, problematic for a variety of reasons.

He had discovered the issue almost by accident, speaking to Pajitnov and his colleagues at the Russian Academy of Sciences about how the computer center could work with Alexinko's organization, Electronorgtechnica, on a completely different software project.

Electronorgtechnica was the mouthful of a name given to a group formed by the Soviet Ministry of Foreign Trade and put in charge of the import and export of technology, including computer hardware and software. But for even the most by-the-book Soviet pencil pushers, the agency was always referred to as ELORG.

Pajitnov was particularly interested in seeing whether there was any commercial potential in a pseudo-artificial-intelligence program he had been working on, Biographer, and whether ELORG could help him sell it internationally.

In the days before ELORG got wind that some pointy-headed academics were forging ahead on their own software licensing deals with Western companies for some homegrown software, the agency was best known for a series of calculators sold under the Electronika brand name. That was a fine business for the days before the personal

computer, when engineers working in Soviet military research institutions could be asked to siphon off some of their time to build
cheap products to bring in a little extra operating income, but it
wasn't the kind of high-tech business the USSR wanted to be in as
the boom years of the 1980s drew to a close.

> Alexey Pajitnov later designed a 3D version of
> Tetris he called Welltris, which is viewed from a
> top-down perspective.

In truth, even the calculator business at times seemed to be a bit
beyond them. Most of the models ELORG sold were essentially
knockoffs of popular American and Japanese scientific calculators,
but something was frequently lost in the translation, and they were
prone to making errors in complex calculations, which pretty much
defeats the purpose of high-end scientific calculators. Software sales,
the organization concluded, might be a better path to pursue.

And then along came Pajitnov, talking about Biographer and casually throwing into conversation that he and AcademySoft, the
computer center's own publishing arm, were having trouble with an
Englishman named Stein, who seemed especially eager to get a signature on a contract for a completely different software program,
named Tetris.

After making sure he wasn't mishearing this entire incredible
story, Alexinko cut the RAS men off. Not only can I not advise you
on this situation, he told them, but the RAS, no matter what Pajitnov and his managers thought, was in no way authorized to enter
into international technology licensing deals, especially with a company from the "other side."

No, there was no doubt about it. To prevent any further damage,
and to protect all involved from the inevitable political fallout when
this entire situation came to light, ELORG would have to take over
the negotiations, immediately.

Alexinko demanded to see any and all paperwork that had passed
between Stein and Pajitnov or AcademySoft. What he saw horrified
him. The trade negotiator found the inexperienced programmer

exchanging loosely worded messages with a clearly savvy foreign businessman. Words had power, and the imprecise language of Pajitnov's communications and the breezy way he offered seemingly positive feedback to Stein could easily be taken the wrong way, either accidentally or deliberately.

In fact, Alexinko deduced, the two parties seemed to be increasingly talking past each other, engaging in parallel but separate conversations. Stein and his Andromeda company kept offering different variations on deal and royalty terms and talked about Tetris as if an agreement had already been reached, even mentioning still other software publishing companies in the UK and the United States that were going to start selling Tetris.

This was a huge mess, but Alexinko could see two potential positives. First, Stein was still asking for a final contract signing, which meant he knew the deal to license Tetris wasn't written in stone, and second, it seemed as if no actual money had yet made its way back to Pajitnov or the RAS, which would have opened a black hole of further trouble.

After all, Pajitnov was not merely a Soviet citizen, working under a system that did not recognize the concept of personal intellectual property exploitation. On top of that, he was a direct employee of a government-sponsored research center, so the idea of any incoming money, especially from a foreign company, getting anywhere near his pockets was so ludicrous to Alexinko as to be unimaginable.

Alexinko took Pajitnov and AcademySoft out of the equation and contacted Stein directly, informing the Englishman that he had been negotiating with the wrong people all along and that any deal he thought might exist was most definitely off. If there was indeed a market for Tetris outside of the USSR, it would be ELORG that would sell it.

On its face, this was a ridiculous position for ELORG to take. The organization could hardly sell questionable scientific calculators to other Communist states. How could it possibly figure out how to break into retail software sales across Europe and the United States?

Robert Stein knew a tough opening stance for negotiations when he heard one. In truth, he probably relished the opportunity to actually work with someone in Russia who was at least somewhat savvy when it came to deal making and, more importantly, could claim to have the actual legal authority to sign on the dotted line.

He sent a warning shot over ELORG's bow, explaining that if Alexinko stopped a commercial deal dead in its tracks, it would make the USSR look unreliable as a trading partner.

It was the era of Gorbachev and perestroika, and Russia wanted nothing more than to be taken seriously in a world where technology was quickly shrinking the distance between nations and commerce— rather than military might—pushed so much of the international agenda.

Forcing Stein to pull Tetris from release, especially given the critical and cultural buzz building around it, could be seen as a huge blunder on the part of ELORG. It was shaping up to be the nation's biggest cultural export, and Alexinko wouldn't want the blame for such a massive international embarrassment to land on his doorstep, all over a few misinterpreted telex messages, Stein suggested.

Political and economic upheaval were coming to the Soviet Union; that much was clear to anyone watching the accelerating pace of change. Alexinko was backed into a corner and he knew it. But that didn't mean he had to make it easy for Robert Stein or that he wouldn't extract every dollar, pound, or ruble he could.

Stein visited ELORG in Moscow as the two sides engaged in a complicated mating dance, circling around each, trading drafts and clauses. By the end of February 1988, a largely complete draft was hammered out, although neither side was entirely happy with it. Some points, such as a rule that ELORG would have final approval over any versions of Tetris to be sold, were meaningless to Stein. Unapproved versions were already on sale, and future sublicensing to software developers and publishers around the world would make keeping up with every version impossible. But they were welcome to try if they wanted.

More important for him was to get the contract to state, as explicitly as possible, that Andromeda had the rights to license Tetris for many different types of computer hardware. The IBM-compatible version that started the negotiations would do him little good in a world where young game players increasingly turned to Apple, Commodore, Amiga, and other computer brands.

But the months continued to drag by, with no sign of the elusive final document both parties were ready to sign. Just when it seemed that February's draft agreement between Andromeda and ELORG would be trapped in a never-ending cycle of Soviet bureaucracy, Stein was told that a final version was ready for ink-on-paper signatures.

It was May 1988, long after he had already sold Tetris licensing rights to Robert Maxwell's Mirrorsoft and Spectrum Holobyte companies, and a newly Westernized version of Tetris was already selling briskly in software stores. But somehow his ambitious plans to monetize Tetris had not derailed the negotiations. Stein was vindicated in playing fast and loose with the standard software licensing model, but it still wasn't enough.

Stein had visions of Tetris in arcade cabinets and on the next wave of living room game consoles that had come roaring back to the forefront of home entertainment, replacing the Atari and Intellivision machines that had died out a few years before.

That would require further negotiations, but at least now he was officially in business with ELORG. Stein confirmed to his partners at Mirrorsoft that the Russian deal had been signed for the computer game they were already selling and assured them that the rights for arcade games, then still quarter-eating profit centers for game publishers, as well as home consoles, which he referred to as "TV games," would be ironed out shortly.

As before, it seemed to all involved that it would be perfectly fine to go ahead booking new business, and the new agreements with the Soviets would eventually sort themselves out. Privately, Stein was less sure of how the Soviets would feel about expanding the licensing agreement into other game platforms. These Russians, with their outdated computers, who could barely get it together to send a telex or fax, knew next to nothing about TV-based game consoles like the Nintendo Entertainment System. At least the Russians knew about arcade games—the late 1970s and early 1980s heyday of Space Invaders, Pac-Man, and Asteroids was impossible to miss, even behind the Iron Curtain. There was even a small but robust local market for rough-looking arcade games that awkwardly echoed Soviet themes.

Even with the initial contract signed, the rights to Tetris were becoming tangled in a web of sublicenses between different companies, each allegedly kicking up a percentage of the profits to their licensor, and finally to Andromeda, where Stein would remit the appropriate amount to ELORG. While Stein was waiting to iron out an arcade deal, Mirrorsoft sublicensed rights to build Tetris arcade games to Atari Games, a spin-off from the one-time video game leader that was in the midst of rebranding itself as a maker and seller of games rather than as a console company. Atari Games in turn had flipped the arcade rights for the Japanese market to Sega, another rising power in the video game world.

Stein's moment of triumph after the first signed contract with ELORG was fleeting. Only a few months later, and he was already in the same difficult situation, trying to get a Russian government agency to sign on the dotted line for Tetris rights that had already been sold and resold by others.

In early July, Stein and Alexinko met again, not in Moscow but in Paris. On the agenda was a stand-alone deal giving Andromeda the right to publish Tetris as an arcade game. Stein walked into the negotiating session with a firm number in mind, a $30,000 advance, plus a standard royalty rate. Surely the cash-strapped Russians would jump at this, he assumed, and probably thank him for such a sizable infusion of Western currency. Everyone would shake hands, drink vodka, and go home happy.

But Alexinko was in no mood to be bought off. Everything about dealing with Stein rubbed him the wrong way, and there was always a catch, an excuse, or a problem when they tried to resolve even the most rudimentary issues.

Alexinko laid into Stein. What was the point of even discussing a hypothetical deal for arcade machine rights, he asked, when the computer version of Tetris has been on sale in the West since January, and ELORG had yet to see any money from the tens of thousands of copies reportedly being sold?

Stein sat back, claiming to be shocked that his Russian sparring partner was unhappy. No one, especially him, was trying to keep ELORG from collecting what was rightfully owed, he insisted. It's just that collecting money from retail sales requires the funds to flow from a store to a distributor to a publisher and so on, and it can take some time for the money to make its way back to where it belongs. It's just the nature of the retail business, he explained.

Alexinko might have been unsatisfied with the explanation, but there was only so much he could do to force the money out of Stein. Frustrated, he demanded revisions to their existing agreement allowing for penalties and interest for late payments. But the ELORG negotiator had more on his mind than just royalty payments. Tetris had also stirred up some political drama at home, and that was potentially more of a problem than any missing money.

The same issue that had so bothered the Russian ambassador at the San Francisco launch of Spectrum Holobyte's Tetris had made its way back to the motherland. International press clippings about the cult hit status of Tetris had been read at the Ministry of Trade. The manner in which Gilman Louie and Phil Adam had dressed up the Western version of the game with Russian scenes and music, especially the reference to Mathias Rust, the young pilot who landed his plane near Red Square the year before, was cause for concern. Some in the Russian government viewed this as a serious insult and reason enough to throw any Tetris negotiations off track.

Pressed on the issue, Stein sensed it was potentially more important to the Russians than the money, and he sent word to Jim Mackonochie at Mirrorsoft requesting tweaks to the Russian cultural references in the next revision of the game. Keep the behind-the-Iron-Curtain feel, he suggested, just get rid of the obvious reference to Rust's plane.

It seemed as if Andromeda and ELORG were back at square one, going from handshakes and signatures to adversaries again, all within the space of a few months. Tetris, however, would not be contained by petty squabbles between trade negotiators. Already a web of licenses and sublicenses was spreading across the globe, including one deal indirectly signed with a small Dutch American programmer and publisher living in Japan named Henk Rogers. More than any of the complex agreements that surrounded the game, this was the single deal Robert Stein would come to regret the most.

13

■ ■ ■ ■ ■

TETRIS TAKES LAS VEGAS

A cacophony of lights and sounds assaults even the most jaded observer. Long halls extend into the distance, disappearing into a sea of tents, tables, signs, and booths. The high ceilings towering above give the entire space the feel of an airplane hangar converted into a bustling bazaar.

And then there are the people. An endless sea of quivering humanity, tens of thousands packed shoulder to shoulder despite the enormity of the space. Some are dressed for business, jackets and ties straining against the Las Vegas heat. Some are engineers or creative types stuffed into extra-large T-shirts. Most fall somewhere in the middle: men in polo shirts with a company name neatly stitched over the left breast, vacantly staring out from assigned stations at their employers' booths or else wandering the massive halls looking for the elusive next big thing.

This strobing hell on earth is the Consumer Electronics Show, or CES, an annual exposition and trade show held in the Las Vegas Convention Center each January since 1978. The brands, trends, and technologies have changed over the decades, but the basic premise remains the same. Electronics makers, retailers, distributors, inventors, and investors all descend on a packed convention center for several days to see the latest and greatest consumer technology.

Some years, it might be hi-fi stereos that generate the buzz; other years it may be 3D televisions or home automation. The modern era of the show is dominated by a handful of major companies hiding inside their own walled microcities, like the grown-up version of a child's fort, complete with meeting rooms, lounges, private showrooms, and even their own security forces. Sony, Samsung, LG, Toshiba, and others act as feudal states, each within a catapult's throw of each other, competing to draw the largest crowds to their presentations. If your neighbor is showing off 80-inch televisions, you had better have 100-inch models.

Today, video games have their own trade show—the equally overpacked, epilepsy-inducing Electronic Entertainment Expo (or E3). But for many years, video games were a big part of CES.

And in 1988, video games and the machines that played them were hot topics at the Consumer Electronics Show. Companies such as Nintendo and Sega seemed to finally have cracked the living room console code, with products like the Nintendo Entertainment System reviving a dormant market once dominated by the now-extinct Atari 2600.

At CES in early 1988, Henk Rogers was standing in a long, slow line, even if he wasn't quite sure why.

Deep queues inevitably formed in front of most of the video games on display at the show as attendees waited for a chance to get a few minutes of hands-on time with a new game. The ritual was reminiscent of how kids would stand in line waiting to play their favorite games in an arcade, only this time, it was a captive audience of industry professionals waiting to play new video games in the name of research. Even better, you didn't need a stack of quarters, just an official show attendee badge.

Something Rogers saw at the Spectrum Holobyte booth grabbed his attention. Up on one of the monitors was a simple geometric pattern of blocks, falling from the top of the screen to the bottom. It looked primitive, even for 1988, and seemed to be aiming for some kind of enforced minimalism.

But despite the lack of flashy graphics and colorful characters, Rogers took note of the long line of people waiting to play. Taking a chance, he settled into the back of the line, peering over the heads in front of him to see what was going on. At the front of the line was a simple gaming setup, with a desktop PC connected to a keyboard and monitor, and Tetris on the screen. Standing next to the Tetris demo station was Spectrum Holobyte president Phil Adam.

Rogers watched as four or five people in front of him stepped up to the game and, with only the most minimal of instructions, started playing. Each in turn seemed to be stacking the different-shaped blocks on top of each other, and sometimes a series of blocks that formed a horizontal row would disappear. Within a few minutes, every player would fill the screen with blocks, causing the game to end.

Up close, Tetris was even more of an enigma. The game didn't even make full use of the screen. Instead, all of the action took place in a narrow vertical well in the center of the screen, with the large areas to the left and right taken up by simple decorative background images and a score counter. The general rule for most games, even puzzle games, was to take advantage of as much of the screen real estate as possible, and certainly not to restrict your game to about one-third of the field.

And then, it was his turn. Henk Rogers leaned over the keyboard as the first tetromino fell, using the keys to rotate and drop it. He repeated the process, awkwardly at first, quickly filling the well and topping out of the game.

The experience was over quickly, and far from being knocked out, Rogers wasn't quite sure what he had just witnessed. He walked away from the kiosk, past Phil Adam, who seemed to be enjoying the level of attention his game was receiving. Rogers thought the strange experience called Tetris really wasn't much of a game at all. Other games at CES, and the other games he typically sought out to license for international distribution, were more graphically intense, more musically intense. They had characters and stories, and if you were lucky, some kind of pop-culture personality to hook an audience.

This was simple. Too simple. And yet, there was still a constant line at least a half-dozen people deep in front of the game. Sometimes a player would finish a round, move aside to let the next person play, and then simply walk right to the back of the line to wait for another chance to play. With so many eye-catching options available at CES, that was unprecedented.

Was this something he could even license? Rogers thought about the potential for international sales, unexpectedly finding himself standing at the back of the line again, waiting to play another round of Tetris.

Henk Rogers had gone through the cycle of waiting in line and playing the game about five times in a row before he realized he was hooked. As many have discovered both before and after, there's an addictive quality to Tetris that sneaks up on the player, something Jeff Goldsmith, the writer who would later chronicle the rise of Tetris for *Wired* magazine, would call a *pharmatronic effect*, the term for a technology that has similar qualities to a drug.

Rogers finally realized why he was so drawn to the this strange-looking little program, over all the flashier and more modern-looking games available on the CES show floor. Tetris reminded him of the classic board game, popular in Japan, called Go. In that game, players compete over a series of black and white stones, while in Tetris, you play with simple four-segment shapes in primary colors. Tetris shapes have the same simplicity as the pieces of Go, he thought, yet it has this great depth to it.

From that moment in 1988, standing in line at the Consumer Electronics Show in Las Vegas waiting for yet another chance to play, Henk Rogers decided to go after Tetris. And in some ways he has never stopped.

After his revelatory experience at CES, Rogers went to work trying to figure out how he could get involved with Tetris. It was too late to get in on the ground floor because the game was already being released commercially for personal computers in two of the biggest software markets in the world. But he operated mainly in Japan, in a culture that had a deep appreciation for both classic puzzles and original, even edgy new video games. It seemed like a perfect match, and ever since the unexpected success of The Black Onyx, his groundbreaking role-playing game, Rogers had moved away from programming and designing and into making distribution and licensing deals, not entirely unlike Robert Stein's business.

It was actually the second Black Onyx game that convinced him to market and sell games rather than make them himself. Despite employing a small team to help him with the inevitable sequel, The Black Onyx II, Rogers still rolled up his sleeves and did a lot of the hands-on work of writing game code. It was 1984, and his team of programmers had been at work on Black Onyx II for several months, but little headway was being made. Looking over their work, based on his own design documents, Rogers was shocked to find that less than 5 percent of the game had been completed. The frustrated programming team simply didn't know all the shortcuts and tricks Rogers had taught himself building the first game on the NEC-8801 computer.

He needed a game to put in stores to build on the success of the original, and the optimal window was closing fast. Rogers programmed day and night, sleeping in a closet at his office at times. The game was completed on time, but he was frustrated with the breakneck pace and never seeing his children. Having gone through the process twice, Rogers told himself he would never put himself through it again.

Instead, he pivoted his company, now called Bullet-Proof Software, and took to traveling the world, looking for games to bring back to Japan. At the time, he noted that American movies were big in Japan, and the hit pop music of the time was a kind of bastardized version of American pop music. For a famously insular culture, the people of Japan seemed suddenly open to accepting entertainment from beyond their shores. Rogers took a chance that video games could fall into the same category and that games being played and enjoyed elsewhere in the world could also be played in Japan.

He looked for games that were already popular in other countries. Because of the language and cultural barriers, he looked for games that were easy to understand and for which he wouldn't have a huge uphill battle to simply teach Japanese gamers how to play.

Once he found a likely candidate, he'd license it and bring the original code back to his team of programmers. While building an ambitious role-playing game from scratch might have been too big a job for them, taking an existing game and tweaking it for the Japanese market, particularly in terms of language, was both easy and cost-effective.

The business model was surprisingly successful because Rogers had become a kind of software anthropologist, adept at seeing games through an international lens and figuring out which concepts would work across barriers of culture and language.

Tetris seemed to fit his template perfectly. It was popular enough at its CES showing to get even a jaded game industry executive like himself to line up multiple times to play, and following that, it had picked up steam as a cult hit among PC gamers. It was also dead simple, requiring little to nothing in terms of translation and localization. The fact that the game had been a success in the West after originating in Russia was further proof of that.

The wheels were turning, and Rogers knew he had to acquire the Japanese rights to Tetris, not only for computers but also for game consoles, arcade machines, and any other platform that might make sense. In fact, it seemed like overkill to use a powerful, expensive desktop computer—his original NEC-8801 had cost the equivalent of $10,000—to play something as simple as Tetris. The game should be available to everyone, and easy to play anywhere.

Jim Mackonochie at Mirrorsoft in the UK had struck the original deal with Robert Stein, a deal that, as far as Mackonochie knew, was wide-ranging enough to cover arcade machines and game consoles—if not on paper, then at least in principle. And if making a sublicensing deal required cleaning up some of the paperwork and dates after the fact, so be it. That seemed to be the order of the day with Tetris so far, and perhaps just a by-product of trying to work across the Iron Curtain.

But it was the team of Phil Adam and Gilman Louie at Spectrum Holobyte, Mirrorsoft's sister company in the United States, that had control of the Japanese rights to Tetris, so Henk Rogers would have to deal with them directly.

After living in America during high school and college, Rogers imagined negotiating with an American company would be easy, and he invited Louie and Adam to Japan, where the trio negotiated a deal for Bullet-Proof Software to publish Tetris. One part of the deal covered computer distribution via floppy disks; another covered living room game consoles. Rights for a coin-operated arcade version of Tetris were stuck in a holding pattern, and Stein was still trying to get ELORG to agree to a separate arcade deal.

But if two sister software companies, both owned by media mogul Robert Maxwell, were trying to simultaneously sell and sublicense the same game at the same time, a turf war was almost unavoidable. When Louie gave Mackonochie a courtesy call to let Mirrorsoft know that Spectrum had successfully made a deal for Tetris in Japan, a key video game market, the Englishman was not happy.

He informed Louie that no matter what the two companies had discussed about who would sell Tetris rights where, Mirrorsoft had seen an opportunity to license new versions of the game to a major player and had taken it. The suitor was Atari Games, and the deal covered an enormous swath of geography and hardware, including living room consoles of all kinds for both North America and Japan.

The Atari brand was traditionally best known as a maker of game console hardware, including the Atari 2600 and its descendants. But in a world dominated by Nintendo and Sega game consoles, the company wanted to be known for its games instead and hoped to sell game cartridges for any and all living room consoles, no matter who made them, as well as arcade games.

By this point what Gen-Xers remember as the classic Atari company founded by Nolan Bushnell, a serial entrepreneur who went on to create the Chuck E. Cheese restaurant chain, had already been split in two after a major video game industry crash in 1984. The successful arcade game division became Atari Games, and the unprofitable console remainder became Atari Corporation, which continued to spiral into obscurity.

To get back into living room games, and signal to hardware companies such as Nintendo that it should be thought of as a partner rather than a competitor, Hide Nakajima, then the Atari Games boss, spun his idea for a console-game-making business off into a subsidiary company called Tengen (also the name of the center square on a Go board). It was the Tengen division of Atari Games that wanted to make Tetris games for consoles and arcades and, more importantly, was about to grab those rights away from Henk Rogers.

Gilman Louie was furious at the idea that instead of the reasonable cash advance Rogers and Bullet-Proof Software was offering, Mirrorsoft was essentially giving away Tetris to Tengen. But even though the computer versions of Tetris from Mirrorsoft and Spectrum Holobyte were doing reasonable business, the game was always a bigger deal in the United States than in the UK. Mirrorsoft's Mackonochie had never really signed on as a true believer in Tetris, and his deal with Tengen turned the game into little more than a bargaining chip.

> Other Tetris-like games conceived by Alexey Pajitnov include Hatris and Faces, which are about stacking parts of hats and faces.

On the other end of that bargain was Randy Broweleit, a video game industry veteran handpicked by Hide Nakajima to launch the Tengen group. As essentially employee number one at Tengen, Broweleit thought he had walked into a dream job. Nakajima had given him free rein to operate, to find a location, to hire a staff. Coming from a smaller niche game maker named Strategic Simulations, or SSI, known for wonky war games such as Panzer General, Broweleit had an exciting opportunity to build a major games business from the ground up. Being anointed by Nakajima carried serious weight; the Japanese executive commanded fierce loyalty from his charges after he helped lead an employee buyout of Atari Games in 1986 from its majority shareholder, Namco, itself a rival game publishing company.

But it was clear early on that the leadership at Atari Games, with their background in the coin-operated arcade game business, knew very little about running a retail publishing operation. Broweleit built a publishing pipeline for getting console games into stores, used the crack engineering and programming staff at Atari Games to create home console versions of the company's biggest arcade games, and sought out new games to publish under the semiautonomous Tengen brand. The idea was a sound one: Tengen would have just enough Atari brand association swagger but would not be held back by any of the company's historical industry baggage.

As had happened many times since Tetris first crossed computer screens in 1984, a deal was put into motion because people started playing the game and couldn't stop. In 1988 a handful of Tengen engineers came to Broweleit, confessing that they had all become addicted to the Spectrum Holobyte version of Tetris. What's more, the engineers suggested, because Spectrum was selling only a computer version, Tengen should convert the game to work on game consoles. That sounded like logical advice to Broweleit, who took the idea up the chain to Nakajima. The Atari Games head agreed that Tetris would make a good console game, especially for the then-hot Nintendo Entertainment System, which was by far the number one console Tengen wanted to sell games for at the time.

As was common in the still-young videogame industry, Nakajima and Jim Mackonochie sealed the deal with a simple verbal agreement. The deal was for Tengen to make and sell non-PC versions of Tetris for the US and Japanese markets, and for Mirrorsoft to get worldwide PC game rights to one of Atari's up-and-coming coin-op arcade games, called Blasteroids.

At least it was up-and-coming according to Atari. Mackonochie thought so as well and willingly gave up a massive chunk of the Tetris rights presumably owned by Mirrorsoft and Spectrum Holobyte in a noncash exchange for Blasteroids. For Gilman Louie and Phil Adam, this was pure madness. Not only was Tetris just beginning what they hoped was a long and profitable career as a must-play game but also this Blasteroids game was an obvious dog.

Released the previous year in arcades by Atari Games, Blasteroids took the classic Asteroids game that helped make that company's reputation in 1979 and updated it with color graphics and new enemies. But eight years later, a handful of graphics upgrades and a tweaked name could only serve to remind people this was essentially the same game as they had played back in the seventies. The basic premise, a triangular ship floating around a flat plane version of outer space and breaking big asteroids into smaller ones, simply hadn't aged well.

Blasteroids was also missing the special touch of the original Asteroids creator Ed Logg, considered one of the greatest classic game programmers of the era. Ironically, Logg would soon get a new assignment from Atari, to work on the Tengen version of Tetris.

But even if Blasteroids had been a decent game, there was no getting around the fact that Mirrorsoft had given away Tetris rights for nothing, and that Henk Rogers, who had a handshake agreement with Gilman Louie for many of the same rights, was going to be left out in the cold, despite offering to put cash on the table.

Louie knew that even if he was right, and Spectrum had the legal right to sublicense Tetris, he'd lose when push came to shove. In Robert Maxwell's eyes, Mirrorsoft was the favored company—the one he'd built—and Spectrum, though he owned it, was merely a foreign acquisition. That was a massive thumb on the scale in favor of Mirrorsoft's deal with Tengen. It also didn't help that Robert Maxwell's son Kevin had been handpicked by his father to oversee Mirrorsoft.

There was no way around it. Tengen was going to get those US and Japanese rights to make new versions of Tetris. Louie argued with Mackonochie that they had to at least offer Henk Rogers some sort of concession, allowing both sides to save face and to avoid damaging any future relationships. Mackonochie gave, just a little, and Henk Rogers was able to keep the Tetris rights for personal computers in Japan. This at least partially allowed Gilman Louie to keep his promise to Rogers to make a deal happen.

The other rights Rogers wanted were going to Tengen, and although there was nothing he could do about it then, that didn't mean he was going to give up on them. His plans to bring Tetris to gamers of all types in his adopted homeland of Japan were just going to require a little more wheeling and dealing.

For Randy Broweleit at Tengen, this all seemed to be good news, at least on the surface, but perhaps a little too good to be true. Getting the rights to Tetris, which his engineering team had practically begged for, was a major win. Even better, the game came at little cost, aside from the rights to the now-forgotten turkey, Blasteroids. But the stories about how the game came from the Soviet Union, through a little-known middleman, and finally to Mirrorsoft were unusual enough to cause concern, especially because all information about the original rights owners from somewhere behind the Iron Curtain were funneled through one man, Robert Stein.

Broweleit had a nagging sense of worry. This was still a young industry, barely fifteen years old, and many of the new companies springing up to capitalize on the second wave of console video games were not particularly well backed or financially stable. But for now, the industry was hot and no one could do any wrong.

If it came from a smaller publisher, the unusual story of Tetris's origins might have stopped Broweleit, but when it came to signing a license with anybody, the company he had most confidence in, in terms of ability to back up a publishing or licensing agreement, was Mirrorsoft. They were a huge company, well-heeled and backed by the reputation of Robert Maxwell. To Broweleit, that made Mirrorsoft the most credible licensor in the industry. It was enough for him to put his concerns aside and go full throttle toward releasing a new version of Tetris.

But while Henk Rogers, Randy Broweleit, Jim Mackonochie, Gilman Louie, Hide Nakajima, Phil Adam, and others horse-traded various Tetris rights around the globe, none of them had any idea that those deals might not be worth the paper they were printed on and that the entire enterprise was built on a tenuous, some would say illusory, foundation that Robert Stein was attempting to shore up behind the scenes.

14

■■■■■

TETRIS INTO INFINITY

Is it possible to "win" a game of Tetris? The idea of what constitutes a winning state is an ongoing source of debate among game theorists. Modern games, with strong narrative elements, characters, virtual actors, and cinematic presentations, are often less about winning and more about reaching the conclusion of a story.

Often there are multiple possible endings, based on in-game performance, moral and ethical decisions made during the course of the game, or a set of indecipherable (except to the programmers) behind-the-scenes metrics, coupled with virtual rolls of the dice for randomness.

Other current-generation games skip the branching storytelling paths and propel the player toward a single monolithic ending. Win enough races, kill enough creatures, and you are presented with a cinematic scene showing your triumph or perhaps just a rote retelling of in-game stats, from the number of cars stolen to an in-game pedometer relaying how far you've run across virtual worlds.

This is where the modern world of video games differs the most from games of the classic era, especially arcade-style games from the 1970s and 1980s. Foundational games like Space Invaders, Pac-Man, and Donkey Kong offer up a dark existentialism. Essentially, these classic games tell players they are born to die, with no hope for reprieve from the churning abyss, and only the chance to forestall inevitable demise through skillful play or, in some cases, a supply of extra quarters.

That's because games of this style, often quick-reflex games with a thin layer of narrative sitting on top of primitive graphics and controls, have no natural end state to strive toward. With limited memory available to programmers, there was little early games could do to provide variety or a developing story within a game. Each level of Donkey Kong or Pac-Man by necessity repeated much of what had come before, recycling the on-screen graphics, sound, and animation. Such was the limited palette available to the first several generations of game designers and programmers that the only option for continued play was to essentially reset the screen after the player reached a predetermined goal and increase the speed of the game to make the following level feel more advanced than the nearly identical one that had come before.

Eventually, no matter how skilled the player, human reflexes reach a point where they can no longer compete with even a primitive computer program. Speed kills, and in early video games the increasing speed of enemies and obstacles whittles away virtual lives until it's game over (or time to insert another quarter).

Or so the theory went. In actuality, the human mind has proven surprisingly skillful at adapting to the increasing speed and challenge of early video games—at least when playing against an opponent that has one hand tied behind its back. Although capable of incredible speed, these vintage games created only the illusion of an artificial intelligence playing against the gamer, countering and parrying and adopting new strategies on the fly. In truth, every bit (literal bits, the most basic subdivision of computer memory) was devoted to handling the blocky graphics and making things on the screen move as expected. These games were incapable of randomness, the true measure of an infinitely adaptable system. (Even today, many argue that computerized random number generators are not truly random.)

Instead of randomness, there was The Pattern. Pac-Man and Donkey Kong are the examples most often cited, but the idea applies to nearly every early twitch-based game. The (sometimes literal) hoops you need to jump through come racing by at increasing speeds but following a predetermined pattern. And it's only fitting that a game system that predetermines your eventual demise would then bring about that end through the careful application of predetermined patterns.

Anyone who came of age in the early 1980s will remember magazine articles and paperback books promising to teach the secrets of almost any arcade game. The most popular being Pac-Man, perhaps Tetris's only true rival as the most important video game of all time.

In that coin-op classic, an unusual creature called Pac-Man, or in the original Japanese, Pakkuman, makes his way through a neon maze, avoiding ghostly apparitions and eating tiny dots. According to his creation myth, Pac-Man is said to have been inspired by the image of a pizza pie with a missing slice. If that is to be believed, he (or it) is literally food eating food, a recursive existence mirrored by the matching exits on each side of the maze, which merely lead to each other, offering no escape from the endless cycle of consumption and destruction. In that way, a Pac-Man maze is like the theory of a curved universe, and going far enough in one direction brings you back to your starting point, a grim confirmation of the born-to-die philosophy of many early video games.

Like blackjack strategy books for Vegas visitors, Pac-Man guides promised success as long as you memorized and followed a prescribed pattern of play. Like playing perfect blackjack strategy, the idea was to make your initial investment (usually a quarter, somewhat less than the minimum at any blackjack table) last as long as possible through rote memorization rather than instinct and insight.

It's not surprising, then, that one of the earliest and most successful arcade game strategy guides was written by Ken Uston, an infamous blackjack player who mastered team card counting and ended up being banned from casinos around the world. First published in 1981, *Mastering Pac-Man* is a classic of the genre, both for its various patterns to memorize and for Uston's playful descriptions of the still-new arcade phenomenon, referring to Pac-Man as "a little yellow fellow who looks like he has a smile on his face."

In truth, the original Pac-Man game was programmed by its creator, Toru Iwatani, to have no ending. The levels repeated themselves with faster, tougher enemies, and the player would eventually succumb or, in theory, continue forever, as long as his or her reactions were fast enough. But the game is a fantastic example of the limitations of computer programming at the time. Once you pass the 255th level (if you can even get that far without falling asleep, because it's essentially the same as the 254 preceding levels), an internal subroutine that keeps track of your progress hits a programming bug, corrupting half of the screen with a jumble of letters and symbols.

It's as if Pac-Man's curved universe is collapsing on itself, a big crunch following the presumed big bang that created the maze, dots, and creatures in the first place. Naturally, gamers being gamers, this end state, also known as a kill screen, has been turned into part of the game itself, and to achieve a perfect score, one must play all the way to the 255th level, encounter this collapsing universe, and consume all the dots on the still-stable half of the screen, before simply acceding to the encroaching entropy.

In that way, Pac-Man is decisively a finite game, and there is a definitive end state beyond which a player cannot proceed. For anyone planning on giving this a shot, that highest possible score is 3,333,360 points, a number first discovered by Billy Mitchell, one of the more colorful members of a loose-knit community of professional and semiprofessional gamers who specialize in pushing vintage arcade machines to their mechanical limits. (This subculture was profiled in part in the excellent 2007 documentary *The King of Kong*, about the race for the best-ever score in Donkey Kong.) Since Mitchell's first perfect Pac-Man score in 1999, only a half-dozen players have reached the same high-water mark, as verified by Twin Galaxies, a scrappy, low-rent organization that has been keeping track of arcade game world records since 1981.

Tetris, which never really existed in one single official form, is somewhat harder to evaluate. Pac-Man, Donkey Kong, Defender, and other vintage games have dozens of official and unofficial versions, but each also exists in a single primary fixed form, typically the original coin-operated arcade game that purists consider the alpha version.

But none of these have the same complicated history as Tetris, where each new version is essentially programmed from scratch, following some basic guidelines but also re-creating itself for the era, the programmer, and the platform. When looking at Tetris strategies for casual gamers, or the math behind the Tetris ecosystem, we must ask: Which Tetris?

As it turns out, this is a subject that has received serious study.

Academic papers on video game topics are usually smartass responses to class assignments and have titles such as "The Heuristic Circle of Real-Time Strategy Process: A StarCraft: Brood War Case Study" or "Popular Music, Narrative, and Dystopia in Bioshock." There are many undoubtedly interesting areas to explore academically, but the majority of work in this area falls into a big gray zone of humanities, examining the culture of game worlds and the lifelike virtual societies that sometimes exist within narrative games.

Research papers touching on Tetris are refreshingly direct in their approach. With no alien cultures to analyze and no overt symbolism hiding inside an army of ravenous zombies, questions are focused on the basic interaction between the gameplay grid and tetrominoes.

For example, Heidi Burgiel at the University of Minnesota asked: "Can you 'win' the game Tetris?" in a 1996 academic paper. More pointedly, Kaitlyn M. Tsuruda at Saint Mary's University asked in a 2010 paper, "If the game is played at a constant speed, does a winning strategy exist such that a perfect player could play indefinitely?"

The basis for these, and other, explorations start with the established baseline game specs. The playing field is always 10 units wide and 20 units tall and starts with a completely blank field soon filled with seven basic tetromino shapes, each the exact size of four of the units, or cells.

An attentive player with lightning-fast reflexes could easily keep the game going for a very long time, but based on the rules established above, is it possible to continue forever? Or, could one program a computer to play with a perfect strategy, such that the computer program displaying the Tetris game and the computer program playing the game would be locked in a never-ending battle, neither able to gain an advantage, continuing in endless conflict until eventual catastrophic hardware failure?

Burgiel says, "Although mathematicians have spent many hours studying Tetris, surprisingly little is known about the mathematical properties of the game." And, in truth, that study is difficult, because the possible variations in game and player behavior are nearly infinite. Seven tetromino shapes across a 10 by 20 grid is enough variation by itself, but add in the player's ability to move the pieces left and right and to accelerate their descent, and the possible patterns explode. But the puzzle pieces don't simply move left and right, they can rotate, spinning through four different positions each, creating a factorial expansion of potential decisions.

In this scenario, some tetrominoes are more friendly to you than others. Long, straight pieces can swap between horizontal and vertical orientations easily, but the troublesome Z piece, known by its zig-zag shape and for the fact that it's rarely helpful to the player, exists in two distinct flavors, the right-hand Z and the left-hand Z. No matter how often you flip the piece around, a right-hand Z will never become a left-hand one. Inevitably, it seems, whichever Z piece you could use to fill a space on the grid to clear a line, you'll get the opposite one.

Taking full advantage of this is a bizarre subgenre of Tetris variants, with aggressive names from Hatetris to Bitch Tetris. In these, the game analyzes the pieces already in play and deliberately sends down the least-helpful tetromino in any given situation. Spend any time playing one these, and the game almost always devolves into a string of Z-shaped pieces, one after the other.

According to Burgiel, even under the best of circumstances, a traditional game of Tetris has a hard cap at around seventy thousand tetrominoes. That's a number that seems mind-boggling, especially if played in real time, but it's a long way from the sought-after infinite game.

The problem comes from those pesky Z-shaped tetrominoes, which wage their own kind of World War Z against the player. In fact, if the game decides to really play hardball and only send Z-shaped pieces down the line, you'll lose after 120 pieces, no matter how perfectly you play. If you consider that, statistically, two out of every seven pieces are the dreaded right- and left-hand Z shapes, enough will eventually appear to end the game, no matter how many lines you clear in the meantime. Burgiel calculates that by the time you reach 69,600 tetrominoes, enough Z shapes will have appeared to reach the top of the game grid.

It's a problem most of us will never have to face, because the average game lasts a few dozen lines at most.

But remember that these calculations apply only to a very traditional version of Tetris, adhering to a set of very specific rules. Countless offshoot versions exist, and some deliberately offer a very different gameplay experience, and others are just subtly different, because they were programmed by different people for different platforms.

> The Classic Tetris World Championship, held annually in Portland, Oregon, still uses the version of Tetris originally published by Nintendo in 1989 for the Nintendo Entertainment System.

Unlike many programs that live on multiple types of devices, Tetris is almost never ported in the traditional sense, where computer code is translated from one language to another. Instead, Tetris is closer to an oral tradition, passed down generation to generation. Whether for eighties IBM computers, Macs, the Nintendo Entertainment System, or your smartphone, almost every version of the game is reprogrammed from scratch, like a mimic of a painting by a Renaissance master artfully copied.

In some cases, this has resulted in a karaoke-like copy of the original, comprising new elements designed to resemble the master copy but still not exactly right. In other cases, you might get a cover version played by the most amazing set of studio musicians available, like the Funk Brothers and MFSB teaming up to produce a soundalike that far surpasses the original. Sometimes, such as the many attempts to make Tetris into a 3D game over the years, all the rules go out the window.

What that means is that we can imagine any number of fanciful variations on the game and model out the math behind each one.

For example, a Tetris game that gave us only square shapes or long bars could easily be played indefinitely.

Mathematician John Brzustowski at the University of Waterloo looked at the problem of "winning" a game of Tetris in a 1992 paper. For Brzustowski, the game takes on the more sinister air of an adversary, actively attempting to wipe the player out. In truth, he claims, there is no chance of maintaining a game indefinitely against a Tetris program that tracks the player's moves and decisions in order to react to them.

But we humans have weapons in our arsenal. One advantage that most academic analyses of Tetris ignore is the "lookahead" piece. Not a part of the original Tetris spec but a staple of nearly every classic version of the game, the lookahead appears in a small window to the right of the 10 by 20 game grid. Like a window into the future, riding on a tachyon beam five seconds hence, the lookahead tells us what the next piece to be dropped on the board will be.

Of course, speaking of competing against seven distinct Tetris shapes does the game a disservice. Each piece can be rotated, either through a button press or touch-screen interaction. Some versions of the game allow for clockwise rotation only, and others let the player use two buttons to spin the shapes 90 degrees in either direction. That's four orientations for each shape, which adds up to twenty-eight shapes to deal with, at least hypothetically.

It's only a small favor to the player, but some shapes end up looking identical from more than one orientation. For example, the square—always a relief to spot one of these during a tough game—works the same no matter how you spin it; the long bar has only two different shapes, either horizontal or vertical; and even the difficult left and right Z shapes really have only two different positions. The final verdict is nineteen total shape variations. Still enough to add a deep level of complexity to Tetris strategy and part of the reason the game has appealed to mathematicians for so many years.

One issue that has bedeviled Tetris scholars for years is the last-minute rotation to cleanly slide a tetromino, usually an L, Z, or long bar, into a slot where it could not have naturally fallen, assuming the world of the game follows the same general rules of physics and gravity as the real world.

This trick works in some, but not all, versions of Tetris. You've seen it in competitive play, in subway commute iPhone sessions, in childhood afternoons in front of a Nintendo console. It's when the rotate button is hit just as a piece hovers exactly over what we'll call an overhang. By rotating at exactly the right moment, you can slide the shape perfectly into place, in the process sliding two units through a space meant to fit only one. It's a back-slapping moment when you pull it off in front of a crowd, but to anyone looking carefully, it's a fishy move at best. But is it a cheat?

Some of these last-minute rotations around overhangs should be impossible to pull off without the falling tetromino bumping into the existing rows of pieces. But some versions of the game allow these moves. Tetris scholars are divided on the legitimacy of these moves, but generally speaking, if the version of the game you're playing allows it, it's all good. That goes back to the golden rule of video games—they just do what they're programmed to, bugs and all. That's something to keep in mind next time you see someone throw a game controller down in disgust, exclaiming that the game was "cheating."

Brzustowski, in his analysis, takes a somewhat stricter view, saying: "Disputes over the validity of rotations in the vicinity of full cells can be resolved by a Euclidian referee. The well and the piece are copied to the plane, and a rotation in the original well is allowed only if it can be performed in the plane without ever having the piece intersect a full cell." In plain English, his position is, even if the game programming allows it, it's still a cheat.

But Brzustowski doesn't necessarily have the last word. Modern video games often brag about their realistic physics (it's literally used as a bullet point on marketing materials), but an Electronica 60 in 1984 had no chance of displaying proper game graphics, much less modeling rates of descent. Nor was it necessarily anyone's goal to make it so. That's why Tetris pieces don't naturally accelerate as they fall, aside from the player's ability to trigger a fast drop when a tetromino is in place.

If you could somehow build a real-life Tetris game in your backyard, you'd see its pieces start to fall at one rate and then fall faster as they neared the bottom of the Tetris chute. (For this thought experiment, let's just agree that a Tetris chute is a real thing and that you made one in your yard.) This is just basic Newtonian physics: the force of Earth's gravity grows stronger the closer you get to the ground. In an infinitely tall Tetris chute, the falling tetrominoes would eventually hit terminal velocity, a speed beyond which they would no longer accelerate, but the neighborhood homeowners association is probably going to have enough trouble with a moderately tall Tetris chute in your backyard, so we won't worry about that just now.

What this tells us is that the universe of a Tetris game, in nearly every variation, doesn't follow the same physical laws as real life. So, any way pieces can slide into place, even if it takes a last-minute magical jog around an awkward overhanging row, should be considered legit.

Still, the game is not completely ignorant of the disparities between its field of play and the real world players are sitting in while playing. Perhaps as a substitute for the physical modeling missing from the game's relatively simple programming, most versions of Tetris start each level with tetrominoes that fall faster than the previous levels. At first, it's a simple test of mental and physical reflexes. With less time to plan and react, the game becomes more difficult, just as later levels of Pac-Man feature faster ghosts.

Eventually, however, the pieces fall faster than human hand-eye coordination can react. In the classic Nintendo Entertainment System version of the game, often used in competitions, the pieces eventually fall so fast that the handheld controller can't input direction and orientation data fast enough to affect the new tetromino, so it just falls straight down, quickly filling the grid to the top and ending the game.

In computer programming terms, this is an example of the age-old question: "Is it a bug or a feature?" Most people consider the point at which Tetris pieces fall too fast to even move them one cell to the left or right to be this game's version of a kill screen. Just as Pac-Man, Donkey Kong, and other classic games fail when they reach a point where the circuits can't properly implement the programming, the too-fast-to-move level of Tetris is just as lethal.

It may be a kill screen, but if you ever get that far, you're already one of the top players in the world. It's a problem very few people ever have to deal with.

Partly as a result of this reality, academic study of winning at Tetris has continued. A trio of MIT students in 2003 summed up the whole discipline in an academic paper titled "Tetris Is Hard, Even to Approximate."

In it, they consider the computational complexity of Tetris—even if the order of the shapes to be played is set in stone before the game starts—to be "NP-complete," to use a scary math term. If you're feeling brave, that means nondeterministic polynomial time and that even the most super of supercomputers would not be able to check every single possibility in a reasonable time.

If you have infinite time to play Tetris, well, good for you. Fortunately, most of us don't have to worry about that, with work, family, food, and sleep preventing a 24/7/365 streak. But the mathematicians who have bravely spent semesters of study and valuable university resources studying the problem remain split on some issues, and they agree on others. Given robotic reflexes and the right combination of tetrominoes or a variant game grid, it is indeed hypothetically possible to keep a specifically tailored Tetris game going indefinitely.

But not the Tetris you and I know. In that case, the final answer takes us all the way back to the early days of simple eight-bit arcade games and the inescapable, hard-coded extinction events that inevitably bring Pac-Mac and Jumpman (Donkey Kong's plumber nemesis, later known as Mario) to the end of the line.

Play for long enough, generating an infinite number of random tetrominoes, and eventually every specific sequence of possible pieces will turn up, including the requisite number of left-Z and right-Z pieces in a row that will end any game. Put another way, if there is a string of shapes that is completely unbeatable, during the course of an infinite game, that sequence is mathematically guaranteed to show up.

So, a classic Tetris game will inevitably end, and mathematicians can do the same thing you and I do when a casual game goes wrong after a dozen pieces—blame those damn Z shapes.

PART III

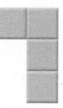

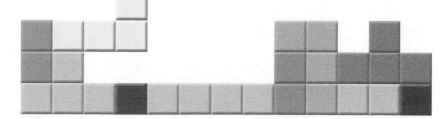

15

■ ■ ■ ■ ■

A BULLETPROOF DEAL

The Tetris rights shuffle continued throughout 1988. Even though he had managed to hold on to the Japanese PC rights, Henk Rogers was far from satisfied. For a small player—Rogers's Bullet-Proof Software was basically a minor software importer, rebranding international games for the Japanese market—that should have been victory enough. But Rogers had a habit of doggedly pursuing what he wanted, no matter the cost. It had brought him to Japan in the first place and pushed him to build the groundbreaking Black Onyx, the first fantasy role-playing game in Japan.

That alone would have been enough to secure him a small but important role in the history of the games industry, but Tetris was a fish he would not let go of until he reeled it in. It still bothered him that The Black Onyx was a flash of prescient brilliance, that he had pioneered a new genre of game for a major market long before any of the industry giants had seen the opportunity, but that those same giants were fast to react once Rogers had a genuine hit on his hands. New role-playing games from Dragon Quest to Final Fantasy were everywhere, and his small team just couldn't keep up.

With Tetris, he got the same premonition of a major force in the making, the tip of an iceberg just peeking from the calm surface of the water, and he wasn't going to let his rivals at Sega, Atari, or anywhere else snatch it away from him.

No matter that both Sega and Atari were already signed on to the Tetris bandwagon or that the game was already a cult hit on personal computers in the United States and the UK. For now, Henk Rogers was just interested in locking down as much of his adopted Japanese homeland as possible, knowing in his gut that Tetris was more than a quirky Cold War curio.

He worked the phones and fax machine, taking his Japanese computer rights and trying to expand them. Gilman Louie had told him about Mirrorsoft's sale of console and arcade rights to Atari's Tengen division, so Rogers went straight to Randy Broweleit.

Tengen's Broweleit didn't get what all the fuss was about. This all seemed like minor-league business to him, swapping the rights to the now-forgotten Blasteroids game to Mirrorsoft in return for some of the Tetris rights that had originally been acquired from Robert Stein and Andromeda. Neither game was high on his list of business priorities at the time.

He had seen Tetris, played Tetris, but didn't feel the same pull toward it as his team of US-based engineers had. "It's because I'm not a hardcore gamer" was the excuse he made, although that wasn't exactly true. He was actually a long-time fan of role-playing games, and when Henk Rogers called to talk Tetris, the two of them would get deep into the details of RPG systems and the great advances Dungeons & Dragons–style games were making.

Rogers used these chats to feel Broweleit out, trying to see whether any of the Tetris rights Tengen had sewn up could be chipped off, particularly when it came to the Japanese market. But try as he might, he was not getting the kind of feedback he wanted. Worse, the arcade machine rights, still a big business at the time, had already been flipped to Sega for the Japanese market, putting them out of Rogers's reach.

Then what about selling me the home console rights just for Japan? Rogers asked. Despite its Japanese leadership, Tengen was primarily concerned with cracking the huge American game market. In Rogers's mind, there was a chance the company would let someone else handle making a Japanese version of Tetris for the popular Nintendo Entertainment System in its homeland (where the console was still called the Famicom).

Broweleit liked talking to Henk Rogers, but he was preoccupied ramping up Tengen's American operations, a task which fell almost entirely on his shoulders. Finding a way to split the company's Tetris rights into narrow geographic slices was far down his list of priorities.

A frustrated Henk Rogers took his case directly to Tengen head Hide Nakajima. That was something easier for Rogers to do than any of the other players in the Tetris drama, because he had the advantage of already living and working in Japan. Although still considered something of an outsider by the Japanese video game industry, he had managed to get at least a hint of a home-field advantage in this negotiation.

Over dinner, Nakajima and Rogers worked out a deal. Rogers would still have to take any version of Tetris he wanted to sell in Japan and get the game's Russian owners to sign off on it, according to the complex licensing agreement he was now a part of. To do that, he'd have to deliver videotaped footage of the game in action to Mirrorsoft, who would handle the Russian approvals from there.

To Rogers, it was just another step in what seemed to be a very complex chain of intellectual property rights. In theory, the chain worked something like this: Robert Stein and Andromeda Software had licensed Tetris for Western and Far East markets from the Soviet Union; Stein had flipped those rights to Mirrorsoft and its sister company, Spectrum Holobyte, both owned by UK media mogul Robert Maxwell; Mirrorsoft had resold various rights, including Japanese PC rights to Henk Rogers and home console and arcade rights to Tengen, the game-publishing arm of Atari Games; and Tengen, while planning to sell Tetris for home consoles in the United States, had also sold the Japanese rights to Sega for arcade machines and to Rogers's Bullet-Proof Software for home consoles.

With personal computer culture thriving around the world, home video game consoles selling tens of millions of units, and arcade machines raking in profits literally quarter by quarter, it was the Wild West era of the electronic entertainment business. Complex deals-within-deals like this wouldn't deter anyone looking to cash in on what looked to be the endless upside of video games.

When Henk Rogers received word that his versions of Tetris had been approved by the game's Soviet owners, he was ready to push his Japanese PC version and, much more importantly, his console version for the Nintendo Famicom. His instincts had been dead-on once again, and the game quickly blew past any business The Black Onyx had ever done. As Japan became the latest country to fall under the spell of Tetris, the console version in particular shot into best-selling territory almost immediately.

> Unauthorized Tetris fan fiction includes the adult-oriented *50 Shades of Tetris* and *Taken by the Tetris Blocks.*

There was only one problem. The Russians had never approved Rogers's Nintendo Famicom version of the game. They had never even seen it. And this was only the tip of the iceberg when it came to what ELORG, the arm of the Soviet government in charge of Tetris, didn't know about its own game and the money it was generating.

16

■ ■ ■ ■ ■

A SECRET PLAN

Hiroshi Yamauchi, Nintendo's all-powerful, much-feared president, had a secret. While the world played Mario and Zelda games by the millions on the Nintendo Entertainment System and its Japanese version, the Nintendo Famicom, his research-and-development team was close to completing work on a project that would rewrite the very DNA of gaming.

From the depths of Nintendo's oldest idea lab, named R&D1, came a prototype that took creative risks no game machine had before. It was to be the signature creation of Gunpei Yokoi, a prolific engineer who started as a simple assembly-line mechanic at Nintendo before impressing Yamauchi during a 1965 factory visit with a toy mechanical arm he had invented in his spare time. For the next twenty years, Yokoi was given free rein to tinker as Nintendo's engineer-in-residence, coming up with games and toys that had a good enough hit-to-miss ratio that he came to head a forty-five-person team at R&D1.

His biggest idea to date had been the Game & Watch series, a handheld digital clock that played tiny versions of Nintendo games. The LCD graphics—simply static images that flashed on and off to simulate movement—were dated, even by the standard of 1980 when the games were introduced. But the miniaturization of video games was an idea with an unexpected amount of cultural cachet, and that inspired his 1987 prototype for a new type of handheld gaming console.

Much like Steve Jobs would later do at Apple, Yokoi stripped the mobile device that would become known as the Nintendo Game Boy of anything extraneous, anything that would draw too much battery or processing power or inflate costs. He rolled back the clock on gaming, shrinking the screen, making it monochromatic, and running the entire thing off of four standard AA batteries.

By all accounts it should have never even gotten out of the gate. Competitors were already planning more powerful handheld devices such as the Atari Lynx, which had a larger, full-color screen, but a higher price and terrible battery life. Instead, Yokoi created hand-held game hardware for the masses, not as powerful, but inexpensive, portable, and able to run for up to thirty hours on a single set of batteries. Nintendo rarely made decisions based on conventional wisdom, and its president at the time was known for his uncanny sixth sense about what would sell and what wouldn't.

Yamauchi, then a severe-looking sixty and known for personally approving every game released on one of his consoles, did the same thing with the Game Boy that he did with all of Yokoi's prototypes. He looked at it, touched it, tried it, and then tried to imagine its place in Nintendo's lineup of consumer products. When it came to pursuing new ideas, even risky ones, he ruled from his gut, rarely seeking input or second opinions. R&D projects, even from established stars such as Yokoi, had a single chance to make an impression and would receive either a thumbs-up or a thumbs-down from the dispassionate leader. It was a nerve-wracking experience for anyone presenting a proposal or prototype, but at least you'd get a definitive final answer in short order.

Something about the Game Boy felt right to Yamauchi. It combined elements of a past success, the Game & Watch series, with Nintendo's current runaway hit living room console. This can sell twenty-five million units within a few years, he guessed. There was no reason not to ramp up production and launch the product.

Even more impressed was one of the next executives to see the top-secret Game Boy prototype. Minoru Arakawa was not only the president of Nintendo of America, the company's increasingly important US-based arm, but also Yamauchi's son-in-law, having been reluctantly pulled into the family business as part of a complicated relationship the two men would have for decades.

Arakawa had broken through to a vast American audience over the past seven years, starting as Nintendo of America's first employee. His wife, Yoko, the daughter of Nintendo president Hiroshi Yamauchi, was employee number two. Arakawa famously managed to pitch the original Nintendo Entertainment System to toy stores in the United States, despite game consoles being cold as ice, in retail terms, at the time. Before that, he pulled in a junior engineer from the Japanese office named Shigeru Miyamoto to help retrofit thousands of unwanted arcade machines collecting dust in a New Jersey warehouse. The game Miyamoto came up with to fix the unsellable machines (originally programmed with a game called Radar Scope) was an unlikely pop-culture pastiche with a nonsensical name, Donkey Kong.

Miyamoto would go on to build his Donkey Kong characters into the Mario Bros. series, and he created the Legend of Zelda games and even Wii Fit, the aerobic tennis and golf game for the best-selling Nintendo Wii console and its motion-control wands.

On the basis of these successes, Arakawa moved from simply being the boss's son-in-law to being the second-most powerful person in the global Nintendo empire.

The Game Boy would sell a hundred million units, Arakawa declared after seeing it, quadrupling the ambitious target set by Yamauchi. But in order to do that, it would need to be more than a clever piece of hardware. Great hardware needed to be paired with great software, almost as if the two were designed from scratch to fit together like a hand and glove.

Just as Tetris had snaked its way through the world by a combination of word of mouth, endlessly copied floppy disks, re-created versions, and labyrinthine licensing deals, so would it invade the Game Boy from several angles at once. *Rashomon*-style, some of these paths seemingly conflict, with recollections fading and claims for credit inflating over the decades.

Henk Rogers was given a peek behind Nintendo's own iron curtain late in 1988. Having moved from programming his own PC games to importing and reworking other titles for use on the NES/ Famicom, he was an outsider with rare access to the inner halls of Nintendo power ever since he talked Nintendo of Japan president Yamauchi into funding a console version of Go. That Rogers had the ear of both Yamauchi and his son-in-law spoke volumes to the unique cross-cultural salesmanship Henk Rogers was already famous for (especially considering Yamauchi ended up hating Rogers's video game version of Go).

The perpetually upbeat Arakawa was the exact opposite of his father-in-law. Hosting Rogers in Kyoto, he could not help but offer his friend an early look at the Game Boy hardware. To Rogers, it looked like a pocket calculator, not a game console, but he was able to see past that, and almost immediately the wheels started turning in his head.

The rights for putting Tetris on something as unique as the Game Boy, he suspected, had never even been considered by anyone down the line, from Tengen to Mirrorsoft to Andromeda all the way back to the Soviets. That meant those rights could be up for grabs. You should include Tetris with the Game Boy package, Rogers told Arakawa.

Many game devices at the time came with a single game inside the box, called a pack-in game. It ensured that anyone buying a device or receiving one as a gift could open it and play something immediately. Like the sample blades that come packed with a new razor, it was an inducement to try one, and then buy more.

It was a risky move, pitching a Tetris game for the Game Boy without already owning the rights to produce the game for handheld devices, but Rogers felt reasonably sure he could go out and get those rights, especially if the Game Boy was still a closely held secret known only by a few Nintendo insiders.

That would be a tough sell to someone like Arakawa. Here he already controlled the biggest brand names in the entire gaming universe, including Mario, Donkey Kong, and Zelda, and now this crazy software publisher was telling him to take a relatively obscure puzzle game (at least compared with Nintendo's biggest hits) and make it the flagship for this already risky new product launch.

"Why should we do that when we already have Mario? All the boys love Mario." Arakawa was genuinely interested in seeing Rogers's thinking behind this.

Of course the legions of adolescent and teenage boys who already worship Nintendo would love a Mario game, Rogers admitted. But, extrapolating out, only those boys will buy the Game Boy if it comes with yet another Mario game in the box. "If you want everyone to play, mothers, fathers, brothers, sisters," he explained, then Tetris was the perfect game for the Game Boy.

Arakawa had to admit he was intrigued, and Rogers had hit upon an important bit of marketing wisdom. It's one thing to be the leading player in your demographic; it's something else entirely to be able to break through to brand-new audiences, something Tetris was already doing for PC gaming around the world.

Rogers knew his pitch was a long shot, but it looked as if the Nintendo of America president might actually buy it. The potential upside for Rogers could range anywhere from a finder's fee to a royalty on every single copy of Tetris sold with a Game Boy.

But he was getting ahead of himself. If Arakawa was truly interested in Tetris as a Game Boy game, the first step would be to dive back into the muddy waters of the game's original rights.

If Arakawa had acted surprised by Rogers's proposal of Tetris as the perfect game for the Game Boy hardware, he was simply playing his cards especially close to the vest. In truth, Tetris was already on his radar and had been for some time. Nintendo's own R&D engineers had pitched Arakawa on the game, and even now, there was work going on to produce a prototype cartridge to discern the feasibility of the game for the Game Boy's small, black-and-white screen.

Months before, at the summer version of the CES trade show, Arakawa had seen Tengen's coin-operated Tetris arcade machine in action. Along with other Nintendo execs, Arakawa was impressed by the game and excited to hear from Tengen's Randy Broweleit that it was coming to Nintendo's living room consoles. At the time, the Game Boy project was still far too secret to breathe a word about, but the paths of Nintendo and Tetris were already intertwined.

Following along with Arakawa at that trade show demo session of the Tetris arcade machine was Howard Lincoln, one of the most important executives in the company's long history. At the time he was the senior vice president and general counsel for Nintendo of America, and later he'd be elevated to chairman before retiring to become the president of the Seattle Mariners baseball team, itself owned and controlled by Nintendo and its chairman, Hiroshi Yamauchi.

Lincoln, forty-eight at the time and looking every bit the stereotypical corporate lawyer, was often the odd man out at video game industry events. He wasn't particularly interested in the games themselves or gaming culture, and his measured monotone and anchorman-like mane of graying hair was a sharp contrast to Arakawa's enthusiasm or Yamauchi's intense focus on product perfection. Yet, beneath that calm exterior, he was Nintendo's legal attack dog, and many opponents, from opposing lawyers to rival company CEOs to congressional committee members, would come face to face with his relentless onslaughts in and out of the courtroom.

Only his most despised foes received the ultimate Howard Lincoln sanction, a personal message of scorn, sometimes even in verse. His most famous may be a short poem directed at Sega president Tom Kalinskie in 1992 after a nasty back-and-forth between the two: "Dear Tom, Roses are red, violets are blue, so you had a bad day, boo hoo hoo hoo. All my best, Howard."

But in 1988, Lincoln was still best known for saving the company's unlikeliest mascot, Donkey Kong, from the all-powerful American film industry during a particularly nasty confrontation.

It was April 1982, and Minoru Arakawa's bet on Donkey Kong was paying off in a major way. Until, that is, Arakawa's boss and father-in-law, Hiroshi Yamauchi, called from Japan to report a threatening telex message from Sid Sheinberg, the president of MCA/Universal, the movie studio head perhaps most famous for "discovering" a young directorial talent named Steven Spielberg.

The language in the telex was unmistakably Sheinberg's aggressive, take-no-prisoners tone. Donkey Kong, a huge hit in bars and arcades around the United States, was a clear violation of Universal's trademark for King Kong, and Yamauchi had forty-eight hours to both turn over any profits from the game to MCA/Universal as well as destroy any arcade machines still in Nintendo's possession. There was no room for negotiation and no time to figure out a workaround. This was a clear attempt by Sheinberg to deliver a killing blow.

Arakawa felt trapped. He had taken the role of Nintendo of America president reluctantly and had since then struggled to establish his own identity and grow the business while keeping one eye over his shoulder on his famous, and famously demanding, father-in-law. This threat from MCA/Universal would be seen back in Japan as a failure of Arakawa's leadership, just as Nintendo of America was starting to grow into an independent, powerful entertainment entity.

> The Nintendo World store in New York has on display a Game Boy handheld that was badly burned in a 1990s Gulf War bombing. It is still powered on and playing Tetris.

As he would many times over the years to come, Howard Lincoln rode to the rescue. After a series of tense negotiations in which Lincoln jousted with Sheinberg and MCA's lawyers, the case ended up in court, which is exactly what he wanted all along. In US District Court in New York, Lincoln was able to show that MCA/Universal had never owned a trademark for the character and that the studio had previously even argued that King Kong was in the public domain in another case it fought against RKO Pictures, which had made the original 1933 film. The judge gave Nintendo a summary judgment in its favor, along with $1.8 million in damages and legal fees from MCA/Universal.

The lesson was clear. Anyone interested in taking Nintendo of America to court would have to face off against Howard Lincoln. By the end of the Donkey Kong case, he was no longer the company's outside council but instead Arakawa's second in command and deeply involved in every major decision the company made.

The next major turning point for Nintendo he was involved with was the battle to put Tetris on the Game Boy. By the time he and Arakawa played the coin-op version of Tetris in the summer of 1988, Lincoln was vaguely aware that Nintendo was working on a handheld product, but he didn't know exactly what it was or that it would be called Game Boy.

When he later put the threads of information together about this potentially revolutionary new product, he almost fell out of his chair, asking, "Why would anyone name a product 'Game Boy'?" But he knew that was typical Nintendo behavior, to rely more on instinct and quirkiness and less on focus groups and marketing experts. He eventually learned to give up arguing about product names.

Howard Lincoln wasn't a gamer by any standard. In fact, games generally bored him, even the instant classics Nintendo was turning out on a regular basis in the late 1980s. But even to him, Tetris was different, so when Arakawa set his sights on figuring out who, if anyone, currently controlled the rights to make Tetris for handheld devices, Lincoln wasn't surprised.

But initial reports from the field were discouraging. Lincoln and Arakawa were frustrated to hear Nintendo lawyer Lynn Hvalsoe report back that she'd run into a dead-end. The convoluted tangle of licenses and sublicenses, with different rights-holders for seemingly every platform in every region, and the fact that no one had thought of specifically carving out handheld rights, in this era prior to smartphones or Game Boys, made it a seemingly impossible task.

There's something screwy going on here, Lincoln concluded, increasingly unsure who exactly legitimately controlled the game. That would be enough to scare most companies off, but Arakawa was becoming more and more convinced that Tetris was indeed the perfect game to pair with the Game Boy.

Arakawa set his in-house engineers to work producing their own prototype version of Tetris to work with the Game Boy hardware. The limitations of the handheld console forced the game back to something closer to its original Soviet version, long before subsequent generations of programmers had re-created it over and over again with new colors, graphics, and features.

On the tiny Game Boy screen, the game was in black and white, or, more accurately, dark gray on green. There were no musical cues or interstitial graphics yet, and even if they could be programmed, they would be of the simplest variety, far from what PC, arcade, and living room console gamers were used to.

Even in this very early, very primitive stage, Arakawa could see that Tetris had survived the translation. The simple geometric shapes were legible even on the small monochromatic screen, and the stripped-down controls—two buttons and a four-way directional pad—were perfectly suited for flipping and shunting tetrominoes.

Arakawa knew from the first playthrough of the prototype that Tetris on the Game Boy would be a hit if only he could work out how to get the rights. It was especially vexing that Tetris seemed to be everywhere already, on different game-playing devices in different countries, and had been covered by everyone from the *New York Times* to CBS News, yet slicing off this one tiny chunk of it for the Game Boy was proving to be such a problem.

According to Nintendo's lawyers, the authority to license Tetris for Game Boy might be hidden well behind the Iron Curtain, and it would be impossible to complete the deal without involving the Soviets.

Arakawa and Lincoln understood the gaming and entertainment markets in the United States, in Japan, and even in Europe, but Russia was still a black hole for Western businesses. Who would they talk to? How much could they expect to pay? Could they even find the original creators of Tetris? Had one of their competitors already made the trip to Russia in search of the same rights?

For a major company like Nintendo to go in blindly would be asking for trouble. At the very least, it could tip off competitors. But Arakawa was forming a plan to find someone outside the company, someone who could navigate this delicate situation without making too much noise.

He informed Howard Lincoln that he planned to ask Henk Rogers to track down the Russian rights on their behalf. To Lincoln, this sounded like a brilliant solution for an intractable problem. He and Arakawa both knew Rogers well from years in the game business, and Lincoln considered him shrewd, even crafty, but above all an entrepreneur who would let nothing—not even a nation still described by politicians as an "Evil Empire"—get in the way of a good deal.

17

. . . . .

THE GATHERING STORM

Like many others before him, Henk Rogers had run into a Robert Stein problem. The rights to make Tetris games for different platforms all eventually traced their way back to this one man before vanishing into the Soviet Union and ELORG.

Here was Rogers, a Westerner living and working in Japan, tasked by Minoru Arakawa, the Japanese businessman running Nintendo of America from Seattle, with securing new rights to Tetris from the Soviet Union. It was a potentially very lucrative deal, and if he succeeded, Nintendo would essentially sublicense the Game Boy rights to Tetris from his company, Bullet-Proof Software, giving Rogers a cut of every cartridge sold.

But for Nintendo to have struck a deal like this instead of going to Russia themselves, Rogers knew the Tetris situation must be more tangled than even he had suspected. Because even the handful of rights he had scooped up for the Japanese market had been the result of negotiations, broken deals, and flips between multiple companies, whatever Nintendo had found in its research was something even its army of lawyers couldn't easily navigate.

All roads ultimately flowed through Stein, who played his cards very close to the vest, working only with Mirrorsoft and using the cover its famous owner, Robert Maxwell, provided to avoid talking directly to other licensees.

At the end of 1988, Rogers fired off a fax to Stein, proposing to pick up the rights for Tetris for portable game devices. A few examples of such gadgets existed at the time, including a handful of credit-card-sized single-game novelties, such as Nintendo's own Game & Watch series, as well as a few clunky, expensive machines without many games available for them. It should be a simple transaction, Rogers thought, especially because no one knows what Nintendo is planning.

But the reaction was anything but the quick thumbs-up Rogers expected. Stein said something about having to check with the Russian trade organization he was working with, ELORG, and that he'd be in touch. Attached to Rogers's offer was a hefty $25,000 advance, and from what he knew about the head of Andromeda Software, turning down guaranteed cash like that was well outside of Stein's established reputation. Rogers was immediately suspicious.

For his part, Robert Stein saw this sudden interest in handheld rights to Tetris as just one more assault on his already shaky position with the game. He consulted with Mirrorsoft's Jim Mackonochie, proclaiming that handheld rights were now a priority and that any inquiries from existing or potential new licensees for those rights should be kept on ice for as long as possible.

> Alexey Pajitnov designed a puzzle game called Hexic for Microsoft that was preinstalled on millions of Xbox 360 consoles.

There was a reason Stein was suddenly so skittish. He'd been able to play ELORG's Sasha Alexinko through multiple rounds of negotiations without breaking a sweat, but now there was a new player on the Soviet side. Still using their outdated telex machines, ELORG informed Stein that he'd now be dealing with someone named Nikoli Belikov. This Belikov was an unknown quantity to Stein, but if he was anything like the other Russian bureaucrats he'd dealt with, this meant nothing but more obstruction and more demands. The worst-case scenario was if the new regime at ELORG looked too closely at the accounting for Tetris and saw that despite selling many copies around the world, very little money had actually made its way back home.

With Henk Rogers sniffing around the handheld rights and a new team of Russians to placate, Stein was on thin ice. Perhaps Tetris enthusiasm had gotten the better of him, and the various Tetris arcade machines around the world weren't actually covered by any deal signed between Andromeda and ELORG. He had always meant to nail down that coin-op deal, it just never happened, and now that Alexinko was gone, those negotiations would probably have to start again from scratch. The better plan was to roll this new handheld issue in with that and try to get a comprehensive deal that covered every form of Tetris imaginable.

The only way to stay one step ahead of everyone else was to go directly to Moscow and meet this new Belikov in person. There he'd use the same flash of Western money that worked so well with Pajitnov, AcademySoft, Alexinko, and others to grab the coin-op, handheld, and any other Tetris rights he could think of. Only after that would he be happy to take Henk Rogers's $25,000, although by that time, the handheld rights might cost a good bit more.

But Stein's stumbling response to Rogers's inquiry got his business partners' attention, and the idea of handheld rights for Tetris was suddenly big talk at Mirrorsoft. Jim Mackonochie reported Stein's sudden interest to his colleagues and caught the ear of both Phil Adams at Spectrum Holobyte and Robert Maxwell's son Kevin, the man in charge of all the Maxwell technology and software companies.

Just shy of thirty, Kevin Maxwell was, like his father, prone to leaving his charges alone for long stretches at a time, and then diving in to meddle with the tiniest details of deals. Tetris had been on his radar for some time, especially after he was forced to intervene in the family squabble between Spectrum and Mirrorsoft over the Tetris rights double-dealt to both Henk Rogers and Tengen. That was trouble enough, but with Stein suddenly acting sketchier than usual, the younger Maxwell decided this was a problem he could solve, and perhaps even use to impress his famous father by scoring a new deal with the Soviets. Mackonochie volunteered to go to Russia to talk to ELORG directly and maybe find a way to sidestep Andromeda completely, but Maxwell told him to stand down.

Back in America, Phil Adam was equally troubled by this new wrinkle in the Tetris situation. Accustomed to operating much more independently from the Mirror Group mothership than Mack-onochie was, he made his own plans to go to Russia to ensure Spectrum Holobyte wasn't going to get cut out of any renegotiated Tetris rights. But word came back from England that he was to stand down as well. Pressing for a reason why, Adam was told his $3,000 plane ticket to Moscow wouldn't be approved. It was an unnecessary expense because Kevin Maxwell was going to Moscow to personally meet with ELORG and solve the Tetris problem.

Adam was frustrated, dismissing the younger Maxwell as someone who didn't know the games industry yet who was now locking him out of the very game he had helped champion. But there was nothing to do at this point except sit back and watch from afar as Robert Stein, Kevin Maxwell, and Henk Rogers each planned a trip to Moscow, each with the same agenda—to get to ELORG and cut the others out.

18

■ ■ ■ ■ ■

THE BIG BET

I n late February 1989, Henk Rogers arrived in Moscow, nearly getting lost in the frigid Russian winter before tracking down the offices of the mysterious ELORG group. After navigating unhelpful hotel staffs, useless maps, and seemingly the entire local Moscow community of Go players and then finally connecting with a local guide who knew her way around town, he was closing in on his quarry.

But he knew that getting in the door (both literally and figuratively) and getting someone at ELORG to even talk to him were only just getting to the starting line. Likely, his competition was already several steps ahead. Both Robert Stein and Kevin Maxwell had been invited to the trade group's offices and had meetings on the books, an important detail in Soviet bureaucracy. For his part, Rogers was in town on a tourist visa; even discussing business with anyone could conceivably put him on the wrong side of the law in a country not known for being especially hospitable to meddling foreigners.

It was remarkable that the grim-faced workers at ELORG, who seemed to have arrived straight from Communist central casting, hadn't kicked Rogers out. He just hoped it was good news, and not the beginning of some governmental nightmare. Even the guide who had miraculously appeared at the last moment to lead him to this otherwise anonymous government building could just mean he was being tracked the entire time.

Rogers pushed these thoughts from his mind, focusing instead on the fact that he was being led to a meeting room rather than being

kicked out on the street. It was time to put on his game face and figure out what he was going to say to the Russian trade negotiators to
convince them to carve out a new set of rights for a handheld version
of Tetris and to license them to Rogers and Bullet-Proof Software
and through him to Nintendo, one of the largest game companies in
the world.

Waiting inside the conference room was Evgeni Nikolaevich Belikov, although Henk Rogers would come to know him simply as
Nikoli. An electrical engineer by training who had never studied English formally, he was brought into the agency in part to clean up the
confusing mess of international Tetris deals and the conspicuous lack
of money coming in from them. Belikov was not the sort to fly off to
Paris for a relaxed negotiating session with Robert Stein over wine
and French food, as his predecessor had done. Instead, he suspected
there was money out there that should be coming into Soviet coffers
and that someone on the other side of the ideological divide between
Communism and capitalism was keeping it all for themselves.

If Belikov distrusted Western companies, from Andromeda to
Mirrorsoft, he had good reason to, and he let his brusque Soviet attitude and tank-like build make up for his lack of practical experience
in business and negotiating. Even though unsavvy about licensing
deals and royalties, he knew that having a new Tetris suitor show up
on his doorstep today could work in his favor, giving him more
leverage to wield against his next two expected guests, Robert Stein
and Kevin Maxwell.

Even letting this newcomer in the front door was major breach of
protocol, but Belikov was intent on sizing up Henk Rogers and seeing whether he was someone who could be of use to him in his plan
to pit his so-called partners, Stein and Maxwell, against each other.
His plan was simple: tell this newcomer to return the next day, by
which time Alexey Pajitnov could be called in from the Russian
Academy of Sciences to make this a more official meeting and to
increase the number of potentially paying suitors to three.

Rogers was welcomed back the following morning and led to one
of ELORG's ornate conference rooms, filled with an imposing lineup
of stone-faced ELORG suits. He had several versions of his pitch

ready to go, and which he would use depended on how familiar Belikov and his men were with the video game industry, software licensing, and international business deals. Most importantly, he had Nintendo's deep pockets, and with that came the ability—he hoped—to outbid anyone else looking to tie up the handheld rights for Tetris.

The room he was led into was large enough for dozens of people, easily. In a city where he had seen little but depressing constructivist architecture and strictly enforced Soviet minimalism, the mere existence of this room felt like a genuine state secret. This was his first experience with anything in Moscow that smacked of conspicuous consumption.

Rogers sat at one end of a long table and looked down at the ELORG team at the far end, like estranged spouses sharing a formal dining room. Seated alongside the obvious Soviet cogs was a slim, bearded man, as calm as he was out of place. He was the man no one in the West had spoken directly to outside of a handful of telexes: Alexey Pajitnov. Belikov had brought Pajitnov, still laboring away at the RAS computer center, to add an air of authority to his planned meetings with Stein and Maxwell. With the game's creator at his side, there was no one in the room who could command more authority about what would be done with Tetris than Belikov.

Rogers and Pajitnov studied each other carefully. If anyone else understood the trials of building a groundbreaking video game almost single-handedly, a project that had almost broken Rogers, it was Pajitnov. The Black Onyx, his reputation-making masterwork, was in a way infinitely more complex than Tetris, yet not nearly as elegant. Just as Rogers had seen his newly created Japanese RPG genre taken over by the major players in the Japanese game market, Pajitnov's perfectly simple game had been taken over by the Soviet government, now hawking it for profit, with its creator wheeled out infrequently, and then only for the sake of appearances.

The ELORG negotiators' stone-faced demeanors were anything but an act. Rogers took the initiative, practically leading the meeting and wondering exactly how unschooled these men were about the deals they were trying to strike. Taking their silence as a cover for inexperience, he played the room much differently from how Kevin

Maxwell or Robert Stein would have. He took his time to explain how international software deals worked and how so many companies were now involved with Tetris in one way or another.

The situation was actually more stark than Rogers even imagined. Despite leading the team responsible for untangling the worldwide mess Tetris rights had become, Belikov was alarmingly unsophisticated about finance. He had no real experience with any kind of modern financial tools, from bank accounts to credit cards, and he even took his ELORG payments in cash.

During a recess in the lengthy session, Rogers made the first approach, walking up to Pajitnov, who had been quietly watching as ELORG officials peppered their visitor with questions. Offering his hand, Rogers told the Russian programmer that he was fascinated by Tetris and very glad to meet him at long last.

For his part, Pajitnov found this foreigner to be smart and agreeable. Rogers was asking for nothing concrete up front and was taking the time to lay out the important definitions and concepts along the way, whereas the back-and-forth telexes and letters with Stein were pushy, demanding, and often changed the terms of the deal from one communication to the next. The men from AcademySoft and ELORG were little better, pulling Tetris away from him with no concern for the creator's rights or needs.

Henk Rogers took Belikov through an improvised Software and Games Industry 101 class, betting that his low-pressure approach would have the opposite effect of Robert Stein's abrasive negotiating style, which he suspected had already rubbed the Russians the wrong way. Whether the approach worked or not, Belikov still needed this newcomer as leverage against Robert Stein and Kevin Maxwell, each of whom was booked for formal Tetris meetings later that week. Deciding that Rogers was at least legit enough to serve a purpose by turning a two-way runoff into a three-way one, Belikov offered the formal invitation Rogers had been waiting for.

Come back tomorrow, he told Rogers, and we will be prepared to hear your formal offer for the rights to Tetris on handheld devices.

Rogers had done well in his initial pitch to ELORG, he knew. But Henk Rogers also knew that the software business, much like the gem business, was built one relationship at a time, person to person.

That was how he had forged a unique connection with Nintendo and its Japanese and American presidents, the father-in-law-and-son-in-law team of Yamauchi and Arakawa, and how he hoped to further cement his case for Tetris.

As the meeting broke up, Rogers and Pajitnov gravitated toward each other. Rogers spoke practically no Russian, Pajitnov just basic English, but the language of programmers and game makers was universal. The two men communicated, haltingly, and Pajitnov ended up as an unofficial tour guide. He led Rogers back to his humble Moscow apartment, where he proudly showed off some of his other software, and they toasted their good fortune at meeting each other the traditional Russian way, with vodka. Both men could sense they were now part of an unspoken alliance, although it was not yet clear against whom and for what purpose.

Rogers spent another sleepless night in his comically unappealing hotel room. The sputtering television had to be unplugged to save him from electrocution, dinner required an advance reservation for the restaurant connected to the hotel, and room service was quite literally a foreign concept. But it didn't matter. This was his chance to do an end-run past them all—from Tengen to Spectrum to Sega—and get his Tetris supply straight from the source.

Arriving early for his meeting, Rogers was prepared for anything, or so he thought. In his briefcase were breakdowns of potential revenue and royalties from the handheld Tetris games he hoped to sell with Nintendo as well as an important visual prop he hoped to impress Belikov with: a copy of his own Bullet-Proof Software version of Tetris for the Nintendo Famicom in Japan, proof that even through the complex maze of rights already circling the globe, Tetris was alive and well and building a fan base.

Seated once again across from Belikov, Rogers danced around the exact nature of the Game Boy device being made by Nintendo. It was a concept the Russians might have had trouble understanding, because the entire Soviet video game culture at the moment consisted of a handful of imported PC games along with a few locally grown ones such as Tetris plus a few hard-to-find arcade machines.

Forget about whatever royalties you're currently getting through Robert Stein, he told them. This is going to top all of that very quickly and bring in a substantial amount of money. He knew to hit this point hard, because it was already clear that the existing master agreement with Stein and Andromeda was trickling in very little money to Moscow, if any.

To drive home that point, Rogers reached into his briefcase and produced the most concrete example he could think of to show his commitment to Tetris, a copy of the game his company had produced for Nintendo's Famicom. It was already a top seller in Japan, where Rogers had successfully sublicensed, to the best of his knowledge, both the PC and home game console rights to Tetris.

The palm-sized rectangular Famicom cartridge was tucked into a red cardboard box and featured a red adhesive label over its gray plastic body. That was the only clue as to the game's national origins, because Rogers's version skipped the backward Cyrillic lettering and Russian iconography of some other publishers' versions.

Rogers scanned Belikov's face as he pushed the game box toward him but saw no glint of recognition. What is this? Belikov asked, completely taken off-guard by the Famicom cartridge. Rogers could feel the pit of his stomach fall. Maybe these Russians just don't know what a game cartridge is or what game systems look like in Japan.

He quickly ran through the tortured history of his involvement as a Tetris licensee, from his own Bullet-Proof Software back through Tengen, Spectrum Holobyte, Mirrorsoft, and Andromeda, and how all these different publishers were already selling their own versions of Tetris for PCs, arcades, or home consoles in every major game market in the world.

The more he went on, the more Rogers realized that Belikov had absolutely no idea what he was talking about, and the more he tried to explain the tangle of interconnected deals, the angrier the Russian grew. What was this, Belikov demanded, some kind of pirated version of Tetris, being sold without permission?

Of course, this was genuine, Rogers pleaded. The box itself gave copyright credit to both Bullet-Proof Software and ELORG, as required by his sublicense through Tengen and Mirrorsoft, and it even gave a creator's credit to Pajitnov, phonetically spelled there as "Alexey Pazhinov."

Rogers explained how he had paid a significant sum to pick up the home console rights for Japan from Tengen. But Belikov didn't budge, insisting he had never heard of Tengen. What's more, he roared, as far as ELORG was concerned, their sole licensor was Robert Stein and Andromeda, and that deal covered nothing but Tetris games for home computers. No arcades, no consoles, no handheld devices.

Wait, Rogers said, you must have seen the videotapes of gameplay footage that each licensee was required to pass up the chain for approval by the people in the this very room. Surely there must be some record of that.

Belikov was hearing none of it. He had seen no videotapes, and he knew of no other deals beyond the first flush of computer games, for which, he added, there was still very little money coming in.

After coming all this way, navigating a strange new country, and talking his way through the front door of this secretive Soviet trade group, Rogers could feel it all slipping away as the seconds ticked by. What was worse, he had two hundred thousand Tetris Famicom cartridges in production, and if the Russians shut him down, his company would be finished. Everything he had built through Bullet-Proof Software was tied up in that inventory. What would Arakawa and the other Nintendo executives think if he came back from Russia not only without the handheld rights for the Game Boy but also having inadvertently shut down Tetris sales for the Famicom and Nintendo Entertainment System?

Belikov could see, despite his anger, that Henk Rogers was genuinely surprised by this revelation. Wanting to definitely show Rogers that all the different Tetris games he was now hearing about could not possibly have been authorized by him or the staff at ELORG, he sent for the file containing the current version of Robert Stein's contract.

He proffered the papers to Rogers, and both men scanned page after page until they found the specific section that outlined the rights granted to Stein and Andromeda. The contract clearly referred to Tetris for computers, with no mention of any other gaming platform.

Rogers understood the wording of the contract better than anyone else in the room, having done countless similar deals himself over the years. Yes, it looked like someone along the way had overstepped their bounds or at least interpreted the terms of the deal very, very loosely.

> A working version of Tetris can be unlocked as an Easter egg on certain Hewlett-Packard oscilloscopes by hitting the right combination of buttons.

Even if he was an unwitting party to it, Rogers was a key player in a long line of Tetris games that the Soviet Union considered unauthorized and illegal. That he had inadvertently revealed this while coming to ELORG, hat in hand, asking for special consideration on handheld game rights made it even worse.

Rogers riffled through the options in his mind while the Russians exchanged angry glances. If there was a way to pull out of this nosedive, now would be the time. What leverage could he possibly have with these people?

Moscow had made an impression on him over the past few days, and it was not an entirely positive one. He had seen the deprivation, the practically nonexistent consumer economy, the lack of basic goods and services. He had heard Belikov and the ELORG negotiators complain about money time and again, especially about the thin trickle of money coming in from Tetris.

That was the key, he realized. These guys weren't part of some massive global superpower; they were victims of the slow but steady decline in the fortunes of the Soviet system, and their backs were against the wall just like everyone else in their country. If he was going to win Belikov over, he'd have to speak in a universal language. Rogers did some quick back-of-the-envelope math and leaned in to Belikov.

I've sold about 130,000 copies of this Tetris game, he explained, pointing toward the red-boxed Famicom game that had gotten the Russians so angry in the first place, and this is how it works out for you. He pushed a hastily written check across the table toward Belikov. It was made out to ELORG and was for just over $40,000.

Belikov was shocked, even if he maintained his normal unyielding expression. In all his direct dealings with Stein and Andromeda, or indirect dealings with Mirrorsoft and others, this was the first time anyone had willingly put money on the table like that. No arm-twisting, no threats, just payment.

Rogers explained that this was ELORG's money, free and clear, a legitimate royalty payment for game cartridges already sold. Both parties could have walked away from the table after that at least slightly satisfied that a wrong had been righted. But, Rogers urged, now that we've cleared the air on this, maybe we can move forward and talk about new opportunities.

Belikov listened as Rogers went over some more details of the existing Andromeda contract, but the Russian was already thinking about the next two meetings he had lined up, one with Kevin Maxwell, the other with Robert Stein. These new revelations about versions of Tetris he considered unauthorized cast both meetings in a whole new light. He now had new levers to work to pressure both men into weak negotiating positions if either one was even worth dealing with now.

In front of him sat Henk Rogers, until a day before a complete stranger. But this stranger had already put $40,000 in his hands. How much more could there be where this came from? He couldn't imagine a partner with deeper pockets than the Mirror Group, but what good would that do if royalty payments were not made in full and on time?

In that moment, Belikov decided that Henk Rogers would be brought into the game and given equal standing to ELORG, Mirrorsoft, and Andromeda. He stated that the only valid Tetris contract at that moment was the one between ELORG and Robert Stein and that it was intended to cover Tetris games for computers rather than for home game consoles such as the ones made by Nintendo. Rogers agreed but realized there was still some wiggle room in the language about what exactly was covered by the definition of a computer.

Would Rogers be able to make a legitimate bid for the rights to produce Tetris for all home video game platforms in addition to the original handheld rights he requested? Belikov asked. It would be expensive, he warned.

More than that, Rogers added, it would make some very big companies very angry, including Mirrorsoft and Tengen, the latter of which was owned by Atari Games, still a major force in the industry. But if it was a question about who could throw more money at the problem, or field a bigger army of lawyers, Rogers was ready to play that game. His partners at Nintendo, he announced, would sweep every other bidder aside and cement a permanent alliance that would enrich all involved.

Belikov liked what he was hearing, at least enough to give Rogers a shot. Excusing himself to prepare for his meetings with the other Tetris suitors, he told Rogers to go back and consult with his Japanese backers and return with an offer. "You have three weeks."

19

■ ■ ■ ■ ■

ENEMIES AT THE GATE

Robert Stein waited for his meeting with Nikoli Belikov to begin, unaware that he was the center of a Tetris sandwich, following on the heels of Henk Rogers and soon to be ushered out on the street to make way for Kevin Maxwell.

If Stein had known Rogers was in Moscow chasing a slice of Tetris for himself, he might have regretted blowing off the $25,000 he had been offered for the thus-far unexploited rights to make Tetris for handheld game machines.

Instead, he was worried about how the brusque Belikov would come at him over any perceived lapses in their dealings. The previous head of the ELORG team was easier to deal with and at least came through with some of the new paperwork Stein needed to keep the flow of Tetris money coming in. Sometimes business operations outran the actual signed contracts, but at least with Alexinko he felt fairly certain he could eventually talk his way into whatever kind of signed contract he required.

And what he needed this time was an on-paper deal for the arcade rights to Tetris and a second one for the handheld rights that he could then resell to Rogers or anyone else who was willing to bid more. The first part of this was especially important, because Tetris arcade machines were already in circulation, although Stein figured it unlikely anyone in Moscow was aware of that.

Enter Belikov. Playing exactly to type, the large Russian pushed a pile of papers toward Stein. It was the original contract from nine months earlier in May 1988, and ELORG was now asking for a list of revisions. This is already a done deal, Stein pleaded. We're here to talk about new business.

But Belikov was having none of it. He ran his finger down the page of contract revisions and highlighted why it was so important for Stein to sign the revised contract. New penalties for late payment of royalties would kick in and in fact be backdated to the original date of the contract.

They were finally coming after Stein for the money. He wouldn't have admitted to withholding anything ELORG was entitled to, at least not in the long run, but if the Russians wanted to stick to a strict payment schedule, Tetris was getting big enough worldwide that it was worth the extra hassle.

Besides, Stein was eager to talk about arcade and handheld games. Nyet, Belikov told him. Sign this amendment first; then we can talk about other deals. From the look on his face, Stein could tell there would be no moving this Russian bear, at least not today.

Best to take these new documents back to his hotel to give them due diligence, Stein figured. So, he returned to his room at the Kosmos, a gaudy gold-colored horseshoe of a hotel built for Moscow's would-be moment of international triumph, the summer 1980 Olympic Games (a moment tarnished when the United States and more than sixty other nations boycotted the games over the USSR's involvement in Afghanistan).

There he went over the contract amendment document more carefully and reluctantly decided to sign it. Some more paperwork and accounting to keep him busy, but a small price to pay to get all his other Tetris rights in order. He grabbed a sheet of paper and a pen and hand-wrote general terms for the arcade and handheld Tetris rights, fully intending to serve the document to Belikov the next day as a binding deal memo, not even waiting to get it properly typed up and duplicated.

Was Stein so caught up in the moment that he failed to notice a subtle language change in the original contract amendment? It was one that would act as a poison pill, designed to blow up all his expectations and put almost all of Tetris back in play.

While Robert Stein was at his hotel reading over the contract amendment, another visitor appeared at the ELORG offices. Kevin Maxwell was the head of both of the Mirror Group's major software publishers, Mirrorsoft and Spectrum Holobyte, but in truth, he had little experience in the video game business. He had pulled rank to take over the Tetris negotiations for reasons that had more to do with family than business.

His father, Robert Maxwell, had long-standing ties to Russia and more importantly had the ear of General Secretary Mikhail Gorbachev. Pulling off a complex deal in the USSR, essentially stealing the Tetris rights away from the troublesome Robert Stein, would no doubt cast Kevin in a good light, a welcome change from the regular power struggles that occurred at the highest levels of the Maxwell empire, both inside and outside the family.

Navigating that particular familial hierarchy was famously difficult, and Kevin felt great pressure to please the elder Maxwell, both as a child and as an employee. Kevin and his brother Ian, the two youngest sons of nine children, each adopted parts of their father's outsized personality. Whereas Ian mirrored Robert Maxwell's charm and flair for salesmanship, down to the bold, eye-catching ties they wore to stand out in meetings, Kevin adopted some of Robert's darker traits. He was drawn to the aggressive business tactics and ruthless drive for empire building that had created the Mirror Group in the first place. For his father's sixty-fifth birthday, just a year before, he had toasted the old man, saying, "Above all, you have given me the sense of excitement of having dozens of balls in the air and the thrill of seeing some of them land right."

That was the gamble Kevin Maxwell took, coming to Moscow to personally oversee Mirrorsoft's attempt to clean up the rights to Tetris. Considering his father's long-standing ties to the Soviet Union as one of the few international tycoons comfortable operating on both sides of the Cold War divide, it would be an egregious mistake to let this particular ball drop.

Meeting with Belikov at ELORG headquarters, Maxwell turned on the mix of charm and power that had worked so well for his father, transitioning from casual chat to demanding a quick settlement of the outstanding issues surrounding rights to Tetris. But Belikov was not going to be cowed by a second-generation tycoon used to getting his way, at least not today.

Since this meeting had first been arranged, two new factors had come into play. Henk Rogers was now Belikov's potentially deep-pocketed backup plan, and Robert Stein had just been sent on his way, seemingly unaware of the ticking time bomb buried in the contract revision he carried. Both men were exactly where Belikov wanted them to be, and now it was time to put Kevin Maxwell in his place.

Cutting Maxwell off, Belikov slid a red box across the table. Inside it was the Famicom version of Tetris that Henk Rogers and Bullet-Proof Software had published, a game that Belikov had newly become aware of. Just as its appearance from Rogers's briefcase had surprised the ELORG negotiators, this was the last thing Kevin Maxwell expected to see.

Just what is this? Belikov demanded of his guest. Maxwell scrambled to figure out what was going on. This looked like a version of Tetris; the packaging was half in Japanese; the design was unfamiliar to him; and this was a cartridge for a home game system, not the PC game that Mirrorsoft was currently selling. Maxwell answered that he had never seen that box or that version of the game before, and he was telling the truth.

Then why, the inquisition continued, was Mirrorsoft's name on the packaging, along with Tengen's, Bullet-Proof Software's, and even ELORG's? The tendrils of Tetris ran through several software publishing companies across multiple countries, and Maxwell was unfamiliar with all but the versions closest to his business. Yes, he knew some rights to the game had been horse-traded to other companies, but he operated at too high a level within the Maxwell organization to be up-to-date on the layers of sublicensing deals.

He scrambled to put the red box in context, to keep from losing the upper hand he felt he had when he walked in the door of this backward agency run by Communists with no head for business. Maxwell chose to bluff the problem away.

This must be a pirated game cartridge, he calmly explained, because Mirrorsoft was not in the business of selling Nintendo cartridges, and this was exactly why ELORG and Mirrorsoft needed to form a tighter bond, so illegal knockoffs such as this could be stamped out.

Maxwell was wrong, of course, and his bluff failed badly. Belikov said nothing. He knew the exact provenance of the Japanese Tetris cartridge, and even had Henk Rogers's check for past royalties owed in his pocket. As far as Belikov was concerned, Maxwell and Stein had, in some combination, sold off the home console rights to Tetris through a series of deals with other software publishers in clear violation of the original agreement.

Maxwell had either walked into this room and lied to his face about it, or else he was so unaware that he assumed it was a pirated game. Either way, this conversation showed Belikov exactly where he stood with Maxwell. The question remained, what to do with this so-called titan of industry? Kicking him out would be satisfying, no doubt, but short-sighted if Mirrorsoft still had the money ready to put into a larger deal. Besides, Robert Maxwell was a well-connected figure in Soviet power circles, and treating his son shabbily, even if it was well deserved, might carry consequences.

> One of the rarest Tetris artifacts is the Sega Genesis version of the game, of which there are only a handful of cartridges known to exist.

Maxwell grew impatient waiting for Belikov to resume the negotiation and launched back into his pitch for the handheld and arcade rights he still assumed were his for the taking. The Russian waved him off, pushed back from the table, grabbed the supposedly pirated Tetris game cartridge, and exited the room, leaving Maxwell stewing.

After an appropriate period of time to throw his visitor off balance, Belikov returned and laid down the new realities of their situation. Things had changed, he explained, but this could still be an opportunity for Maxwell to clean up all the available rights. Nothing could be finalized today, he said, at least until the mystery of the

pirated game is cleared up, but Maxwell would now be given a limited right of first refusal on new Tetris rights and would be expected
to come back shortly with an offer for the console game rights as
well.

For Belikov, this last part was especially important. Maxwell had
disavowed the already published versions of Tetris for home game
consoles, and if he now accepted an offer to bid on the console rights,
he would cement the concept that those rights had yet to be assigned
to anyone by ELORG.

But that was not to be the end of it. Belikov twisted the knife just
a little more, as he watched Maxwell realize there would be no licensing deal signed that day. In return for this very generous right
of first refusal, ELORG would need something of value. Today's
bounty was the Russian rights to some of Maxwell Communications'
library of reference publications. It was a demand completely outside
of the software issues he had come to discuss, but Maxwell was ready
to agree to anything, having just ping-ponged from being accused of
piracy to being offered the chance to take the ultimate prize, the
potentially very valuable console rights for Tetris.

Belikov walked out of the meeting with new reference book publishing rights, a small victory, but more importantly, he now had two
potential bidders waiting to throw money at him for Tetris. For his
part, Kevin Maxwell walked out with only a piece of paper labeled as
a "protocol agreement," which was potentially worth millions or, just
as easily, could be completely worthless.

Belikov would have been more than satisfied with this as a day's
work, but there was still an important loose thread hanging out, one
that could threaten the entire enterprise. He would have to wait until the following day to see whether Robert Stein would return with
the signed contract additions, and he hoped Stein would not have
read the fine print too carefully.

That evening, Henk Rogers met up with Alexey Pajitnov again.
This time, instead of Pajitnov's apartment, the pair retired to Rogers's minimalist hotel room, where he said he had something very
special to show his new friend. Rogers rolled out a small portable
television he had brought along from Japan. It seemed incredibly

high-tech to Pajitnov, although Rogers explained that it was useless for actually watching television here, because Russia and Japan used different broadcast standards. In the background, Rogers's own hotel room TV sat unplugged, its frayed power cable too dangerous to leave connected to a power outlet.

No, the portable TV was for Rogers's personal Nintendo Famicom. Alexey Pajitnov was about to get his first opportunity to play Tetris on a home gaming console. He was buzzing with excitement, at least at first.

Rogers slipped the red cartridge into the machine and turned it on. As the television came to life in a warm glow, Pajitnov squinted at the small screen. The Tetris graphics seemed fuzzy and indistinct to him, a victim of the low-resolution signal put out by the console. As a computer guy, he was used to higher resolutions and sharper graphics, even in something simple like Tetris. He shrugged; there was just no way around the technical limitations of playing a game on a soft-focus television screen instead of a crisp professional computer monitor.

Gripping the rectangular gamepad that controlled every Famicom game, Pajitnov struggled through a few rounds of Tetris. As the bricks piled up toward the top of the screen, he wondered why he wasn't doing better. Being the game's creator should give him some kind of edge, right? This game played faster than his original version, but not so much that he should top out so quickly.

He realized it was the gamepad. On the computer version, he needed only one hand to play, using the arrow keys on the right side of the keyboard to control the game. It was a perfect system for right-handed players like himself. But the Nintendo gamepad required using both hands, and the most important controls, the ones for moving and dropping the tetrominoes, were under his left thumb.

Pajitnov wasn't sure how to react. He didn't want to insult his new friend and ally, but the console version of Tetris just didn't feel right. The timing was off, dropping tetrominoes too quickly, and the gamepad controls were awkward, favoring the left hand too much. He complimented Rogers on his achievement as sincerely as he could, but inside he was less than impressed. Still, just knowing

Tetris was this far out into the world already was a heady feeling, and if no one else could program a version of Tetris as perfectly tuned as his original, that was certainly understandable.

The next morning, Robert Stein arrived back at the ELORG offices, ready to turn the tide of the negotiations back in his favor by pushing both the amended agreement and his own handwritten deal memo for the handheld and arcade rights at Belikov as a tit-for-tat deal. Belikov looked over Stein's proposed deal, but this was a pretense; the handheld rights were already almost certainly going to Henk Rogers and it was just a matter of seeing which party would end up with the potentially bigger deal for home consoles.

But Belikov sensed Stein had been pushed close to his limit, and getting that signed contract amendment was vital for Belikov's plans. We're not ready to sign off on the handheld rights, Belikov told Stein, keeping the idea in play, if just out of reach. But to keep his target intrigued, he dangled something else: rights to the coin-op arcade machine version.

Stein knew new Tetris arcade machines were already in operation in Japan and the United States, so he needed those rights on paper before someone else nabbed them and left him in a very tight spot. So, fine, he'd sign the amendment for his original Tetris contract and deal with the new penalties for late royalty payments. He was happy to get that outstanding issue nailed down, but less happy when Belikov told him he had six weeks to come up with a $150,000 advance against arcade game royalties.

With the high advance, the late payment penalties, and the now-you-see-them-now-you-don't handheld rights, it's little wonder Robert Stein missed the entire point of his meetings with ELORG. A subtle change in wording was included in the backdated amendment to the previous year's contract. It read that the deal covered not simply Tetris games on computers but also "PC computers which consist of a processor, monitor, disk drive(s), keyboard, and operating system."

It was this more specific definition within the deal, now backdated to its original date, that would later prove so pivotal in a courtroom on the other side of the world. For now, however, it was simply a trump card Belikov could save and play at the right moment.

For a bunch of Soviet bureaucrats who not too long ago could barely handle selling defective calculators to Eastern Bloc nations, Nikoli Belikov and his ELORG crew were suddenly wheeling and dealing like experienced technology salesmen. Perhaps some of Henk Rogers's entrepreneurial spirit had rubbed off on them; perhaps they were tired of being treated like backwoods rubes by everyone who wanted a slice of the Tetris action. Over the course of a few days, Belikov had managed to get a $40,000 check from Henk Rogers as well as a promise of a potentially multi-million-dollar deal from Rogers's mysterious backers at some company called Nintendo; he had sent Kevin Maxwell away with next to nothing, while keeping the media company heir in play as a second bidder for the console rights to Tetris; and finally, he had exacted a small measure of revenge on Robert Stein, who would at the very least have to finally start paying ELORG on time and who might even come up with $150,000 in advance for arcade game rights.

Back at his hotel room, Henk Rogers was now part of a much larger game than he expected. Far from a midsize deal for handheld Tetris games, he now had a chance to broker a master deal between ELORG and Nintendo for nearly everything. Just his small cut of a deal like that could be worth countless millions, and he knew he had to act fast. The Russians would not wait around forever, and, to seal a deal like that, he would have to coax the top leadership of Nintendo into action and drag at least a few of the most powerful executives in the video game business back to Moscow with him.

He was sure of one silver lining: no one at ELORG, at Mirrorsoft, or anywhere else outside of himself and perhaps Minoru Arakawa, understood just what a massive product the Nintendo Game Boy would be, especially if paired with Tetris. He could make it all happen, but it had to be now.

20

■ ■ ■ ■ ■

"MEET AT THE CHICKEN"

Howard Lincoln couldn't believe what he was hearing. He could live with the fact that Henk Rogers had returned from Moscow reporting that some Soviet trade group with a name right out of a James Bond film was in charge of the rights to Tetris. And he was downright happy to hear that ELORG was getting jerked around by several other video game companies and was ready to drop them all in favor of Nintendo. But there was one fact that made him furious: one of the main rivals in question was the Atari Games subsidiary named Tengen, and Tengen was planning a major release of Tetris for the Nintendo Entertainment System.

Lincoln, along with the rest of the top tier of executives at Nintendo of Japan and Nintendo of America, was locked in a long-term legal battle with Atari Games and its charismatic leader, Hide Nakajima. Once close allies, but now bitter enemies, the two companies had a falling out over Tengen's attempts to hack a lockout chip system built into Nintendo consoles and games. The system, called 10NES, was put into place by Nintendo to keep tight control over who made games for the NES, and a version of the digital lock-and-key system has been in place on virtually every game system since then, including PlayStation and Xbox consoles.

The basic technology in question was simple. Program a game, make it into a cartridge, plug it into a Nintendo console, and then hit the power button. Nothing happens. That's because you don't have a special microchip inside the cartridge that acts as a key. The console looks for this chip, sometimes known as a lockout chip, and if it detects one, the game starts. If it doesn't, nothing happens.

Nintendo made the proprietary lockout chips for its consoles, and if you wanted to make a game for the NES, you had to buy these special chips directly from Nintendo. And you could only do that if you agreed to Nintendo's standard terms for royalty rates and gave the company the right to sign off on the actual content of your game. Nintendo tightly controlled the supply of chips, essentially limiting what games other companies could publish and how many copies of each game they could manufacture.

> Guinness World Records has declared a version of Tetris projected on the side of a twenty-nine-story building in Philadelphia in 2014 to be the "Largest architectural video game display."

For Nakajima, the problem was not so much the copy protection built into the lockout chip system but instead the stock publishing agreement Nintendo presented to him when he came calling on Lincoln and Arakawa at Nintendo of America's offices in Redmond.

Arakawa went to great lengths to explain the many demands Nintendo made of its publishing partners, and why these deals needed to be exactly the same for everyone, no matter who was involved. Besides, Arakawa explained to Nakajima, it's not just the contract details that are important, it's your relationship with Nintendo, and if you needed any help getting into Walmart or Sears or Kmart, our sales guys could help you.

Lincoln could see his boss was going out of his way to help make the partnership happen, and both he and Arakawa considered Nakajima a friend, someone they knew very well in a close-knit industry.

Nakajima had walked into the meeting assuming that as a major player in the games business with deep personal connections at the highest levels, he could appeal for more favorable terms. No, Arakawa told him, it was the same deal for everyone, and he could either take it or leave it.

Frustrated, Nakajima started down two parallel roads. First, in 1987, he signed on as an official Nintendo licensee, agreeing to what he considered to be a bad deal, just to get the first round of Tengen games into stores and onto Nintendo systems. At the same time, Tengen set up a special engineering unit to find a way to reverse-engineer the Nintendo 10NES security system. The goal was to build a game cartridge that would play in a Nintendo console without the special lockout chips Nintendo held a monopoly on and to cut Nintendo out of the loop entirely.

Tengen engineers quickly claimed they had made a breakthrough and had discovered a way to bypass the Nintendo technology. The company prepared to release a slew of games that would play on the NES without the need for Nintendo's custom lockout chip.

It was the day after Nintendo of America's 1988 Christmas party that Howard Lincoln discovered what Nakajima was up to: he woke up to Tengen's public claims of reverse-engineering the 10NES system in order to publish NES games entirely on its own. They've turned on us, he thought. It was no longer a business issue, it was personal, and both he and Arakawa felt they had been betrayed by a friend.

Adding insult to injury, Tengen followed with a lawsuit accusing Nintendo of monopolistic practices. The back-and-forth lawsuits over this copy protection circumvention poisoned the relationship between the companies and their executives from that point on.

The reality of Nakajima's ability to hack the Nintendo system was somewhat more complex than the company let on. Tengen's Randy Broweleit had spent the previous year smoothing over any tension between Nintendo and Tengen over Nakajima's original fight for better publishing terms. For Broweleit, that meant accepting whatever Nintendo demanded and making sure Tengen and parent Atari Games were being good corporate citizens.

Despite initial apprehensions, Broweleit found that once he got his teammates accustomed to following Nintendo's strict rules, the Japanese gaming giant was surprisingly easy to work with. Tengen's first wave of games was hot, and Nintendo wanted more of the same. Being one of the public faces of Tengen when defending the company's controversial reverse engineering of the Nintendo lockout chip was not a task he looked forward to. Still, reverse-engineering existing technology was a well-established legal right in most cases, and Broweleit felt confident in saying that Tengen had figured out the secret to bypassing Nintendo's technology honestly.

It was only later that he came to suspect that the story might have had other angles. It turned out that Tengen lawyers had gone to the US Patent and Trademark Office and talked their way into obtaining a copy of Nintendo's trade secret patent documents, claiming they were needed for their own legal filings. With the actual proprietary schematics for 10NES under the same roof as the engineers working on reverse-engineering the system, the company's efforts were tainted. Even though Tengen maintained that this happened entirely independently from the in-house reverse-engineering plan, it was too late—it would eventually all come to be seen as fruit from a poisoned tree.

Broweleit soon became worried that his team had not done a clean job of reverse-engineering the Nintendo lockout chips, especially because he had been quoted widely, from the *New York Times* to the *Wall Street Journal*, defending Tengen's honor. Like Lincoln and Arakawa, he would also come to feel betrayed by people he considered close friends, even mentors. But for now, the push to release new chip-free Nintendo games, including a new NES version of Tetris, continued.

For Lincoln and Arakawa, it was galvanizing to hear that Tengen was also mixed up in the Tetris negotiations. Rogers might as well have waved a red cape in front of two bulls. Lincoln, by nature the more aggressive of the two, was especially determined to go for the throat. Only a week after Rogers had made his sojourn into Russia, Howard Lincoln packed for his own trip to Moscow, this time with a new purpose: find a way to take down Tengen.

Rogers had succeeded beyond anyone's wildest dreams, bringing back the handheld rights he was originally looking for and a chance to snatch up the rights to make Tetris games for living room consoles around the world. If the global fever for Tetris continued its slow but steady spread across these new platforms, that could be a deal worth tens of millions. As it turned out, he was wrong: it was worth significantly more.

Not wanting to lose the thread, Arakawa had sent Rogers right back to Moscow, this time with a New York lawyer named John Huhs, who had the perfect résumé for the job—he had worked in the Soviet Union previously, was fluent in Russian, and had put in time with mercurial, oppressive regimes, having worked in the Nixon administration. With Rogers as the video game expert and Huhs on board to translate his ideas into legal language the ELORG negotiators could more easily understand, the pair had Belikov itching to sign the master deal, thanks to the deep pockets of Nintendo and the reported $5 million minimum guaranteed payment the pair had been authorized to offer.

It was an amazing amount of money for the Russians, who until then had been picking up smaller sums, from $150,000 for Robert Stein's arcade game rights to $40,000 from Rogers for royalties on his Japanese NES cartridges. Nikolai Belikov did not want to let this opportunity slip through his fingers—it could be the crowning achievement of his time at ELORG and a chance to lay down an important marker during a time when accelerating change and upheaval were the order of the day in the USSR.

But Belikov still had one wild card hanging over his head. In dismissing Kevin Maxwell weeks before, he had given Mirrorsoft what effectively amounted to a right of first refusal on any deal for Tetris console rights, and that needed to be cleared off the table before he could take Nintendo's money.

Cutting out a major player like the Maxwell family carried risks, but Belikov was determined to minimize them. A fact that worked in his favor was that Maxwell and Mirrorsoft had not followed up on the initial Moscow meeting with their own offer for the console rights, so the game was clearly not top of mind to them. Because Kevin Maxwell had missed his own deadline for submitting an initial bid, Belikov decided to give him only the thinnest possible pretense of a chance to respond to Nintendo's offer, as required by their protocol agreement.

A fax sent on March 15, 1989, gave Mirrorsoft until the next day to respond, and when, as Belikov predicted, no reply came, he indicated to Rogers and Huhs that he was ready to sign the deal. But, although Rogers and Huhs were perfectly legitimate in making proposals and negotiating, neither one was actually a Nintendo employee. For a deal this big, the leadership of Nintendo of America would have to come to Moscow in person to sign on the dotted line.

As Lincoln packed, so did Arakawa. But both had to do so in near-total secrecy. Only a handful of trusted advisers knew of their true destination, and most of the staff at Nintendo of America thought their two bosses were going to Japan for typical company business. The reason for the deception was to avoid alerting Nakajima and Atari, whom they were already fighting in court over the lockout chip issue. To scuttle Atari/Tengen's Tetris plans would be a major victory in the battle between the two companies, but until the Tetris rights had been secured, they did not want to tip their hand and give Nakajima a chance to cause further havoc.

Arranging a last-minute trip to the Soviet Union in the late 1980s was about as easy as getting into a war zone. Lincoln and Arakawa flew first from Seattle to Los Angeles, and then took an overnight flight to Washington, DC, where they expected to find prearranged visas waiting at the Soviet embassy. Of course, despite Huhs's assurances, there were no visas, and no one at the consulate seemed to have any idea what Lincoln was talking about. By late afternoon, a new telex had arrived from Moscow, and the pair could continue on the next two legs of their journey, flying first to London, where they would have to stay overnight before boarding the final flight to Moscow.

The trouble at the Soviet consulate in Washington was all but forgotten by the time the pair landed in the USSR, if only because they barely made their flight for the final leg of trip, with Lincoln oversleeping in his London hotel and he and Arakawa racing to the airport and hustling his disheveled self through security just in the nick of time.

When they disembarked from the airplane to find Rogers waiting for them, it hardly seemed as if this was only Henk Rogers's second visit to Russia. Ever at ease across different cultures, Rogers picked the two Nintendo executives up at the airport in a rented Mercedes and already came off like an old hand at showing newcomers around Moscow.

It was March, and Arakawa marveled at the extreme weather and how legions of Muscovites roared over the snow-covered roads in old cars without snow tires. Rogers seems to know his way around, Lincoln thought, impressed at how quickly their host had taken to Russian living. He was less impressed with their hotel complex, immediately labeling it "a dump."

He and Arakawa did not even get to enjoy the modest charms of that dump. They were shunted off to a secondary building next door, more like a Soviet condo complex, used when the hotel's regular rooms were either full or in too extreme a state of disrepair for human habitation. Walking into a supposed luxury apartment, the two men found a single sparse bedroom—the second bed would be the living room couch—and a collection of kitchen appliances that was apparently just for show—nothing was hooked up to the water or gas lines. Lincoln took one look and said, "God, this is just awful, but it's probably the best hotel they've got."

Retiring for the night after a brief sojourn in the city streets for supplies, Arakawa marveled at just how different Moscow was from the United States and Japan. The few stores that seemed to have anything worth buying only accepted US dollars, which he took to mean that these were set up purely to service the small but financially important contingent of foreign businesspeople living in or visiting the city and were off-limits to locals.

Lincoln woke the following morning in the condo's sole bedroom, and Arakawa stirred on the couch down the hall. He recalled the instructions Henk Rogers had given him for how the team was to assemble for a breakfast meeting before heading to the ELORG offices: "Meet at the chicken."

In the center of the lobby of the hotel—the hotel they were supposed to be staying at instead of the overflow building next door—was an unexplained piece of sculpture that looked to everyone involved like a chicken. So, "meet at the chicken" became the easiest way to get everyone together.

Eating in Moscow was still a challenge. Reservations had to be made, usually a day in advance, or diners would be turned away even if they carried precious foreign currency. Rogers had learned from his first trip to the city and arranged a four-person breakfast reservation at the hotel's dining room for himself, Huhs, Lincoln, and Arakawa.

"When I take you up for breakfast, don't panic," Rogers warned the others as they rode the hotel elevator to the dining floor. "Because you're going to smell stuff that you couldn't believe."

How bad could it really be? Lincoln asked himself. But as soon as the elevator doors slid open, the smell of the place was just appalling. Russian breakfasts at the time could include anything from meat stews made of pig's trotters and offal to boiled dumplings stuffed with a variety of pungent meats. The iron-fisted reservation system at local restaurants prevented them from fleeing for a better breakfast option, so they stayed but consumed little more than toast that morning.

The foursome assembled later that morning with the ELORG team. Lincoln and Arakawa were the fresh faces; at this point Rogers, Huhs, Pajitnov, and Belikov were familiar enough with each other to have established a kind of joking camaraderie. The Russians sized up the newcomers, and the Nintendo execs did the same.

Arakawa zeroed in on Pajitnov. In Nintendo's culture of video games driven by auteur-like designers, a one-man creative force like Pajitnov was a concept he was familiar with, and Tetris's inventor came off as quiet and gentlemanly.

Lincoln focused on Belikov as the primary decision maker in the room. Forming the right bond with him would be key and, based on what Rogers had told him about the state of Tetris deals before now, trust was a major issue.

These guys resent being treated like a bunch of rubes, Lincoln reasoned. He pegged Belikov as not particularly business-savvy but at least admirably upfront about the troubles he'd had to date. Look, we're a legitimate company, Lincoln explained. We're not going to play games with you, and we're going to pay you a lot of money.

In his head he added, Well, maybe not a lot of money for us, but a lot for you.

Arakawa sat quietly as Lincoln talked, watching each of the players. The Russians surprised him with their questions. He got the impression that they had very little experience dealing with people from the West and found they still required some very elementary tutorials about the structure of business deals and contracts.

Lincoln was more concerned about the earlier Tetris deals. It was all well and good to say that the console rights for Tetris were available for purchase, but there were already Tetris console games either for sale or coming onto the market soon, so clearly other software publishers disagreed with ELORG's interpretation of the current state of Tetris rights.

Belikov went back to the case file, laying reams of paperwork out in front of Lincoln and Arakawa. They sifted through the contracts and faxes, all the way back to the original telex messages from Robert Stein. In all the mess there was one key document that made the case crystal clear.

It was the contract amendment signed just a month before by Robert Stein. For Stein, it was about penalties for late payments and royalty rates. But Lincoln understood Belikov's real intention almost immediately. The revised definition in that amendment defined a computer, for which Stein and his sublicensees still had a legitimate claim, as having a monitor, disk drive, keyboard, and operating system. Such a list could describe many types of devices, but it would certainly not describe a living room game console such as the Nintendo Entertainment System.

That was the smoking gun they were looking for, and it confirmed to their satisfaction that the console rights they were about to buy were legally available. Lincoln knew that, if they got those rights, he and Arakawa could really go after Nakajima and Tengen, an idea both men relished.

Nintendo's base of operations moved to the offices of a Japanese trading company in Moscow, where Rogers, Lincoln, Huhs, and Arakawa worked on the basic outline of the deal. Suspecting that simple tools they took for granted in the West might be hard to come by in Russia, Arakawa arranged for a basic suite of office technology to be delivered from the United States, including a computer, fax machine, and printer, which enabled the team to go through contract revisions quickly.

The days dragged on, with the Russians concerned about vetting each section to make sure they were not being taken for another ride, and the Nintendo execs primarily concerned with establishing that ELORG would stand by the deal during the inevitable legal challenges to follow. We know there's going to be litigation and Tengen isn't going to roll over, Lincoln explained to Belikov. This is going to be expensive. Nintendo is going to pay you a lot of money, but we're also going to spend a lot of money defending our rights and going after Tengen.

Beyond the language and culture gaps, negotiations never got especially contentious, at least until Lincoln brought up one very sensitive issue. Alexey Pajitnov, even though on hand to act as the face of Tetris, would not actually be receiving any of the money coming in from his creation. In the United States and Japan, video game creators were well compensated, and some of the top names were even entitled to a cut of sales or royalties. A handful, including Nintendo's Miyamoto, were genuine rock stars to a generation of gamers.

When Lincoln suggested cutting Pajitnov in on the action, he could see right away that Belikov thought the idea was out of bounds. The shocked look on the Russian's face said that anyone who would even suggest such as thing was nuts. "No, no, no," he roared, "that's not appropriate."

These exchanges about what Pajitnov was and was not entitled to did not go unnoticed by Rogers, nor did the fact that Pajitnov had, on paper, granted the Russian Academy of Sciences and ELORG control over Tetris for a ten-year span, which would end in 1995. That was still years away, but with Gorbachev and glasnost changing the Soviet Union from the inside, it was impossible not to think that the situation might not look very different in five or six years. Rogers filed that particular piece of information away for later use.

One thing was true the world over: business deals were not restricted to office hours and official meetings. Rogers was determined to further develop the friendship he had formed with Pajitnov during his first trip to Moscow. He invited the Russian programmer to join him, Lincoln, and Arakawa at the closest thing to a respectable eating establishment they could find.

Unlike the unbearable breakfast service, this was a legitimate dining spot, and even more unexpectedly, it was a Japanese restaurant, perhaps the only one in Moscow at the time. The restaurant could not have asked for a more demanding audience than a pair of executives from a Japanese company and a Westerner who had lived in Japan for years.

Arakawa found the food surprisingly good, especially compared with some of the other meals the team had endured. The secret was that the restaurant received a delivery of fresh fish every day, flown in on a Japan Air Lines flight. The cuisine was considered authentic, which was known to cause some problems because sushi was not universally well known outside of Japan at the time and was only starting to become popular in the United States. Incredulous servers at the restaurant had learned to deal with Western and Russian businessmen who demanded bread with their meals by discreetly slipping it to them wrapped in cloth napkins.

Marveling over the entire surreal experience as they ordered sushi, Lincoln wondered why Pajitnov still hadn't arrived. It seemed unlike the polite programmer to blow off an invitation. Eventually, he wandered out the front door to the street and found his missing dinner guest cooling his heels on the sidewalk.

The entrance to the restaurant was guarded by a couple of bouncers in leather jackets, and they seemed to control the flow of who was allowed in. Pajitnov found his entrance blocked, and not without reason. Like most of the other higher-end stores and amenities in Moscow, the restaurant was intended only for moneyed foreigners and the upper reaches of Moscow's business class, and Pajitnov's unshined Russian-style shoes immediately pegged him as an ordinary Muscovite, and therefore not welcome.

"He's with us," Lincoln said, motioning toward Pajitnov and hoping his meaning was understood. Grudgingly, the bouncers allowed Pajitnov to pass so he could join the rest of the party.

On another nighttime excursion Rogers drove his colleagues through the center of Moscow, and Lincoln wondered how the man had managed to become such an expert on navigating the tangled streets of the city so quickly. Rogers hadn't led them astray yet. They eventually parked in front of a building on a street of identical-looking buildings on a block among endless blocks of similar structures around the city, each place rising up with a single entry door on the sidewalk that was invariably crowded by a bunch of people hanging out.

Somewhere in this anonymous tower was the apartment where Alexey Pajitnov lived with his wife, Nina, and their children, Peter and Dmitri. Rogers had been there before on his last trip to the city, but for Lincoln and Arakawa, it was a new experience. They rode the elevator up, trying not to look down through the wide gaps in the floor through which they could see the shaft descending below.

After this inauspicious start, Lincoln was surprised to find what seemed like a fairly nice middle-class apartment, and the group bonded over vodka. The Pajitnov children were amazed to see a Game Boy unit Arakawa had brought, making them some of the first people outside of Nintendo to play with the new game system.

This was the first time Pajitnov had a chance to see Lincoln and Arakawa as ordinary people, not the distant businessmen they presented themselves as during the ELORG negotiating sessions. Before this, he considered them cold and closed off, as if they were from another planet, and completely unlike Henk Rogers, whom he recognized as a kindred spirit almost immediately. Alexey Pajitnov may have been fully on Nintendo's side at this point, but he wasn't the one making the final decisions.

As the writing of the licensing deal drew to a close, Belikov seemed to get cold feet, throwing a handful of last-minute roadblocks in the way. First, he wanted to renegotiate the royalty details, and then he was visibly unnerved by Mirrorsoft's response to his right-of-first-refusal fax from the previous week. In the latest reply, Mirrorsoft's Jim Mackonochie informed ELORG that as far as the Maxwell-owned company was concerned, it already controlled those rights, no matter what Kevin Maxwell had said in person during his contentious visit to the ELORG offices the previous month.

It wasn't enough to derail the signing, but even as Arakawa, Belikov, and Pajitnov put pen to paper on the final contract, it was clear this fight was far from over.

The overall air of tension continued into the evening hours, because there was precious little to do in Moscow for uninitiated visitors. Lincoln had grown weary of trying to find decent restaurants, at one point saying to Rogers, "It would really be nice to see the Bolshoi," referring to the famous theater and opera company that represented Russian culture to much of the outside world.

Not long after, Rogers pulled Lincoln aside. "I've got you and Arakawa tickets to go to the Bolshoi Theater." He drove his two partners to the theater that night in his flashy rented Mercedes, dropping them off right in front of the Roman-style pillars at the main entrance. "I'll pick you both up right here after the show," he promised, before pulling away into the night.

Lincoln and Arakawa entered the hallowed theater, originally built in 1821 to house expansive opera and ballet companies, not knowing exactly what to expect. Despite being acquired at the last minute, their tickets were far from back-row tourist seats, and the two men were amazed to find themselves escorted to an upstairs box overlooking the entire audience. It was just more Henk Rogers magic as far as they were concerned.

Lincoln looked down over the crowd as the performance was about to start. An imposing, nearly bald-headed figure strode through the center aisle, instantly recognizable, even from behind. Leaning over to Arakawa, Lincoln motioned toward the man taking his seat, "Hey, that's Gorbachev."

Arakawa strained to see for himself, while another man who had been sitting silently in the same box inserted himself into their conversation, confirming the identity of the famous audience member. From his demeanor and dress, Lincoln deduced their seatmate was a member of the Russian equivalent of the Secret Service. Below, Gorbachev sat by himself briefly, until a long line of official-looking men marched up the aisle and joined him in the same row, leaving the entire row behind them empty. The government agent explained that the group the general secretary sat with were all members of the Central Committee.

Sitting in their premium seats, Lincoln and Arakawa realized they had no idea what the night's entertainment would be. They had simply wanted to attend a performance at the Bolshoi and had never bothered to ask Rogers what show the tickets were actually for. The printed theater program was no help either, written entirely in Russian. As the performance started, a few musical cues gave it away for Lincoln—it was to be an evening in celebration of the nineteenth-century Russian composer Modest Mussorgsky.

But as the orchestra played, Lincoln's mood soured. He was already dreading his exit strategy with a head of state sitting in the same theater. He whispered to Arakawa, "There's no way we'll ever find Henk Rogers again."

Arakawa smiled. "Oh, yes. He'll be right outside. He said he'd pick us up."

"That's the general secretary of the Communist Party, the head of state. Do you think that they're going to let Henk Rogers anywhere near the entrance to the Bolshoi? There's no way we're ever going to find him."

"Oh, yes, not a problem," Arakawa insisted.

As the last strains of music faded, Lincoln and Arakawa made a break for the front entrance to the theater just as the applause began to swell. They raced down from their box to try to get ahead of the crowd and burst through the front door to find a line of limousines waiting. One nearly at the head of the line was especially extravagant looking and sat low to the ground, as if weighed down by internal armored plating. That must be Gorbachev's limo, Lincoln guessed.

And parked directly in front of it was Henk Rogers's Mercedes.

I have no idea how he did that, Lincoln thought. But it hardly mattered. He and Arakawa dove into the back seat and Rogers sped away, tearing through Red Square late at night as if the country were his to buy and sell.

21

■ ■ ■ ■ ■

A TALE OF TWO TETRISES

The final agreement between ELORG and Nintendo for the console game rights to Tetris had been signed, but the battle over who actually controlled the increasingly popular game was about to enter a dangerous new phase.

Ironically, the handheld rights to Tetris, which would in time become the most valuable piece of that pie, went down virtually without a fight. ELORG had granted those rights to Henk Rogers, who had sublicensed them to Nintendo for use with the new Game Boy handheld system. Only Robert Stein was really put out over this, and he had only been seeking those rights in order to resell them to Rogers at a profit.

At the time, living room game consoles such as the Nintendo Entertainment System and Sega Genesis were king, and outside of optimistic projections from Nintendo's Yamauchi and Arakawa, no one thought handheld gaming would one day trump them all. It turned out that even those best-case projections were off by an order of magnitude, and the Game Boy would eventually sell nearly 120 million units worldwide, around 40 million of which came bundled with a Tetris cartridge.

But on March 22, 1989, all eyes were on the now-final deal for living room console rights. At the same time as Arakawa, Pajitnov, and Belikov were signing the master document, a telex was sent to Mirrorsoft in reply to Mackonochie's claim to already control the console rights. In it, Belikov reported that the rights Kevin Maxwell had promised to bid on were no longer available because they had been granted to Nintendo. A flurry of back-and-forth communiqués followed between the major players, each threatening the other with legal action or claiming to hold rights to some part of the Tetris pie.

Kevin Maxwell himself dived right back in immediately after the Nintendo deal was signed. He threatened Belikov: "You are now in grave breach twice over of our agreements with you," adding that his father's company already controlled "worldwide rights to Tetris on the Nintendo Family Computer" and that the matter would be taken up with the Soviet authorities.

The Maxwells, father and son, were a true wild card because of their deep pockets and because of Robert Maxwell's purported personal connections with General Secretary Gorbachev. Still, it was surprising how quickly Kevin Maxwell had escalated to the nuclear option, essentially threatening to get his dad to call Belikov's boss.

And this was far from an empty threat. Robert Maxwell and Gorbachev were, if not close friends, at least members of a cross-cultural alliance that had served both sides well. Maxwell, with his roots in Eastern Europe and left-leaning politics, was taken more seriously as a newsman when he could get the leader of the USSR to return his phone calls, and Gorbachev benefited from having an influential Western ally who bought ink by the barrel, especially as he was attempting to rewrite the very economic foundations of the Soviet Union, a plan that would soon spiral far out of his control.

As Lincoln, Arakawa, and Rogers prepared to leave Moscow, it was Arakawa who was especially glad to be putting the experience behind him. The deal had been signed—a small miracle in itself—but doing so while simultaneously preparing to fight off the other Tetris suitors and essentially teaching the ELORG negotiators about the basics of software licensing was an extraordinarily taxing feat.

Once the extent of Nintendo's potential investment became clear, the Russians started seeing dollar signs (or ruble signs) everywhere. If you like Tetris, we have many other fine Soviet games you could buy, they offered—as if a team of Russian programmers had been sequestered in a secret computer lab for months to churn out the next Tetris. Or, our giant factories can produce Nintendo consoles here in Russia or manufacture the actual cartridges. Arakawa had seen enough of the institutional dysfunction in Moscow to stay far away from any deeper entanglements.

The Russian flair for the theatrical came to a head during one negotiation session, when Lincoln and Arakawa were introduced to a Soviet cosmonaut, trotted into the room to sell them on a very Western-sounding branding idea. Imagine, they were told, the launch of a glorious Soyuz spacecraft, the pinnacle of Soviet space technology, rising up from the launch pad with the Nintendo name painted on the side. In disbelief, Lincoln cut them off and said Nintendo would have to think about it.

Between that and his third-world hotel accommodations, Arakawa had had enough and vowed never to return to Moscow. If any follow-up meetings were required, Howard Lincoln would have to handle them.

And Lincoln did indeed return to Moscow three more times. One area the Russians were not eager to let go of was the potential tie-in between Nintendo and the Russian space program. On a visit later that year, Belikov escorted Lincoln, accompanied by Lincoln's seventeen-year-old son Brad, to the heart of Russia's space training program, Star City. Officially designated as Closed Military Townlet No. 1, it was the highly secure site outside of Moscow where cosmonauts had trained since the 1960s.

Star City was home to the Yuri Gagarin Cosmonaut Training Center, named after the first man in space, and over the years it grew from a small training facility to a fully formed company town, housing the families of more than 250 full-time employees. Apartment blocks sprang up around the training grounds, as did a post office, high school, and movie theater. In later years, Star City would host international groups from other space programs, participate in an exchange program with American high school students, and even erect a statue of a small dog atop a rocket in tribute to Laika, the ill-fated first dog to orbit the earth in 1957 on the *Sputnik 2* spacecraft. But at the tail end of the Cold War, this was still an area far off-limits to tourists, especially Americans.

Except, of course, to Howard Lincoln, who was given a grand tour by another cosmonaut. He was escorted into a gigantic round room, where a narrow ring of walkways surrounded a deep circular pool. Through the clear water, he marveled at the submerged space equipment, including a mockup of a full-sized spacecraft. It was in these underwater environments that cosmonauts trained for the zero-gravity environment of space. One level down, trainers could observe through portals as cosmonauts, tethered to oxygen tubes and lowered into the water by cranes, went through mock missions.

Lincoln's next stop was a full-size replica of a Soyuz space capsule. He squeezed inside to see what the interior of a Soviet spacecraft looked like. Far from treating it like a state secret, the Russians were incredibly open about the equipment, handling it like a typical tourist attraction. "Do you have a camera? Take all the photos you like," he was told.

Despite the VIP tour, Nintendo never did end up sponsoring the Soviet space program.

But the bearlike Belikov and the refined, lawyerly Lincoln did strike up an unlikely friendship. During the same trip, which was to deliver a load of Game Boy handhelds for a Russian charity, Belikov, having learned that they were both avid fishermen, invited Lincoln and his son on a fishing expedition.

This will be great, Lincoln thought. A camp on a lake, a fishing lodge probably used by high-ranking government officials. But his dreams of a relaxing fishing trip evaporated almost immediately as he and Brad piled into a waiting car with Belikov. Their driver raced through the hundred-mile trip as if his life depended on it, hitting eighty or ninety miles per hour on single-lane roads running through thick birch forests. Along the side of the road, Lincoln watched as Russian women cut long grass with large scythes and piled it in the carts with wooden wheels they pulled behind them. It was as if they had left the Moscow city limits and traveled several decades back in time.

The fishing lodge was little better, with father and son trapped in a small hut, surrounded by Belikov and a gang of Russians who looked like they were ready for a wild weekend of fishing and drinking (but mostly the latter). Lincoln followed a short path behind the hut through the woods to where he was told the shower facilities were and found a dilapidated pool filled with what seemed to him like a hundred years' worth of crud and mosquitos. If the Soviet elite had a weekend escape spot, this was not it.

An impromptu party broke out the first night, which consisted of everyone stripping down to towels to sit in a giant steam-filled room and gather around a selection of vodka and cheese on a table. One of the Russians cut hunks of cheese with a pocket knife while mosquitos swarmed inside and out. Lincoln saw his son scratching at mosquito bites and looking miserable, so he administered the only remedy available. "Here, drink some vodka and you'll feel better."

At five the next morning, the group assembled at a nearby dock to wait for their fishing boat. As a small craft motored up to the dock, Lincoln hesitated. Taking one look at their stumbling pilot and fishing guide, he thought, This guy is clearly drunk. But it was too late to back out, already a hundred miles from civilization, deep in the woods. The boat puttered out to the middle of the lake, but the fishermen had little luck pulling in a catch.

Something didn't feel right to the experienced fisherman, and Lincoln started to wonder how deep the lake actually was. As if to answer his question, a group of locals wandered past the boat, literally wading through the middle of the lake right beside them. Like almost everything else he had seen in Russia, this was a facade stretched over a threadbare reality. It was little wonder Nintendo's millions were so sought after.

Back at the ELORG offices, Lincoln saw Belikov was deeply disturbed by something. The Maxwell family had been pushing the Tetris issue with levels of government far above ELORG, and pressure was leading to a lot of uncomfortable questions. "Mr. Lincoln, we're going to honor our commitment," Belikov assured him. "We have a contract, and we're going to honor it."

Behind the scenes, the situation was more severe than Belikov was letting on. Throughout the spring of 1989, a series of faxes and telexes was traded between the major players, which only seemed to antagonize everyone involved.

ELORG telexed both Mirrorsoft and Robert Stein, finally informing them that they "were forced to conclude the contract concerning Tetris for handheld with another firm." Tetris would indeed be coming to the Game Boy through the license granted to Henk Rogers and sublicensed to Nintendo.

Adding fuel to the fire, Howard Lincoln gleefully sent a fax to Hide Nakajima of Atari Games, parent company of Tengen, on March 31, ordering the company to "cease and desist" any activity related to Tetris for the NES—a move directly targeting the tens of thousands of NES Tetris cartridges Tengen was said to be preparing for sale in the United States along with a massive advertising campaign. If Tengen did have to drop its Tetris plans, that would lead to a significant financial loss for the company, which would be stuck with warehouses full of product it couldn't sell.

Sending a personal fax to the head of the company, rather than dealing through lawyers, was in keeping with Lincoln's combative style, similar to how he went directly at Sid Sheinberg at MCA/Universal over the King Kong–Donkey Kong dispute. But for both Lincoln and Arakawa, this was more than just a business deal—it was personal. There was a real anger at the way they felt Nakajima had betrayed them, and that motivated this full-frontal assault. Once they were sure they had the home console rights locked down, they went for the throat.

In early April, Tengen responded to Nintendo, claiming the console rights the company had received from Mirrorsoft were "clear and unequivocal."

If the plan was to force Nakajima and Tengen into firing the first shot in what could be a costly legal battle, it succeeded. In early April, Atari Games filed a US copyright application for the Tengen version of Tetris. The company then filed a preemptive lawsuit against Nintendo to establish its claim over Tetris.

At the same time, Robert Maxwell, patriarch of the Mirror Group, had taken a new interest in Tetris. Debriefed by his son Kevin, the elder Maxwell went straight to the top, taking his case to General Secretary Gorbachev.

Phil Adam, the president of Spectrum Holobyte, was one of the many industry figures now scrambling to deal with ELORG and hold on to whatever Tetris rights he had. In the case of Spectrum and Mirrorsoft, the PC game rights did not seem to be in any danger, but Adam was dispatched to Moscow to shore up that part of the relationship and hand-deliver a royalty check. After originally being denied a chance to negotiate with ELORG in favor of Kevin Maxwell, he was also entrusted with a vital new mission: to personally deliver a letter from Robert Maxwell intended for Gorbachev.

But in a comedy of errors, the letter was never signed. Adam waited in vain in England for Maxwell to meet him and sign the letter, but Maxwell instead took off in his private helicopter for a dental emergency. Adam instead went to Moscow empty handed, and when he arrived, the tension at the ELORG offices was obvious.

During their meeting, standing at attention about ten feet behind Belikov in a half-dark room were two military men. Adam tried to ignore them, but in the poor lighting he could still tell each was stiffly holding something by his side. Only after he left the room did he realize the men were armed with rifles.

Robert Maxwell eventually did reach Gorbachev directly, after lodging complaints through both the British and Russian governments. But the Soviet leader was too distracted to focus his efforts on a video game. The economic reforms he had kick-started were picking up steam but also pulling the nation toward political reform and weakening his grip on power. These economic and political earthquakes were matched by a real earthquake in Armenia that stole Gorbachev's attention away from the in-person meeting Maxwell had finally managed to arrange. In the end, Gorbachev paid the matter only lip service, famously telling Maxwell that he "should no longer worry about the Japanese company."

But even if the supreme leader of the Soviet Union was not going to follow through and get personally involved, plenty of people throughout the chain of command got the message that a close ally of Gorbachev's was not happy with how ELORG was handling business. Belikov got the worst of it, being questioned by prosecutors and having his files searched. He assumed he was under constant surveillance.

To prepare for their countersuit against Tengen and Atari Games, Lincoln carefully went through all of ELORG's paperwork on Tetris with the help of a bevy of Nintendo lawyers, including John Huhs and John Kirby, who had been instrumental in the case against MCA over King Kong. The team focused on the definition of a "computer" in the amended contract with Andromeda and conducted detailed interviews with Belikov, Pajitnov, and others on the Russian side.

Lincoln was worried about one thing in particular. As part of the agreement between Nintendo and ELORG, the Russians were required to send anyone necessary to the United States to testify in court. It was now looking increasingly likely that Nintendo and Atari Games/Tengen would end up in a courtroom showdown, but with Belikov and ELORG suddenly out of favor with the Soviet government, he was afraid his witnesses would run into bureaucratic roadblocks just getting out of the country.

Racing against the clock, Hide Nakajima and Randy Broweleit plowed ahead toward an American release of their Tetris game for the Nintendo Entertainment System, hoping to beat Nintendo's own version to market and to establish themselves as the legitimate NES version of Tetris.

They had every reason to believe their plan for Tetris domination would be successful. Not only did Atari lawyers assure them that the Tetris rights they had acquired from Mirrorsoft were legitimate, but they had one of the most talented game programmers in the industry creating an entirely new version of the game, finely tuned for Nintendo's popular console.

Ed Logg, best known as the designer or codesigner of massive arcade hits like Asteroids, Centipede, and Gauntlet, was one of Atari Games' star staffers and an early proponent of Tetris. In just six weeks after receiving the assignment to re-create the PC version of Tetris for consoles, he had a prototype up and running.

An easygoing native Californian with a shock of blond hair, Logg was known as a closer since his early days at Atari. He had come on board when that company was still a freewheeling seventies start-up. His specialty wasn't so much groundbreaking original ideas as taking existing ideas and distilling them into the perfect addictive form.

For Tetris, he started over from scratch, without the source code or art assets from any of the PC versions of the game, and what he created has come to be known as the definitive version of Tetris on consoles. As you play it, the game's speed gradually increases but so subtly that it takes you by surprise. Logg's secret was his mastery of logarithmic tuning. He figured out that if you want a level to be twice as difficult, you can't just make it twice as fast. Instead, you increase the speed slowly, because just a small bump in speed makes for a much more challenging game experience.

A series of two-player Tetris modes created by Logg were years ahead of their time, allowing a pair of gamers to compete head to head on the same television screen or to work together, juggling two tetrominoes at the same time. The NES version of Tetris Henk Rogers was already selling in Japan, which would become the basis for Nintendo's eventual American release, lacked these innovative features and never felt as finely tuned as Logg's creation.

Nakajima ordered an advertising blitz, including a full-page color ad in *USA Today* and ads in other newspapers and magazines (one read in part, "You'll wish you had ten hands—and ten brains!"), and Broweleit prepared for a media launch party, inviting journalists to New York's Russian Tea Room to play Tetris in a Russian-themed atmosphere. The tagline for the party, for which Tengen employees dressed in black tie, was "The Tetris Affair." For Broweleit, it was the pinnacle of his career at Tengen. In a few months he would be gone, a victim of the brutal legal battle between Atari Games and Nintendo.

May 17, 1989, was the first day American console gamers could buy a copy of Tetris for their Nintendo Entertainment Systems. This Tengen version of the game followed in the footsteps of its PC predecessors, featuring box art that played up the game's Russian roots, including the inverted letter *R* and the phrase "The Soviet Mind Game." A distinctive airbrushed painting (by illustrator Marc Ericksen, a game art veteran behind iconic images of Galaga, Mega Man, and other games) featured Saint Basil's Cathedral in Red Square sitting on top of a gray stone base that slowly fell away into Tetris pieces.

Tengen sold tens of thousands of copies of Tetris in the first few weeks, but the good times would not last. The very next month, in

June 1989, the reciprocal lawsuits between Nintendo and Atari entered the US District Court for the Northern District of California courtroom of Judge Fern Smith. Smith was familiar with the players, having presided over much of the ongoing courtroom drama between the two companies over Atari's reverse-engineering of Nintendo's lockout chips.

Both companies filed injunctions, each seeking to prohibit the other from selling its version of Tetris, and on June 15, Judge Smith considered the competing motions. The argument from Atari's side was that ELORG and the Soviet Government were double-dealing the same rights after discovering Nintendo would pay more for them than the original licensee. If there was any dispute about the exact meaning of a computer in the contract, that was merely a semantic loophole. After all, Nintendo's popular console, which controlled more than 80 percent of the world home video game market, was officially called the Family Computer in its home country of Japan.

Judge Smith reviewed the competing piles of paperwork during the second half of June. The most compelling evidence, she concluded, was the signed statements from Belikov and other ELORG officials and from Pajitnov, all of which claimed that the only rights they ever intended to grant to Robert Stein and Andromeda—from which all the subsequent licenses grew—were for versions of the game to be played on home computers. The alliance formed between Nintendo, ELORG, Rogers, and Pajitnov during those weeks in Moscow held strong. When combined with the clear language in Stein's amended contract that defined a computer as a device with a keyboard, monitor, disk drive, and operating system, she concluded that the weight of the evidence favored one side.

On June 22, Judge Smith issued a preliminary injunction, barring Tengen and Atari Games from selling its version of Tetris. The Associated Press covered the news under the headline "Nintendo Zaps Atari."

SAN FRANCISCO (AP) A federal judge awarded Nintendo Co. a potentially lucrative victory over video rival Atari Games Corp. on Wednesday, ruling that Nintendo could market a home video version of the Soviet-designed video game "Tetris."

U.S. District Judge Fern Smith issued a preliminary injunction prohibiting Tengen Inc., an Atari Games subsidiary, from continuing to sell a home video version of Tetris that it started marketing last month. She denied Tengen's request for a similar injunction against Nintendo, which is due out with its own version of the game in August.

John Kirby, Nintendo's lead lawyer in the case and one of the lawyers who had recorded depositions with potential Russian witnesses, told the press at the time, "We are very pleased that the judge, after reviewing the evidence, concluded that the Soviets were correctly describing their position that they had not granted the rights for home video production indirectly to Tengen and that they were very angry that Tengen was purporting to exercise those rights."

Tengen's spokesperson, David Ellis, could only tell the AP that the company "in good faith understood it had the rights for Tetris under the Nintendo video game format."

The effect of the judge's ruling was immediate. Less than four weeks after Tengen's version of Tetris had gone on sale, it was pulled from store shelves. The remaining inventory was locked away in a warehouse and never officially seen again. The fate of those remaining cartridges remains a mystery today.

The most likely theory is that they were bulldozed under a landfill, which would not be the first time that grim fate befell a pile of unsellable video games. Years before, the original Atari company, which eventually begat Atari Games and Tengen, buried millions of copies of its unsuccessful E.T. movie tie-in game in a landfill in New Mexico. The exact location of those game cartridges was a matter of speculation for decades until a 2014 excavation in the town of Alamogordo uncovered some of the lost copies of the E.T. game.

Before June 22, however, around a hundred thousand copies of Tengen's Tetris had shipped, and many remain in the wild today, traded among collectors or sold on eBay. Concerned the excellent Tengen version of the game would vanish forever, fans would rent copies in stock at Blockbuster video rental stores, and then fail to return them, paying whatever the replacement fee was in order to hold on to the cartridge.

Even with the injunction in place, the case was technically still alive, pending a trial. But Atari Games was losing money every day its Tetris cartridges were under lock and key. Randy Broweleit admitted in a deposition for the case that Tengen had invested in three hundred thousand copies of Tetris at a raw cost of $3 million before advertising and marketing.

> Gaming giant Electronic Arts currently makes eight different versions of Tetris for various mobile platforms.

With Tengen's version of the game effectively banished, the runway was clear for Nintendo to launch its own version of Tetris in July, which quickly sold three million copies; it continued to sell for years afterward. More importantly, Nintendo's Game Boy and Tetris bundle was finally released on July 31, 1989. This pocket-sized one-two punch was an incredibly successful example of hardware and software synergy. People bought the Game Boy just so they could play Tetris, and the most dedicated fans would actually glue the game cartridge into its slot in the machine, ensuring that the Game Boy would never be unfaithful to its lifetime partner.

This led to a secondary problem: many nongamers who became addicted to Tetris on the Game Boy never bothered to buy another game, throwing a wrench in the razor-and-blade model, where game hardware is sold at a slim profit, if any, and the real money comes from ongoing game sales. But, with 120 million Game Boy units eventually sold, no one at Nintendo could say they were unsatisfied with how the new platform was received.

Even with Tengen's game off the market and Nintendo's NES and Game Boy versions selling briskly, the legal case wasn't over. Howard Lincoln, Minoru Arakawa, and the Nintendo legal team were prepared for a long haul and a trial full of complex testimony about technology definitions and Soviet trade practices.

Despite his concerns, and the pressure on ELORG from Robert Maxwell's allies in the Kremlin, Belikov was granted permission to leave the country. He flew to California, where Nintendo kept him in the wings, ready to testify. While waiting, Lincoln brought the Russian home to the Seattle suburbs to have dinner with his family and see some of what the country had to offer. Like every 1980s cliché about Russians encountering American excess, Lincoln stood back and watched as Belikov marveled at the size and selection at QFC, a large grocery store on Mercer Island outside of Seattle. The Russian admitted he had never seen anything like it in his life.

But Lincoln's hand-wringing over bringing Belikov, Pajitnov, and any other required players to California was unnecessary. Through John Kirby, Nintendo had petitioned for a summary judgment, effectively asking the judge to end the trial before it even began, on the basis of what it said was clear and compelling evidence.

Howard Lincoln didn't think this sounded terribly likely, especially as these two companies had a long and tortured history in court together. He didn't think it would go all the way to a jury trial but assumed there would at least be some testimony in front of Judge Smith, particularly from Belikov, whom he had imported from Russia for exactly that reason. Getting a summary judgment without going to trial was, in his experience as a lawyer, what he would call "a tough haul."

But Judge Fern Smith short-circuited everyone's plans for a trial, issuing a summary judgment on November 13, 1989, just before the case was set to begin.

SAN FRANCISCO (AP) The home video rights to a Soviet-designed video game called Tetris belong to Nintendo rather than rival Atari Games Corp., a federal judge said Monday. U.S. District Judge Fern Smith cancelled a scheduled trial and said she would rule that Nintendo owned the rights to the game.

The legal skirmishes between Nintendo and Atari Games/Tengen would hobble along for a few years to come, over both Tetris and the reverse engineering of the 10NES lockout chip system, but the eventual conclusion was already obvious to everyone involved.

Nintendo's official versions of Tetris were the only ones gamers could play on their Nintendo living room consoles or Game Boy handhelds. If the PC and arcade versions of Tetris had made the game a cult hit, the widespread American console release made it part of our everyday vocabulary. Tetris, in all its variations, would go on to sell more than 170 million physical copies and 425 million mobile phone and tablet downloads.

The game that everyone wanted a part of had fulfilled its mission. Tetris could now be played by everyone, everywhere; for the next several years, it was inescapable. In the twenty-five years since Judge Smith's decision, Tetris has become a rite of passage for new game platforms and a benchmark for smartphones, smart watches, tablets, and any other new technology hardware to measure whether it is truly capable of being a mainstream entertainment device. Today, Tetris lives on iPhones and Facebook and on the latest Xbox One and PlayStation 4 consoles.

The 1989 trial ended before it began, with Nintendo essentially sweeping the table, but the result meant little to Alexey Pajitnov. Back in Moscow, he could only sit back and watch dollars from the game flow into seemingly every pocket but his own. In most tales of a creator forced to watch his work take flight without him, this would be considered game over. For Alexey Pajitnov, there was to be an unexpected coda to the story of Tetris.

22

■ ■ ■ ■ ■

THE COGNITIVE VACCINE

The subjects are led, one by one, into a silent, featureless room. Seated, they are left alone, their minds open to input.

A screen on the far wall flickers to life. All the subjects know that what they are about to experience is outside the norm, that they will see and hear unpleasant things. The medical researchers who recruited them admitted as much, but no more. But even the hardiest among them cannot be fully prepared for what follows. Scene after scene is presented on the screen, each more gruesome than the last. Car crashes and their aftermaths, bloody news footage, human surgeries.

The scenes blend into each other in a haze of blood and gore, even as the viewers know this is no slick late-night fright film but real-life death and destruction of the kind only rarely caught by shaky hand-held cameras. The loop of film clips lasts only twelve minutes, but it feels endless.

When the lights come back on, each participant is justifiably traumatized. How could any normal person not feel disturbed after nearly a dozen snuff-film-like clips played out right in front of them? But the effect is very deliberate. This collection of on-screen carnage is part of an experimental technique known as the trauma film paradigm, and the forty participants in this study have all volunteered to be subjected to it in the name of medical research.

The use of real-life film footage of dangerous and deadly scenes is designed to trigger a particularly intense reaction in nearly everyone who sees it. It's the closest scientists can come to approximating the effects of post-traumatic stress, without actually putting test subjects in harm's way. To the impressionable human mind, viewing a dozen or so on-screen examples of death and destruction they know to be real can evoke an emotional injury similar to actually being involved in a traffic accident or other traumatic life event.

After being exposed to the trauma film paradigm, subjects can expect to experience involuntary emotional memories, also known as flashbacks, mental scenes of the horror they have witnessed. It's the same effect, if not to the same degree, experienced by soldiers and survivors of violent crimes. These flashbacks, if untreated, can cause long-term harm to individuals, from an inability to concentrate to a complete mental breakdown.

For a long time, PTSD was considered a condition that could be treated only well after the fact. Months or years later, victims of PTSD could be treated through a combination of medication and therapy, not in the immediate aftermath of a traumatic event. The most popular treatments, including cognitive behavioral therapy, which is a kind of action-oriented, problem-solving short-term therapy, can't be applied to PTSD until the disorder fully blooms.

But was there a better way? Professor Emily Holmes and her colleagues at the Department of Psychiatry at Oxford University in England asked this question back in 2010. The period when memories, such as those formed by being injured in a war zone or accident, deeply implant in the brain occurs relatively quickly after the trauma. All the more-established therapies were predicated on the concept that the harm had already been done and the only fix available was to treat the symptoms much later on.

Holmes had studied PTSD for years, fascinated by how traumatic experiences can come back in the form of mental images, forcing victims to relive the pictures again and again in the mind's eye. Memory acted as a kind of vehicle for carrying that mental imagery. But what if you could change how that vehicle operated?

Not with a drug, like she knew the American military had been trying to develop to erase memories of trauma. Instead, she theorized, ideally after a trauma you would want someone to still be able to remember what happened, and even testify in court, but without the debilitating effects of PTSD. The best-case scenario would be to leave people with a sense of memory, a narrative of the difficult events, but one that they can choose to remember when it's needed without it intruding on their thoughts and emotions all the time.

For a long time, she and other researchers tried using the standard tools in the researcher's toolkit to soak up that mental imagery. They would ask subjects to type letter patterns on a pretend keyboard, hoping to disrupt the imprinting of traumatic memories.

> A 2014 study showed that playing Tetris reduces cravings in smokers and drinkers by about 24 percent.

But that wasn't much good in the real world, where trauma victims don't have access to clinicians administering abstract test regimens. Instead, she gathered her team for a brainstorming session, asking, "Where does this take us? Wouldn't it be amazing if we could actually use these sorts of things in the real world?"

The group, consisting of student clinicians, neuroscientists, psychologists, and psychiatrists, started throwing out ideas. Someone suggested knitting, which involves pattern, color, shape, form, and movement. Another student proposed using something like worry beads, involving manipulating colors, space, and shapes.

One of the younger members of the lab group asked, "What about computer games?" Holmes wasn't all that familiar with computer games but liked the idea. "That's great. That could be something we could try."

But what game would fit the bill? It needed to be something without a verbal narrative, she explained, because that would affect the wrong part of the brain. Someone pitched Tetris: it doesn't have a story, the way a lot of computer games have. It's very visual. It's very colorful. It's very spatial. You can calibrate it. It appeals equally to men and women.

That was more than enough for Holmes. It seemed to have all the properties they were looking for. "Brilliant. Let's try Tetris."

And so the experiment took shape. Oxford is a university town, and it was easy enough to put up advertisements asking people if they'd like to be involved in a medical experiment. Under clinical trial rules Holmes couldn't pay participants but could offer a few pounds per hour to cover travel costs and expenses, and she quickly ended up with a few dozen volunteers, ranging in age from eighteen to forty-seven.

People came into the lab one at time, whenever their schedules allowed, over the course of weeks. The experimenters quickly became acclimated to the trauma film, administering it over and over again, but for each participant, it was a fresh, shocking experience. Holmes thought of the small, sparse room the subjects sat in to view the film clips as "the office you don't really want to have," and the lack of visual distraction made the on-screen horror all that much more effective.

After the film clips had created a traumatic atmosphere for the volunteers, each was given a simple mood test, and then set to work at a handful of time-killing busywork tasks for thirty minutes, roughly twice the time they spent watching the film loop. That was just enough time for the memories of what they witnessed to start the consolidation process in their brains, whereby recent memories are essentially transferred from short-term memory, which is constantly in flux, filling up with and dumping information, to the long-term storage that acts as the brain's permanent hard drive.

How this information is transferred and rewritten determines how we'll recall and reexperience life events later on. For victims of trauma, terrible life-changing events can literally be seared into the brain, stamped so deeply that they bubble to the surface with uncontrollable frequency in the form of debilitating flashbacks.

The next step in this experiment was key, and timing was crucial. Medical science suggests that memories undergo much of this consolidation process over the course of six hours following exposure to trauma. At the same time, the pathways used by the brain to transfer that experience are actually quite limited in bandwidth, as if you're trying to download an online movie over a slow dial-up Internet connection. It will eventually get downloaded, but if other traffic gets in the way and interrupts the process, you may hit the limit of your six-hour window.

That's why Holmes's experiment was carefully timed. After 12 minutes of on-screen carnage, and 30 minutes to give memories time to begin forming, the test subjects were randomly selected to join one of two groups. One group was allowed to sit quietly in another bare room. Given nothing to distract themselves with, they were told to make a note of the number of flashbacks to the film footage they experienced over the next 10 minutes. During that relatively short period of time, the experimental subjects who were left to their own devices and whose brains were allowed to consolidate the memories of what they had seen reported an average of 12.8 flashbacks, more than one per minute.

The other group of subjects experienced a very different second half of the test. They were led to a similar room, but this one had a desktop computer set up and waiting for them. Each subject was directed to the computer and told to watch the screen.

What they saw was at once familiar—very much so to some, a faint pop-culture echo to others. It was the iconic falling tetromino blocks of Tetris. Told to play the game in front of them for the next 10 minutes, the test subjects required no further instruction. The moves, using the cursor keys to slide the tetromino pieces left and right and rotating them end over end, were as natural as riding a bicycle, even if it had been years since they last played.

During these 10 minutes, players periodically paused to note any flashbacks they had to the trauma film footage, just as the control group had done. Playing Tetris was a distraction from such unpleasant involuntary memories to be sure, but it was not a cure-all. Still, rather than recording more than one flashback per minute, the Tetris players only experienced 4.6 flashbacks during the entire second half of the test.

Interesting information, to be sure, but certainly something that could be chalked up to simple distraction. Once the game was over, a mere 10 minutes later, there was a good chance the flashbacks could come on just as strongly as they had for the group that did not play Tetris.

Either way, the results would reveal something about how the human brain processes information and the unique inherent properties of Tetris. With its perfectly proportioned flow of visuospatial tasks, Tetris was able to occupy the same data transfer lines in the brain as would have been used in the consolidation of traumatic memories to a person's mental hard drive.

Holmes was testing the operative theory, if you overwhelm that limited mental bandwidth with Tetris, the traumatic memories cannot be written to the brain's long-term memory in a way that leads to excessive flashbacks. Behind that theory was a bold objective. To take an incredibly difficult-to-manage mental condition, post-traumatic stress disorder, and create a cognitive vaccine for traumatic flashbacks.

The next step after keeping the subjects sequestered viewing the trauma film paradigm and then either playing Tetris or doing nothing and recording the short-term frequency of flashbacks was to send all the subjects away for a longer period of time.

The forty participants were all given a diary to take with them and then were sent home for a one-week period. During that time, they were instructed to record the frequency of flashbacks they experienced over the next seven days, just as they had in the laboratory.

Upon their return, the two groups, those who played Tetris and those who didn't, were given two distinct mental examinations. First, they underwent a clinical assessment of their PTSD symptoms, if any, using a tool called the Impact of Event Scale, which is essentially a lengthy questionnaire that measures distress in a patient. As one might imagine, the control group, left to quietly marinate in the horror of the gruesome series of film clips they had been forced to view, scored relatively high on this test. The Tetris players, while still registering a recordable score, were judged to be not as affected as the other participants.

Everyone involved was also given a second test, called a recognition memory test, which was a quiz that measured recall of the specific events in the film loop. This was to test what Holmes called "voluntary memory retrieval." Meaning that, even if you've managed to disrupt the formation of involuntary flashbacks by playing Tetris or performing some other visuospatial task in the hours after a traumatic incident, you still have the ability to dispassionately recall the actual events.

Subjects were shown statements of alleged facts about the film clips, such as "Three cars were involved in the crash," and were asked to label them as true or false. Both the Tetris players and nonplayers could accurately recall facts about the film to the same level, with hardly any difference between the two groups. That was really key to this experiment and strongly suggested that using Tetris as a cognitive vaccine against PTSD flashbacks didn't actually block the memories from forming but instead blocked how they formed and how they could affect the subject later in life.

Since then, Holmes has continued her work, extending the time frame in which the Tetris vaccine concept can work from hours to days. The next step is pushing for the game to be made available in hospital emergency rooms as an inexpensive but effective medical treatment, and one that allows you to recall the facts of what happened without as much of the trauma. "Tetris only affects the visual intrusions of the memory. It doesn't affect your ability to remember what happened," she says, "which is so fascinating in terms of memory theory. Actually, it contradicts mainstream memory theory that you can even do that. It's just so beautifully elegant that you can."

EPILOGUE

■ ■ ■ ■ ■

THE FINAL BRICKS

The ocean air was warm early in the morning of November 5, 1991. Too warm for Robert Maxwell, founding father of a vast and tangled media empire that included newspapers, book publishers, and software companies. At 4:45 a.m., he called up to the crew of his luxury yacht, the *Lady Ghislaine*, and demanded they crank up the air conditioning.

It was the last conversation anyone ever had with the millionaire tycoon.

The boat sailed on toward the Canary Islands, but Maxwell was never seen alive again. The following morning, docked at the town of Los Cristianos on the island of Tenerife, a crewman went to rouse Maxwell. After knocking on the cabin door, he heard no response. Worried about his aged, out-of-shape employer, the crewman let himself in, but Maxwell was not in his room. The man scanned the decks with increasing panic. Still no Maxwell. He alerted the rest of the crew, and an intensive search effort was launched.

At the time, Maxwell and his son Kevin were still smarting over the loss of valuable Tetris rights they were convinced they had nailed down years before. In the two years since Judge Fern Smith shut the door on any claim besides Nintendo's to home console rights for Tetris, the pair could only sit back and watch as Nintendo sold tens of millions of copies of the now-iconic game.

But beyond being cut out of the loop on a huge global hit, Robert Maxwell had much bigger problems in front of him by the end of

1991. His companies were more than $3 billion in debt, and he had been forced to sell off strategic assets. Worse, hundreds of millions of pounds from his own companies' pension funds had been illegally siphoned off to support failing parts of his empire and his own lavish lifestyle. The blame for the missing money would fall squarely at his feet.

In recent months, Maxwell had also faced a new kind of challenge. Rumors surfaced that he had been a Mossad agent, or at least an asset, and had played a role in the Israeli capture and conviction of a rogue nuclear scientist. For Maxwell, a former member of British Parliament and confidant to many world leaders, being labeled a spy was a damaging insinuation. He went to great lengths to keep the story, which he called "ludicrous, a total invention," from being covered in the British press.

A fishing boat about a hundred miles from where the *Lady Ghislaine* had passed the night before spotted Maxwell's body floating in the Atlantic. The sixty-eight-year-old Maxwell had grown from a handsome war hero to a three-hundred-pound senior citizen with serious heart and lung problems. It took a Spanish helicopter to lift his body from the water.

Theories behind Maxwell's death are numerous. Some say he had a heart attack and fell overboard. Others, that this was a suicide brought on by impending financial doom. Conspiracy theorists point to the many enemies he had made over the years in the bruising world of media and politics, or his alleged spy activities, and claim a late-night assassination.

Whatever the cause, Maxwell's collection of media companies soon followed him to the grave. His sons Kevin and Ian tried to keep the ship afloat as wary creditors called in loans, but once it became clear that the elder Maxwell had stolen from his own workers' pension funds to support his foundering empire, it was all over. The Maxwell companies jointly filed for bankruptcy in 1992.

Kevin Maxwell was left holding the bag after his father's death and went on trial for fraud over the company's collapse. He was acquitted but soon after filed for the largest personal bankruptcy in British history, with debts of more than 400 million pounds.

His subsequent public life has been tabloid fodder, with failed businesses, a failed marriage, and continuing squabbles over the Maxwell legacy. Following an investigation into the failure of yet another of his business ventures in 2011, Kevin Maxwell was barred from serving as a company director in the UK for eight years.

■ ■ ■

After Judge Smith's ruling, the game was essentially over for Atari Games and Tengen. Randy Broweleit had already left the company by that time, hoping to avoid the fallout over the ongoing lockout chip patent dispute. Atari Games continued to release games, mostly for Sega systems, but the brands were shut down by Time Warner after that media conglomerate acquired the remains of the company in 1993.

Spectrum Holobyte lost its dynamic partnership when Phil Adam and Gilman Louie went their separate ways, and the company itself was soon subsumed in the Maxwell collapse. Adam would move on to other game publishers, including Interplay, where we worked on entries in classic games series such as Fallout and Descent. Louie, after a stint finding technology partners for the CIA, became a key member of Silicon Valley's venture capital class. Both men still prominently list their connection to Tetris in their bios on LinkedIn or for speaking engagements.

Robert Stein eventually lost even the last slice of PC game rights he had managed to hold on to for Tetris. By his own estimate, he probably made from $200,000 to $250,000 from the game, but played a different way, it could have been tens of millions. He largely withdrew from the industry after a 2007 heart attack.

■ ■ ■

Minoru Arakawa and his father-in-law, Hiroshi Yamauchi, continued to sustain Nintendo's stratospheric success from opposite sides of the globe, perfectly in keeping with their arm's-length relationship. Arakawa announced his retirement from Nintendo of

America in 2002, after it became clear he would never lead Nintendo of Japan, and he retired to Hawaii at the relatively young age of fifty-five. Henk Rogers had also moved his base of operations back to Hawaii by that time, and it wasn't long before they worked together again.

■ ■ ■

Howard Lincoln moved up to become chairman of Nintendo of America in 1994, before retiring in 2000. But he didn't go far; instead, he set up shop across town as chairman and CEO of the Seattle Mariners baseball team.

It wasn't an entirely random move. The team's principal owner since 1992 was Nintendo of Japan chairman Hiroshi Yamauchi, who later transferred his ownership stake to Nintendo of America after his 2002 retirement (just five months after his son-in-law's). Yamauchi died in 2013, having never once come to see his American baseball team play.

■ ■ ■

Vladimir Pokhilko, the Moscow medical researcher and friend of Alexey Pajitnov who first saw the clinical applications of Tetris, cofounded a 3D software company called AnimaTek with Pajitnov and later emigrated to the United States. But he didn't find the dotcom-boom success he hoped for, and in 1998, said to be facing intense financial pressure, Pokhilko murdered his wife and son in their Palo Alto home before taking his own life.

Vadim Gerasimov, the high school student who so brilliantly translated Pajitnov's original version of Tetris to work on IBM-compatible computers, and who occasionally shared cocreator credit, earned a PhD from the Massachusetts Institute of Technology before moving to Australia, where he works as an engineer for Google.

■ ■ ■

The global success of Tetris made Alexey Pajitnov a minor celebrity on the technology and video game circuit. Over the next couple of years, he attended the Consumer Electronics Show in Las Vegas and other trade events as a guest of Tetris's various licensees, but he was still considered a bystander to his own creation.

Henk Rogers, however, made millions from Tetris in the first few years after the ELORG deal was signed. Rather than taking his winnings and moving on, he never forgot the bond he formed with Pajitnov in Moscow over nights of vodka and game design talk. In 1991, he helped Pajitnov and his family emigrate to the United States, where the programmer set up shop in Seattle and worked on new software ideas before signing up for several years with the only other organization besides the Soviet Union regularly referred to as an "Evil Empire": Microsoft.

During the upheaval and confusion caused by the collapse of the Soviet Union in 1991, public and private resources became blurred, changing hands quickly, often to the benefit of a new class of market-minded converts to the capitalist ideal. ELORG, the state-run trade group, became a private organization. The idea of owning and profiting from ideas and innovations was no longer forbidden, and everyone suddenly seemed to be on a massive grab for cash and resources.

One of Russia's formerly state-owned resources was the rights to Tetris. When the original ten-year agreement Pajitnov had signed expired at the end of 1995, Henk Rogers was right there to help his friend make a successful claim to at least part ownership of Tetris. Pajitnov and Rogers would form a new organization, today called The Tetris Company, to own and administer the rights to the game, finally giving Tetris's creator a share of the game's financial success.

Owing to the Wild West approach to free markets in the early 1990s in the former Soviet Union, Nikoli Belikov effectively ended up dealing himself a portion of those same rights, forming his own private company, called ELORG LLC. After years of an uneasy partnership with Rogers and Pajitnov in The Tetris Company, Belikov sold his share of Tetris back to them in 2005. According to court documents, he received $15 million to exit the Tetris business once and for all.

After years of living and working in Japan, Henk Rogers was drawn back to his last American home, Hawaii. He realized his children, growing up in Japan, had little connection to American culture and in fact spoke little English. Taking the entire family to Hawaii, he gave the children the same sort of language immersion that he experienced when he had arrived in New York as a child. His daughter Maya followed him into the video game business, working for Sony's PlayStation division before taking over as the CEO of The Tetris Company in 2014.

A sister company, Tetris Online, was founded in 2006 to create versions of the game for Facebook and other Internet-powered platforms. The cofounders were Rogers, Pajitnov, and Rogers's Hawaii neighbor Minoru Arakawa, who took over as president and CEO.

Arakawa had moved to Maui upon retiring from Nintendo of America, building himself and his wife a palatial home, and Henk Rogers lived a couple of islands to the west in Honolulu. Despite walking away from one of the biggest brands in gaming, Arakawa couldn't stay away entirely and would host annual gatherings of old industry friends, which he called simply The Arakawa Meeting. He joked that his wife was tired of him being home all the time and had suggested he find a job. Rogers was more than happy to comply, bringing three of the major players in the Tetris saga together once again.

The continued financial success of Tetris has allowed both Pajitnov and Rogers to pursue their passions. Alexey Pajitnov continues to design games and acts as an ambassador for the Tetris brand, and Henk Rogers has founded a new company, called Blue Planet Energy, to create green energy technology.

■ ■ ■

Today, Tetris is everything from a cultural shorthand for crowded elevators, closets, and parking lots to the first game many people download on their new tablets and smartphones. Maya Rogers is even working on a full-scale narrative science-fiction movie based on the game, hoping to strike the same pop-culture nerve as the Transformers and Lego films.

It's hard to overstate the impact Tetris has had on the world over the past thirty years. Sales of authorized copies have brought in nearly $1 billion to date, with countless millions more pocketed over the years from unofficial versions.

> Including free versions, Tetris has been downloaded more than five hundred million times on mobile devices.

Tetris is a unique example of an idea, a product, and an era coming together at exactly the right moment. In the still-nascent category of interactive entertainment, Tetris made the leap from niche hobby for computer nerds to the heights of mainstream crossover appeal in a way no game has since Pong invaded living rooms and bars in the 1970s. Your parents played Tetris, your kids have played Tetris, you've played Tetris, and you'll encounter the same story in nearly every country on Earth.

Tetris has permeated popular and artistic culture. It has been included in a MoMA Applied Design collection, has been adapted as interactive public art installations projected onto the sides of buildings, and is the subject of an annual World Championship competition.

More than three decades after it first crawled along the monochromatic screen of Alexey Pajitnov's Electronica 60 computer, Tetris lives on in tablets, laptops, smartphones, and game consoles, but Tetris also serves as a harsh reminder that the lines of code that make up a video game, or any type of digital media, are ephemeral. They weigh nothing; they cost little to endlessly reproduce. With such a perfect combination of widespread dissemination, psychological triggers, and basic human greed, it's not surprising that Tetris was the one of the world's first "viral" hits.

But in the end, we come back again and again to the core of the game in its original, unadulterated form. There may be new colors, new multiplayer modes, or new theme music, but the basic idea of fitting tetromino shapes together with the speed and accuracy of a master builder remains unchanged. Tetris is bringing order to disorder. It's the eternal struggle against the nonstop onslaught of daily life, in all its colorful randomness, seeming to fall on you from the sky.

ACKNOWLEDGMENTS

This book would not have been possible without the support of my terrific agent, Kirsten Neuhaus, who patiently worked with me through numerous false starts before we zeroed in on the perfect story. At PublicAffairs, editor Ben Adams employed a deft but light touch to pull out more humanity and drama from this first-time author's manuscript.

I'm indebted to the many people connected with the history of Tetris who spoke to me, both on and off the record, including Alexey Pajitnov, Henk Rogers, Howard Lincoln, Minoru Arakawa, Phil Adam, Randy Broweleit, Jeff Goldsmith, Emily Holmes, Richard Haier, and Maya Rogers. Video game industry veterans Perrin Kaplan and Sean Maggard were instrumental in putting some of these interviews together.

A special thanks to my many colleagues at CNET over the past ten-plus years, and especially to executive editor John Falcone and editor-in-chief Lindsey Turrentine for allowing me to take advantage of this opportunity.

And, finally, none of this would be possible without my personal and professional partner of nearly twenty years, Libe Ackerman, who deserves a coauthor credit on nearly everything I've ever written professionally.

SELECTED BIBLIOGRAPHY

The complex history of Tetris has been covered many times over the years, although never as the sole subject of a full-length book. Instead, Tetris has occupied at most a few chapters in other works devoted to the big-picture history of video games, which typically cast a very wide net, covering everything from the very beginnings of electronic games in the 1960s through the smartphone and app-based games of today.

Many of these books tell a version of at least part of the Tetris story. The most comprehensive of these is *Game Over: How Nintendo Conquered the Word* by David Sheff, first published in 1994 and revised several times since. It has become a go-to resource for many reporters and authors and was instrumental in sketching out the timeline for many of the events detailed here. It's an especially valuable contemporaneous account, because it was written just a few years after the major events it covers.

Different accounts of the main Tetris timeline, from creation to commercial triumph, are also retold in *All Your Base Are Belong to Us* (2011) by Harold Goldberg, a long-time friend and fellow member of the New York technology and video game journalism scene; *The Ultimate History of Video Games* (2001) by Steven Kent; and *Replay: The History of Video Games* (2010) by Tristan Donovan. All of these works provided valuable insight and background information.

Each of the books cited above tells the story of Tetris with the big beats intact but often conflict on details, dates, and other specifics. Many events covered here occurred between twenty-five and forty-five years ago, so it's not surprising that memories can change over time or that business rivals on opposite sides may recall events differently.

In cases where the historical record is unclear, or when my interviews conflicted with previously published accounts, I've attempted to recount the most likely version of what happened, based on research and my own conversations with many of the primary participants. A certain amount of historical interpolation was required to offer a clear narrative understanding, including into the thought processes and motivations of those involved.

Also especially valuable in understanding Tetris are the numerous interviews granted over the past few decades by many of the people behind the game, especially Alexey Pajitnov and Henk Rogers. Over time, they've told and retold parts of the Tetris story for different online and print publications, although as the years wore on, these interviews have tended to downplay some of the conflict between rival factions.

Key examples of informative Alexey Pajitnov interviews include "Catching Up Casually: A Chat with Alexey Pajitnov," published on Gamesutra.com in 2008; "Mr. Tetris Explains Why the Puzzle Game Is Still Popular After Three Decades," from VentureBeat.com in 2014; and "The Man Who Made Tetris," published in 2015 by Motherboard, the technology news section of Vice.com.

Henk Rogers detailed the creation of his groundbreaking Japanese role-playing game, The Black Onyx, in a 2013 interview for the now-defunct gaming website Edge-Online.com. "The Making Of: The Black Onyx" is no longer online, but a cached version can be found at Archive.org. Gamasutra also conducted a long, informative interview with Rogers in a 2009 feature titled "The Man Who Won Tetris."

Even at the beginning of Tetris's commercial life, the game, and the people behind it, garnered plenty of contemporary media coverage in newspapers and magazines. "New Software Game: It Comes from Soviet," by Peter H. Lewis in the January 29, 1988, issue of the *New York Times*, was one of the first major news articles about Tetris (the awkward headline seems to have been truncated to fit a narrow newspaper column width). Similar mainstream coverage can be found in early 1988 articles from the *Chicago Tribune* ("Glasnost Reaches Computer Games, and Tetris Is Terrific" from June 10, 1988) and Reuters ("Soviets Play Capitalist Game with New Computer Puzzle," from January 28, 1988).

The 1994 *Wired* magazine article "This Is Your Brain on Tetris" was so important, it influenced an entire section of this book, including an interview with its author, Jeff Goldsmith.

A detailed interview with games programmer Ed Logg on the website AtariHQ.com was instrumental in understanding his work on the game and offered further insight into the conflict between Nintendo and Tengen.

Considering the protracted legal battles around Tetris, an excellent source of background information not often cited in other accounts comes from publicly available legal documents. *Atari Games Corp. and Tengen, Inc. v. Nintendo of America Inc. and Nintendo Co., Ltd.* explains much of the bad blood between Tengen and Nintendo; *Blue Planet Software, Inc. v. Games Intern., LLC* and *Belikov et al. v. Huhs et al.* offer insight into the various parties who ended up owning a chunk of the rights to Tetris and how much those rights were bought and sold for.

Tetris has also been the subject of several films and television programs over the years. The best known is the BBC-produced documentary *Tetris: From Russia with Love,* which first aired in 2004. Its hour-long runtime can only scratch the surface of this complex story, but the film is notable for offering some of the only on-camera interviews with Nikoli Belikov and Robert Stein as well as for giving voice to the late Jim Mackonochie. *Ecstasy of Order: The Tetris Masters,* an independent documentary from 2011, looks at the cultural impact of Tetris and follows several players seeking to capture the top spot at the annual Classic Tetris World Championship.

Finally, my own introduction to the story of Tetris came in an episode of the cult favorite online video series *Play Value,* a talking-head documentary program about the history of video games. I was a cast member for this series, produced by OnNetworks and directed and created by Jeremiah Black. The 2007 episode "Tetris: Splitting the Iron Curtain" offered a brisk recounting of the major story beats and remains one of the series' most popular episodes. OnNetworks is no more, but PlayValue episodes are easy to find on YouTube.

INDEX

251

Credit: Sarah Tew

New York native **Dan Ackerman** is a former radio DJ turned journalist. An editor at leading technology news website CNET, he writes about hot-button consumer technology topics, from virtual reality to cybersecurity, and appears regularly as in-house tech expert on *CBS This Morning*. He lives in Brooklyn with his family and a large collection of vinyl records.

PublicAffairs is a publishing house founded in 1997. It is a tribute to the standards, values, and flair of three persons who have served as mentors to countless reporters, writers, editors, and book people of all kinds, including me.

I. F. STONE, proprietor of *I. F. Stone's Weekly*, combined a commitment to the First Amendment with entrepreneurial zeal and reporting skill and became one of the great independent journalists in American history. At the age of eighty, Izzy published *The Trial of Socrates*, which was a national bestseller. He wrote the book after he taught himself ancient Greek.

BENJAMIN C. BRADLEE was for nearly thirty years the charismatic editorial leader of *The Washington Post*. It was Ben who gave the *Post* the range and courage to pursue such historic issues as Watergate. He supported his reporters with a tenacity that made them fearless and it is no accident that so many became authors of influential, best-selling books.

ROBERT L. BERNSTEIN, the chief executive of Random House for more than a quarter century, guided one of the nation's premier publishing houses. Bob was personally responsible for many books of political dissent and argument that challenged tyranny around the globe. He is also the founder and longtime chair of Human Rights Watch, one of the most respected human rights organizations in the world.

·   ·   ·

For fifty years, the banner of Public Affairs Press was carried by its owner Morris B. Schnapper, who published Gandhi, Nasser, Toynbee, Truman, and about 1,500 other authors. In 1983, Schnapper was described by *The Washington Post* as "a redoubtable gadfly." His legacy will endure in the books to come.

Peter Osnos, *Founder and Editor-at-Large*